Amélie

Amélie

The Story of Lady Jakobovits

——◄◦►——

Gloria Tessler

VALLENTINE MITCHELL
LONDON • PORTLAND, OR

First published in 1999 in Great Britain by
VALLENTINE MITCHELL
Newbury House, 900 Eastern Avenue
London IG2 7HH

and in the United States of America by
VALLENTINE MITCHELL
c/o ISBS, 5804 N.E. Hassalo Street
Portland, Oregon 97213-3644

Website http://www.vmbooks.com

British Library Cataloguing in Publication Data

Tessler, Gloria
  Amélie : the story of Lady Jakobovits
  1. Jakobovits, Lady Amélie 2. Jewish women – Great Britain –
  Biography 3. Jewish women – France – Biography 4. Rabbis'
  spouses – Great Britain – Biography 5. Jewish women –
  Religious life – Great Britain
  I. Title
  941'.085'092

             ISBN 0 85303 340 4 (cloth)

      Library of Congress Cataloging-in-Publication Data

Tessler, Gloria.
  Amélie: the story of Lady Jakobovits / Gloria Tessler.
    p.   cm.
  Includes index.
  ISBN 0-85303-340-4 (cloth)
    1. Jakobovits, Amélie, Lady, 1928–   . 2. Rabbis' spouses–Great
  Britain–Biography. 3. Jewish women–Great Britain–Biography.
  4. Jakobovits, Immanuel, Sir, 1921–   . I. Title.
  BM755.J279T47 1998
  296.8'32'092–dc21
  [b]   98-43095
                                                              CIP

Typeset by Vitaset, Paddock Wood, Kent
Printed in Great Britain by
Creative Print and Design (Wales), Ebbw Vale

For my Parents

Contents

Contents

List of Illustrations

Acknowledgements

OF THE many who gave of their time, advice, moral and actual support in the research and creative process of this book, I want first to acknowledge the Rev. Reuben Turner, whose suggestion it was and whose interest and concern remained constant throughout. I would like to thank Kerryn Vincent for her enduring patience and invaluable help with tape transcriptions, Alan Radnor, Soli Daruwalla and Ronald Channing, all of whom were sources of guidance and support during the book's creation. I also appreciate the help given to me by the Jewish Chronicle Library, particularly Linda Greenlick and Anna Charin. I am grateful to Barbara Falter for additional research in Germany and Lex Crofton for his help with translations. Also thanks go to my editors Hilary Hewitt, Rachel Joseph and Linda Osband. Especial thanks go to my husband, Richard Sherrington, the first to read the manuscript, for his endless encouragement both legal and literary. Last, but not least, none of it could have happened without the love and patience of my three children, Daliah, Donna and Rami.

I silently thank an army of family and friends, too numerous to mention, whose good wishes and loving interest spurred the book on its way. My final tribute is to the spirit and energy of Amélie's remarkable father, Rabbi Elie Munk, whose inspiration was never far away.

Prologue

SHE KNOWS how to enter a room. There is a housewifely bustle about her and an old European charm, but with all that softness something jars; a hint of sharpness, a slightly granular edge to her voice. She can be penetrating and profound. When she addresses a room or a conference, she is always intimate; her French accent is caressive and challenging, and she will reduce everything she wants to say to personal experience with an innocence that can hush a crowd. Her eyes are an unusual turquoise: they reflect vivacity and sadness – a certain knowledge. With the strength of her beliefs, she can lead women's seminars on the meaning of Jewish law and ritual, and flip through the pages of *Hello!* magazine asking how so and so can *possibly* wear that dress, while sorrowing simultaneously over the British divorce figures.

Amélie Jakobovits rose to prominence in Anglo-Jewish circles and beyond in a vicarious role that she has transformed into something personal and extraordinary. It would be a rags to riches story were it a simple, secular tale of a young girl who married well and made good, the eternal fantasy that transcends political creeds whether socialist or feminist. But this is the story of a woman from a respected, religious family whose life was spared by many miracles.

Her own mystique is that she is a consort, not a queen, emerging from a threatened Jewish patriarchy to reflect the European experiences of her people in her time. Daughter of a great rabbinic thinker and writer, Rabbi Elie Munk, she married an enigmatic and ascetic man who achieved the office of Chief Rabbi of Great Britain and the Commonwealth. Immanuel Jakobovits won the respect of Margaret Thatcher, the Prime Minister of his day, for his intrinsically Jewish ideas on self-help

xiii

politics and medical ethics. He has steadfastly clung to his principles, whether on homosexuality, the Palestinian refugees or the issue of family purity, no matter how unpopular they have sometimes made him.

When he is not required in the pulpit or the House of Lords, Lord Jakobovits would prefer to remain in his reflective privacy. Sometimes that privacy is invaded by an inquisitorial public interest from which his wife has tried fiercely to protect him. She cannot understand how anyone can criticise him for, to her, he is beyond reproach. He, too, will face his critics with surprise that their spirits are made of different stuff. Sometimes the protector herself turns bully and she will goad him from his shyness to face his community, although she undertakes much of the pastoral work with a gusto that once provoked the comment that she, too, like the late Princess Diana, is a Queen of Hearts.

Certainly she is astute enough to get to the heart of the matter. Her definitions are clear: the woman must put husband and family first. This stance, the ultimate preserve of Jewish Orthodoxy, defines her own femininity and gives her the parameters of her freedom. It is a freedom in which a woman's gifts are driven by and curtailed by the home environment. With a nod and a wink to the Deity, she has drawn up her own Ten Commandments for a happy marriage. Stick to these, she says, and life will be happier; you will reap a rich harvest that will transcend the immediate thrills of first-stage love.

At a time when the polarities of feminism and religious funda-mentalism place the *new woman* under such stress, Amélie sails in calm waters. For her, the diurnal ritual of religious imperative both protects and illuminates. She remains saddened but un-threatened by the challenges the couple face both from within the Jewish community and outside. With her husband's retirement and the advent of a new British Chief Rabbi, Jonathan Sacks, the bowing out has not been easy. Amélie, who was once told by her prospective mother-in-law that she would never make a lady, may remain 'a Queen of Hearts' to her people, but the modern demands of this office are arguably colder, less comforting, more distanced and more English. They reflect the demise of the traditional European ethos in Anglo-Jewish society, with all its sighs and longings, its *haute bourgeoisie,* its knowledge of pain and its bitter laughter.

In writing this book, the image of Amélie I retain most is the atmosphere around her. She is rarely contained and always generating a particular emotion, a certain sensitivity. Sometimes she will burst in, upset at something in the media, seeking confirmation of her righteous indignation, and then her anger will subside into a kind of reflective grief. She is never vengeful but often profoundly shocked, unable to believe that the world can behave in the way it has done, although she knows its ways better than most. At other times she will enter quietly, obsessed with some family worry – and with such a large family there is always something to worry about – but then her faith and natural optimism will pull her out of depression. Frequently she is amused at something that has been said to her, and then she is at her most French; her laughter is gutsy, contagious and earth-bound, because in humour you see the earthiness of the person, never mind how questing and upwardly mobile her spirit.

The Almighty is always in her voice and constantly invoked. Yet her natural, unquestioning conviction is balanced with a sense of realism. She is often on the edge of being mannered, taking herself too seriously, but her natural humanity holds this in check. She speaks too quickly, partly because she is French and partly because her natural temperament is upbeat and on the move.

People are always asking, how does she do it? How does she fit so much into her day? The answer is will and also skill. She uses her Gallic wit to push a conversation her way; when it is finished for her, she has the art of closing, as the Americans might say, swiftly moving in with a timely farewell. During the course of our interviews, she preferred my home to hers believing – often wrongly – that there would be less bustle and telephone interference at my place. She rejected the lounge for the kitchen from where she could see for herself the life and spirit of the house. Her eyes, always sharp, missed nothing.

A biography is an engagement of two people, the writer and the subject. Yet Amélie was always acutely sensitive to the writer's condition, understanding every nuance of my own feelings, helpful and patient – though she believes she is not – empathetic, pre-emptive of my mood and what I sought from her.

Shakespeare might have said of her: *She is a woman: Take her for all in all*. This is the story of a woman of her time, who is also, according to the proverb, 'serene before the time to come'.

Gloria Tessler
London, 1998

Beloved and respected, by the fortunate many
Who have been recipients of her abundant bounty
Of her caring and overflowing heart
Where so many others share a part
Her every deed, so noble and wise
How much thought, behind each one lies?!
A listening ear, a hearty smile
A comforting word, they stretch over a mile
Her special sixth sense, her deeper insight
Has brought to the world, so much warmth and light
May the Almighty's guiding light illuminate her days
And give her much strength to continue in her golden ways

Eli Kernkraut

Amélie

I slept and dreamed
that life was joy,

I awoke and saw
that life was duty,

I acted, and behold
duty was joy.

Tagore

An inscription presented to Amélie on her birthday by Nicole Davoud who was awarded an OBE for her contribution to the educational needs of young people struck by Multiple Sclerosis.

1   *Grandfather Goldberger*

PARIS, 1936. The city was enjoying its last few years of freedom before falling to the Nazi invaders. An eight-year-old Jewish girl who had just arrived with her family from the Bavarian town of Ansbach, near Nuremberg – where Nazi anti-Semitism had turned increasingly vicious – was enduring her own silent torment. She had become terrified of the dark. Night-time to her was like entering a tunnel in which she could find no ray of light.

It was worse when her parents went out. Taking care not to awaken her younger brother and sister, Amélie Munk silently dressed and waited in the street for that moment of exquisite relief when her parents suddenly reappeared on the horizon. Often she would wait for three hours, going upstairs occasionally with a torch in her hand to check on the younger children. Her prevailing thought was one of jealousy: why were *they* sleeping when she couldn't?

Only days before, Amélie and her family had been picked up at the station in Paris by a close friend of her father, Samuel Kohn, a businessman and lay leader of the Parisian pre-war Orthodox community, and given temporary sanctuary in the apartment which he shared with his wife. But the child's insomnia on the first few nights forced her to get up in the dark, feel her way wall by wall into the Kohn's bedroom and then slip into bed beside the indulgent couple.

Perhaps her childish terror symbolised the long dark night into which the European soul was soon to be engulfed. Either way, Amélie Munk's life had entered a phase of adventure and danger which would take her way beyond the early years she had spent in Ansbach with its picturesque brown-and-yellow houses, its festooned markets and small-town pageantry. And yet she had already sensed the nightmare within the dream, tinged as it was with shades of a Grimm's fairy-tale: Ansbach, as she knew it, was dying a little each day, poisoned by a viral hatred that gradually infected the entire continent.

* * *

BERLIN, 1926. Elie Munk, a Parisian rabbinic student and leader of the popular Orthodox religious and cultural youth movement, Ezra, was addressing one of its seminars when his mind wandered over to a very attractive girl who happened to blush whenever she caught his eye. It did not take the gentle-featured young man, with the mild, yet penetrating, blue gaze, long to make the girl's acquaintance. Her name was Fanny Goldberger. She was nineteen years old and was the second of four daughters. When, with equal alacrity, he proposed to her, Fanny told him that, according to time-honoured tradition, he must first speak to her father.

Mr Natan Goldberger, a Nuremberg textile merchant who came from a long line of Orthodox German–Jewish businessmen, frowned and said, 'I really don't know. She's never mentioned your name to me.'

Elie Munk was told to telephone in a day or two, by which time the father of his intended bride would have spoken to her. Yet the reaction from his would-be love was not at all what he anticipated. Mr Goldberger's daughter received the news of the proposal with amazement. 'I've never met him,' she insisted. 'I don't know what you're talking about.'

Mr Goldberger had wrongly assumed that it was his elder daughter, Malie, whom the young rabbi had in mind. It was rare within Orthodox Jewish tradition that a younger daughter should marry before her elder sister. However, when the confusion was clarified and it became obvious that Fanny and Elie were in love, the laws of matrimonial hierarchy were relaxed and the wedding was celebrated amidst great excitement. Elie had married a woman who would match his sense of *joie de vivre* with her own instinctive intelligence for life.

A symbol of the endurance of their union, despite many hardships, came in an unexpected way some six decades later when their first child, Amélie, was mysteriously handed a gift at a London reception by a stranger, who told her not to open it until she reached home. It proved to be the immaculately preserved prayer book, embossed with the names of Fanny and Elie Munk, given to them by Fanny's parents on their wedding day in 1927.

In the dynastic and scholarly rabbinic world from which Elie Munk hailed, he was already demonstrating an unusual depth and insight. The second of three brothers, his traditional background was the Germanic *Mitnagdim*, which supported an intellectual interpretation of religious teaching common to Central Europe. However, the young Munk was a romantic and the more emotional Chassidic tradition, rooted in Eastern Europe, had begun to attract him. He was particularly fascinated by the mystical world of the Kabbalah. Such leanings were regarded by his contemporaries as dangerous, way beyond the scope of current Orthodox thinking. For Rabbi Munk, however, they were to prove the basis of a profound scholarship and a quest for the expanding spirituality of Jewish values. By the mid 1930s, his views were to draw fire from some members of his own circle.

This was the man who was one day to write in his Kabbalistic work, *Ascent to Harmony*:

> To be pure is to follow the path of nature: to be holy means to conquer nature. The way of Judaism is dynamic, not just static; holy, not just pure. When G-d created nature He wanted mankind to rise to a state of holiness by continuing with the work of creation, improving on nature. This applies to the nature of the physical world: it also applies to the natural state of human society that an individual may find when he appears on the scene.

Believing that Christianity 'had accepted the "kingdom of Caesar" as society formed it', that Buddhism had shown an earthly disinterest and that Islam was philosophical in its acceptance of evil and misery, Rabbi Munk wrote that Judaism accepted that the will of man was stronger than fate, that the power of justice could transform society and that moral values could sanctify life on earth. He came to believe that the role of the nations was to build great civilisations along the lines laid down in the 'Covenant with G-d', while the role of Judaism was to help man recognise Divine Law and bring about *Tikkun* – restoration, unification and brotherhood. But this was still in the future.

Munk's first calling was to take over the Ansbach ministry of Rabbi Kohn, a founder of the Agudah Movement in Ansbach, which was near his bride's Nuremberg home. In the course of his ministry he visited all the smaller Jewish communities dotted around Bavaria, many of whose inhabitants bore the names of the little towns of their origin, such as Ansbacher or Hamburger. In 1928 Fanny gave birth to their first child and they named her Amélie after Elie's mother, who had died young.

Zipporah Stefansky, who was fourteen years old at the time and a young student of Rabbi Munk, recalls her teacher as kind and tolerant; she remembers his wife as a lively, good-humoured, down-to-earth person, who could adapt to any situation and gave much of her time to the Jewish youth movement. 'Fanny organised plays, gave advice and counselling to the members, trained them and studied with them. She was a popular lady.'

When baby Amélie came along, she proved to be a central attraction, the cynosure of all eyes, fussed over and indulged by a community ardently seeking to renew itself. 'She was a very sweet baby. I remember her blue eyes and everyone wanting to take her out for walks in the pram,' said Zipporah. 'There were not so many Jewish babies, there was always anti-Semitism, even before Hitler.'

Nevertheless, Jewish life in Ansbach prospered under the lay leadership of Municipal Councillor Ludwig Dietenhoefer, who headed the Jewish Agency from 1903 to 1922. Despite the early rumblings of anti-Semitism, it was something of a golden age for religious, communal and cultural affairs. The community possessed a Baroque synagogue built by the eighteenth-century Italian architect, Leopoldo Retty, a community house, a ritual bath, a schoolroom and a cemetery. It was a very vigorous mercantile community strongly based on the cattle trade. A local centre offered facilities for 'Germans of the Jewish persuasion', and there was a military branch of the Zionist Association for Jewish frontliners, a Keren Kayemet and clubs for the study of Jewish history and literature.

Ansbach's somewhat turbulent Jewish history dates back to the beginning of the fourteenth century. The community had suffered a wholesale massacre in 1349 during the Black Death, was expelled in 1561 and readmitted in 1609. During the seventeenth century, two leading Jewish families, the Models and the Fraenkels, were active in the town's economic and administrative affairs. Ansbach's famous rabbis included Abraham Merzbacher and Pinchas Kohn.*

The Munks and their baby daughter, Amélie, settled at No. 33, Maximilian Strasse, site of a famous cigarette manufacturer, Ceslanski, which gave the street its particular ring – the Ceslanski corner, as it was known. The entire area resonated with the thrust of small-town Jewish enterprise. Here, too, was a perfect confluence of the rural and the urban. At the approach to Mount Triesdorfer stood Kupfer's, the silk thread factory, and at Karolinenstrasse, Wallersteiners Antiques rubbed shoulders with Weissmanns, cattle dealers. There were more cattle dealers in the neighbouring Alten Postrasse and Sonnenstrasse, while the main shopping street, the Uzstrasse, buzzed with the trade generated by its well-patronised Jewish shops. The Herriede Gate through which the young Amélie Munk passed on her way to synagogue led to the market-place – the nerve-centre of Ansbach – where the wool and linen merchants, Moses Mahlers, and the clothiers, Leopold Wittkowsky, were based. Across the road stood Jakob Weil, working-men's outfitters. There were shoe shops like Lebrecht's and Krebs', not far from Frau Weiss' men's and boys' outfitters, flaunting their maritime insignia – '*Zum Matrosen!*' – while at the Endersstrasse was the clothiers, Michelsohn's. Finally, in Nurnbergerstrasse was Joel's ready-to-wear men's shop, whose prices were so competitive that much later the proprietor was fined 5,000 Reichsmarks because he had failed to observe the average resale price maintenance.

These names fronted a life rich with anecdote and full of small-town market haggling. It was a sort of commercial Anatevka, an intensely vibrant Jewish society into which the Munks introduced their growing family. After Amélie in 1928 came her brother, Jacki, born during Chanucah eighteen months later; and eighteen months after that another daughter, Ruth, was born. Amélie

*Source: Diana Fitz, *Ansbach unterm Hakenkreuz*, Ansbach: Stadt Ansbach, 1994.

was just old enough to remember Ruth's birth at home and her first cry.

To the young rabbi and his family, the Ansbach community offered all the pezzaz of Jewish commercial energy within a classical Bavarian landscape. The buildings were Gothic and Baroque with grand rococo interiors, suggesting a mental and spiritual generosity in conflict with the rigid, rejectionist Nazi thinking that loomed ahead. The steepled symmetry of the town itself was bordered by the rich green of the Steigerwald forest.

By 1933, Rabbi Munk's community represented nine per cent of the town's 23,000 population. Twenty-four Jews owned 480,000 dms worth of property, forming a vital part of the town's industrial life. Up till then, the Jewish businessmen were perceived by their compatriots as friendly and helpful, no matter how petty the transaction. These Jewish retailers enjoyed great popularity because their goods were usually a little cheaper than their competitors', and they did not mind giving credit.

However, this popularity was both seductive and dangerous. For a long time, the Jews of Ansbach had begun to sense a slow yet incipient anti-Semitism. Posters declaring them a national enemy had appeared as early as 1923. Four years later Jewish cemeteries were being desecrated. Even before the National Socialists came to power, local Jews had had to endure anti-Semitic jibes prompted by the Streichers' Nazi weekly, *Der Sturmer*. Bavaria was the centrifugal point of Nazi anti-Semitism and the Streicher presence in this small Bavarian town provoked intense anti-Jewish measures.

Yet, on the whole, the people of Ansbach did not take part in the official nationwide boycott of Jewish shops on 2 April 1933. SS stormtroopers found other, more insidious means of frightening off Ansbach's citizens from purchasing at Jewish shops. They planted themselves ominously outside and took the names of prospective customers.

Most threatening of all was the Nazi attempt – rejected by the Ansbach local authority on 14 November 1933 but implemented four days later – to ban Jews from access to the cattle markets, a branch of the economy which had been very slack until 1925 when Jewish initiative boosted the trade into prosperity, winning great influence with the farmers, who were paid cash and offered better prices. It was not long before the Nazi councillors began to prohibit Jews from entering Ansbach from the smaller towns out of fear that they might choose to settle there.

Against this background, Amélie's first years at school were, in her own words, 'absolutely horrendous'. The kindergarten which she attended at the age of four was already under the influence of the Nazis. Amélie's teacher, Fraulein Lemline, wore a black dress up to the neck and down to the ankles, and had very tightly braided hair: an appearance terrifying to a small child. She would come over to the Jewish pupils, order them to stand up, and then she would rap them on the head and over the knuckles with a ruler. Amélie and other Jewish children would be punished just for not being able to answer a question. It was a humiliating pain which entered the child's psyche and remained permanently with the woman she was to become.

Every morning Amélie would wake up with a sinking feeling, anticipating the terrible ordeal that lay ahead. 'I felt sick in the tummy simply because I realised that I was Jewish and that I was going to be treated like a dirty little Jewish girl for doing absolutely nothing offensive.'

To try to forget the horrors of school life, Amélie would go ice-skating on the lake. But little by little such pleasures were prohibited to the Jews. The Nazis began forbidding 'Jewish children and dogs' to enter certain parts of the villages, so that Amélie could no longer play in the village gardens. Notices banning Jewish children from playing in the parks of Ansbach also appeared overnight. So Amélie used to wander into the nearby Steigerwald forest, where she could smell the pine, which she never encountered again apart from a sudden whiff, many years later, when she visited Atlanta with her husband and, walking through the forest at night, caught the sharp smell which reminded her of the home to which she had long vowed never to return.

Gradually the covert anti-Semitism became more exposed. By 1934, laws were passed forbidding Jews to congregate in groups of more than three. A banner floated across the entry to the town that proclaimed: 'The Jews are our Misfortune.' One day, Amélie discovered that the father of her closest friend, Erica, who lived in the upstairs apartment, had become a member of the SS. This was unthinkable because the family was so pleasant to her. Each time something bothered Amélie at home, she would run upstairs to play with Erica.

One day Erica's mother accused Amélie of stealing half a crown which had fallen beneath the dresser. She denied it to her father, but in fact it was true. She had seen the money fall underneath the dresser and had gone after it. Because she had lied, her father slapped her around the face. His slap landed on her eye and, recoiling from the shock, Amélie heard her mother, Fanny, reprove him: 'Well, you didn't have to hit her on the eye.' Amélie had always regarded her father as a very tolerant and sweet man, slow to anger. This was why the memory of his blow, like the teacher's rap over the knuckles, stayed with her all her life.

Many years later Amélie asked one of her granddaughters: 'How come that each one of your brothers and sisters appears to be an only child?' The nine-year-old girl thought for a moment and then replied: 'I think it is because Daddy and Mummy are very consistent in their love and discipline. They really love us and they tell us so and they hug us and kiss us, but if we have to be punished because we did something naughty, they do it and they stick to it and they tell us to go upstairs. We're not allowed up for Kiddush* because we did something terrible, and I think that this love and the discipline is what makes us the way we are.'

If the words of the child echoed Amélie's own upbringing, there was another, perhaps softer, dimension to her life in Germany: her relationship with her grandfather, Natan Goldberger. The two had an unusual rapport, which Amélie later attributed to her being his first grandchild. 'As a result of that he spoiled me stiff,' she said. Their friendship also insulated her against the possibility of feeling any sibling rivalry with her younger brother and sister.

Nearly every Friday afternoon, from the age of two and a half, Amélie was sent off to meet her grandfather at Nuremberg station. Mme Munk actually considered it a miracle that Amélie turned out the way she did after having been so spoiled by her maternal grandfather. The relationship between them clearly had something

---

*A reception with wine and food which usually follows a Shabbat service.

of the feel of two children at play – two eternally youthful spirits – and yet it went far deeper than that because even now she never does anything of major consequence in life without first asking herself what her grandfather would have done in the same situation.

After meeting Amélie at the station, Grandfather Goldberger would take the child to what was, in her eyes, an enormous textile shop, a four-storey building emblazoned with his name and coat of arms, in the centre of Nuremberg. On the way he would ask her, 'What shall we go and buy for you today?'

'If he could have given me the moon, he would have done so,' she remembers. On an earthier plane, Amélie would at the very least receive the most expensive toy possible.

In the sanctuary of what seemed to her the endless expanse of his workplace, she was made to feel more valued than the most important customer. 'I was always being told that I had priority over them and he would simply ask them to wait.'

Once he took her on an overnight trip by car and Amélie, always a bad sleeper – 'it wasted time' – could not be induced into slumber. 'He stopped at every inn he could to buy me another glass of beer, and then I insisted on combing his head, which had no hair. He started bleeding. I really was a devil,' says Amélie, 'but I was allowed to get away with it. I was allowed to do anything I wanted. My grandmother was more severe; she didn't really approve of this, but she couldn't change it!'

'Anyone who does something to my Amélie will get into trouble with me,' her grandfather would threaten others in front of the child. Far from being bored in the clothier's store, Amélie was fascinated by the great bales of material which were delivered into the shop and placed on a low trolley. When she came in, every yard of material had to be removed so that she could glide on her tummy on the trolley going backwards and forwards, while her grandfather roared, 'Everybody get out of the way. *She* comes first!'

The bond between Amélie and Grandfather Goldberger was so powerful that Amélie did not really develop a close mother/daughter relationship until much later. There is no doubt that she was over-indulged by her grandfather and his staff, who would have been in trouble had they neglected her every need. A modern parent might well be irritated, but in this case it is almost as though Goldberger sensed that he must give her everything he had because her childhood and their unusual relationship would prove so short. His affection for her began to nurture a certain charisma in the young Amélie and even a lingering sense of the cherished child, which were to remain with her into adult life.

Amélie became aware that her mother seemed closer to her younger brother Jack and her sister Ruth. In fact, Ruth was so close to her mother that she felt no need of friends until her late teens, when she went to a seminary in Gateshead. 'I wouldn't say Maman rejected me,' says Amélie, 'but she felt that my grandfather took over.'

On her last visit to Nuremberg in 1933, Grandfather Goldberger turned to her for the last time and asked, as he met her at the station, as he had done so many times before, 'What can I get you today?' The teasing, affectionate words are burned into Amélie's memory. For not long after this the Nazis walked into Nuremberg and ordered the swastika flag to be raised over all the main buildings overnight.

Goldberger was president of the Jewish community in Nuremberg, which was housed in a listed building with a huge green dome, suggestive of the London Planetarium. He called in his council for an emergency meeting to resolve the dilemma. Everyone sensed that this was a no-win situation. If they raised the swastika flag on a Jewish place of worship, it would probably cause trouble with the Nazis, but if they did not, they would be in equal trouble. After much soul searching, it was decided that the lesser of the two evils was probably to obey the decree and put up the flag.

At 2 a.m. that morning four towering Nazis came for the president of the Jewish community. As Natan Goldberger opened the door, they arrested him for defiling the flag by putting it up on a Jewish building. They ordered him to get dressed and to go with them to take the flag down. When Goldberger left the house, his wife saw him to the door and asked, 'Natan, do you have everything you need?'

'Yes,' he sighed, 'I have my tefillin in one pocket and a picture of Amélie in the other. That's all I need.'

He was ordered to climb up to the roof alone and remove the

swastika. Despite the physical danger and his advanced years, he managed to do so and miraculously slid down the roof without being hurt, holding the flag in his hands. He was surrounded by a dozen Nazis, who told him to kneel down in the synagogue courtyard. 'Whatever you call prayers, you dirty Jew, say them now, because this is the end of your life,' they jeered. They drew their guns and pointed them at the old man. Whatever prayers may have been in Natan Goldberger's heart during those few terrible moments, the Nazis changed their minds. After kicking him mercilessly, they let him go. Grandfather Goldberger survived the ordeal, but died of a heart attack a few months later.

Amélie was told the news by her paternal grandfather, Shmuel Munk. He sat her on his lap and started telling her about life and death. It meant nothing to the child. She was not particularly shocked by his ruminations. He then revealed that Grandfather Goldberger was no longer on this earth but had gone to another world altogether. Amélie remained unconcerned. 'I was convinced that the world had come to an end, but it didn't worry me very much because I felt I was going to sleep now and when I woke up, I'd be together with my grandfather. I wasn't worried.' Amélie was four years old then. She never went into shock over her grandfather's death, but it stayed with her – the yearning, the missing him. Even today she says, 'I feel he is absolutely alive. He's just hovering over me whatever I do, wherever I am.'

The loss began to forge embryonic spiritual ideas within Amélie. Born to a deeply religious family, she herself developed her own view of a world that exists in three stages: the womb, this earth and the world to come. Spiritual survival was an unquestioned belief that no rational or agnostic challenge could move.

'My grandfather has never left me,' she says. 'He might have left me physically, but he actually has never *left* me. He comes in dreams. The dreams give me the feeling that he is just standing next to me.' Years later, when Amélie herself had become a grandmother, these esoteric thoughts filtered through to her eldest daughter, Esther, when she celebrated her child's wedding. 'As I walked up the aisle holding my child's hand,' Esther confided to her, 'I could see my grandparents walking in front of me and I was so very moved.'

Meanwhile, in Ansbach, Jewish life was being squeezed out. Rabbi Munk's young student, Zipporah, recalls the hardship, the narrowing down of opportunity. Soon it was forbidden for Jews to buy groceries at their local shops. Zipporah's parents' cleaner had to shop for them, and she would be apprehended the moment she tried to post a letter on their behalf. By 1938, the community had to rely on a traveller to bring in provisions from Nuremberg, forty minutes away. The Jews of Ansbach reacted – as so many did – like mime artists in a dream.

'Nobody could really believe it was happening. The Gestapo were brought in from out of town to do the dirty work. People were very worried whenever there was a Gestapo march past their homes. They always feared they were coming for them.'

On Seder night* 1938, the marchers, imported from the Bavarian cradle of anti-Semitism, chanted out their hope that only Jewish blood should splash from the diners' knives. 'That was the first Seder night no one stayed to drink red wine,' says Zipporah, grimly. 'They wrote on our house, "We don't need any Jews here, rabbi go to the devil."'

A few months later, on *Kristallnacht*,** the Mayor of Ansbach saved the synagogue by the brilliant coup of staging a mock-fire there. But the Munk family was spared the nightmare that became Ansbach.

---

*The first night of Passover at which a ritual meal is eaten as part of the celebration of the Jewish exodus from Egyptian slavery.

**On the night of 9 November 1938, the Nazis burned down 200 synagogues (including the noted Fasenenstrasse in Berlin, where Immanuel Jakobovits' father, Julius, was rabbi) and arrested thousands of Jews in reprisal for the assassination of a German diplomat in Paris by a young German Jew whose parents had been deported to Poland.

2   *The French Connection*

PARIS, 1936. As life deteriorated for the Jews of Ansbach, Rabbi Elie Munk received calls to lead two different communities: one in Cologne and the other in Paris. The Rue Cadet community in Paris had the sentimental call of his roots – he had been born there – and, on a more practical level, it seemed a good idea to leave Germany. He was expected to succeed Rabbi Weiskopf, who had died in office one week before his 100th birthday. The community to which the young boy now returned as its rabbi comprised some 350 families, mostly third-generation Parisians, the roots of an Orthodox migration to Paris after the Franco-Prussian War. Rabbi Munk found them both unswerving in their faith and rigidly anti-assimilationist – in fact, a bastion of religious belief in a country in which eighty-five per cent of French Jews were entirely secularised and liable to view their more observant co-religionists with some disdain. A similar contempt was reserved by the French for refugees in general, yet it was in the style of a typical Frenchman that Amélie remembers her father doffing his hat and bowing each time he passed the street where he was born.

'Everyone who was in contact with my father would realise that he was an extremely gentle person, a very tolerant person in every sense of the word,' Amélie describes him. 'He had enormous faith, a perpetual smile, wonderful softness and kindness of heart, and yet all this disguised a very strong willpower and an immense amount of courage.'

Among his congregants were the Reichmann family who found him to be a staunch traditionalist – a 'seamless composite of French and German rabbinical traditions'. In his biography, *The Reichmanns*, Anthony Bianco expands: Rabbi Munk, he says, was 'Germanic in outlook, in his studiousness and the rigour of his religious observance', while at the same time proud to remain a true Frenchman. The Reichmanns themselves found 'a measure of solace and protection within Rabbi Munk's extraordinarily tight-knit congregation,' adds their biographer.

The community rented an apartment for the Munk family at No. 18, Rue Notre Dame de Lorette in Paris 9. Amélie, fortunately brought up to speak French – 'though I was always told off in German' – was trained by her father to be his little spy. After services at the Rue Cadet Synagogue, the worshippers used to gather socially in the courtyard. The main membership body of this synagogue was largely comprised of two different clans. One was the large Klein family, and the other, the Levy Bamberger family. The two rarely saw eye to eye and frequently played one off against the other. Rabbi Munk was endlessly called on to arbitrate in the course of their grievances, which usually centred on arguments over which passages to say and which to leave out in the prayer book.

'Papa would listen to both and smile and then say, "I'll let you know tomorrow what I think about it." I don't think the answers ever came through, but it went on like that for years, each one believing that the rabbi agreed with him.' Thus Amélie discovered the art of rabbinic diplomacy, and the charm or otherwise of communal foibles. They gave the Paris community its warmth, its idiosyncrasies, its essential humanity. The only Paris restaurant under Rabbi Munk's supervision was Ringer's on Rue Buffaut, around the corner from the synagogue. This venue was the hub of local Jewish society, frequented by the Reichmanns and several of their Austro-Hungarian refugee friends as well as tourists.

Although the Rue Cadet community had held tightly together in the face of assimilationist French Jewry, Rabbi Munk still had to endure his own rite of passage. One day he declared from the pulpit that the Jewish law against carrying anything on Shabbat must be enforced, even to the exclusion of carrying an umbrella. The community was up in arms. There was uproar in the courtyard. Rabbi Munk asked his daughter on the way home what reactions she had overheard. 'I tell you what they said,' she replied: 'Oh, that little refugee, who needs him as a rabbi? *What* does he think he is? *Who* does he think he is? We've been carrying personal belongings on Shabbat all this time and now, suddenly, we are not allowed to carry? I think we'll send him right back where he came from.' But they did not send the rabbi back to Germany. In the end they listened to him and accepted his exhortation to keep the Sabbath to the letter of the law.

Despite their carping in the courtyard, the community of those days had tremendous respect for rabbinical authority. Clearly this adoption of the moral high ground on the part of Rabbi Munk represented, if not a power struggle, something of an initiation ceremony for him. Consequently, a deep bond developed between her father and the community which he had returned to lead.

It made its mark on Amélie, too. She saw it as 'the most emotional relationship between a rabbi and his community. It was a very wonderful experience. I never again came across a community where I felt so much at home, so relaxed, so much part of one family as I did in the Rue Cadet before the war and also after the war when a few of us came back.'

This feeling of acceptance filtered into her educational life, too. Amélie's school experiences in Paris were a dream compared to the anti-Semitism she had suffered in Germany. There were very few Jewish schools in France at that time, so Amélie went to a public school in Rue la Martine. The relief at being able to wake up in the morning without fear of humiliation or unjust punishment simply for being Jewish was indescribable. The next few years proved a time of greater security than she had previously known.

In 1939, however, Rabbi Munk was drafted into the army and Mme Munk, who had put on a great deal of weight after the birth of her second daughter, Ruth, was surprised to find herself pregnant for the fourth time. She was very afraid of being alone without her husband by her side. This anxiety, plus her awareness of the German advance in Europe, caused her to shed those extra pounds in a very short time. On 3 September France declared war on Germany and, despite his French birth, Elie Munk was interned as an 'undesirable alien' (of German origin). After that he was sent to an 'assigned residence'.

In November, as the German bombs started falling, Mme Munk gave birth to a girl, who weighed a mere three pounds. The clinic's medical staff became so afraid of the German bombing campaign that the babies were kept in a cellar and only had one change of nappy a day. Consequently, when Mme Munk brought her tiny daughter home one week later, her body was in a terrible state, with sores all over; however, she grew up to be one of the strongest of the family, destined to bear nine children herself. After the birth of this child, Fanny Munk never asked any new mother the weight of her baby. She simply asked whether there were ten fingers and ten toes. There was already a tacit acknowledgement that times were getting tougher for everyone, and yet even the frailest new baby with the will to survive could do so, provided all its vital organs were healthy.

Meanwhile, Amélie was at school in Paris and developing new friendships. One of them was with Edith, the daughter of the cantor at the Rue Cadet Synagogue, who was the same age as Amélie. They grew up together and remained close friends until the war, when the trauma that Edith was to experience in Auschwitz radically altered and deepened their relationship. The emotions they were to share were symbolic of the changing relationships among the people she knew as carefree children in Paris who survived the war to pick up the tentative threads of old friendships.

The two often dissenting 'ruling' families which comprised the Rue Cadet community, meanwhile, provided a social life that was vibrant, full of energy, argument and spirit. The younger generation of Rue Cadet were the nucleus of the embryonic Yeshurun youth movement, which was eventually to provide Amélie with the experiences and opportunities she would need to develop the personality of a rabbi's wife. Mireille Warshawski, *née* Metzger, now living in Jerusalem, was a member of this youth group and lived in the Munk family's apartment for a short while during the war. 'Amélie was always laughing and was always the same person,' she says. 'She used to talk quite a lot, but always very kindly.'

Yet, despite Amélie's new sense of freedom and friendships, the first years in Paris were turbulent. The family had arrived as German refugees and there was a pervasive sense of the German advance. Too young to understand it, she and her friends turned the experience into a game of 'fooling the enemy', as she puts it. 'The whole thing was to defeat the enemy and to get the better of him by fooling him, and so there was a sense of enormous adventure rather than fear, because our age didn't allow us to realise the dangers. I'm talking about a child's fantasy of running away from the bombs, running away from the Germans. I felt very proud and very full of myself that I was able to find a cellar or a little farmer who took me in and therefore I defeated the enemy. I was never frightened. I was just always very heroic. I was the heroine of the game.'

But while Amélie was fighting off the German army, her mother was concerned with more down-to-earth business. She was preoccupied with naming her new baby. She couldn't reach her husband for advice, so it was to her family doctor that she turned. With true Parisian sang-froid, the doctor recommended the name Françoise Victoire, to reflect political optimism in the face of a somewhat harsher reality. So the child who, in normal circumstances, would have been given the name of an ancestor, became Françoise, named for this difficult period of history into which she had been born. And she was, as Amélie piquantly describes her, 'the sweet and honey of the family'. But, sadly, Françoise Victoire, although a beautiful name for a girl, represented a futile hope for the Munk family, as it did for the rest of France. The war moved in the Germans' favour and they invaded France on 15 May 1940.

Amélie walked down the streets one day to find huge posters calling on Jews to register with the local mayor and produce identification papers. The shadow of Ansbach suddenly returned to haunt her in the cosmopolitan French capital and became still more ominous the next day. The local streets were plastered with notices forbidding Jews to visit certain parks in Paris, forcing them to register once a week and to wear the yellow star. Rabbi Munk had already volunteered to join the Foreign Legion and was sent to a training camp in the south. Sam Levy, the president of the Rue Cadet community, telephoned Fanny Munk and urged her to take the children and leave town.

Fortunately, Mme Munk had had a call from another member of the community and close family friend, Maître Mathieu Muller, who offered her his country home near Orléans. So Fanny Munk took the family to the Gare de l'Est, along with thousands of other refugees, Jews and non-Jews, who were attempting to flee the incoming Nazi power. The Munk family just managed to catch the very last carriage of the last train as it pulled out of Paris two hours before the German bombs rained down on the French capital. The train was supposed to take all the refugees down to Spain, travelling through France over the Pyrenees. However, it stopped many times at different places, sometimes deep in the countryside, letting people off so that more people could get on. What was remarkable was that at each stop, either in the country, a main town or a village, there were highly organised groups of volunteers – Scouts or Brownies, the Red Cross or the Salvation Army – who handed in food to the refugees through the windows.

The journey itself was a such terrible experience that, to this day, Amélie wonders how they survived. 'You couldn't budge. You just couldn't move at all. There were thousands of people in each carriage and I remember being caught near a toilet whose door was open, and where I sat just like everybody else on that train. Wherever you stood, you remained, and if you actually came into the train and sat down, then you couldn't get up, and if you stood, you couldn't sit down because we were squashed in tight as though we were in a tin of sardines.'

There were many incidents on this journey, but one particular one occurred on the third day after the Munk family left Paris. Amélie could not see her mother and guessed that she was at the other end of the carriage. Suddenly Amélie heard a loud scream followed by the sound of crying. It was a voice she immediately identified as her mother's, but she could not get to her. Instead, she decided to send word down from person to person to find out whether the lady who was crying was a certain Madame Munk. Word came back in the affirmative. The reason for her mother's panic was that she had suddenly lost baby Françoise, who was then only a few months old, and who was lying in her arms. Whether the exhausted mother had suddenly dozed off, no-one knew, but one moment the baby was in her arms and the next she had completely disappeared! Amélie, desperate to help her, could not move for the sheer pressure of people. 'I said out aloud at that moment, "Who could possibly kidnap a baby at this time? You can't move. You can't get out of the train."'

Everyone was starving and tempers were beginning to fray. Gazing at the irritable people around her, random surreal thoughts assailed Amélie. How much, for instance, did it take to turn people into cannibals? She tried to brush away these ideas born of fear and exhaustion. But where was baby Françoise? At last her mother stopped crying and word came back to Amélie that a baby had been found lying contentedly asleep on the paws of a dog under the bench! It was a poignant memory that was to remain with Amélie and affect her for the rest of her life.

Accompanying her mother and younger siblings on the train was her maternal grandmother, who had joined the family from Nuremberg in 1938. Her paternal grandfather and his second wife, Esther, had moved to Nuremberg when her parents left Ansbach. Although he was not an ordained rabbi, Shmuel Munk held a rabbinic diploma and had volunteered to look after the Nuremberg community when its incumbent, Rabbi Klein, was eventually deported. His son, Elie, had tried desperately to persuade him to leave Germany and join his family in France in 1939, but Shmuel had simply sent back a postcard which read: 'A captain cannot leave a sinking ship.' Munk the elder may or may not have understood the full significance of his stand: that he was set to perform the ultimate act of Jewish sanctification – that of *kiddush Hashem*, or martyrdom for the sake of Judaism. He died in Theresienstadt soon after.

Meanwhile, despite the strain and tension of the cramped train journey, Amélie discovered that she had misjudged her fellow travellers. A great camaraderie developed among them which dissolved her earlier fears during the time of baby Françoise's disappearance. It was a friendship born of a single common factor: they were all French people fleeing tyranny. Religion became irrelevant. 'For as long as everyone was together on that train,' Amélie recalls, 'people were very kind to each other.'

Mme Munk had packed a small case of food for each of the children. She had even taken some silver cutlery with her, as well as her husband's kiddush cup, one of their wedding presents which is still in Amélie's possession. Years later, on the birth of a grandchild, the baby was named after Elie Munk and that very kiddush cup was used at his circumcision. The combination of having a grandchild named after her father, and the use of the kiddush cup that had been used at her parents' wedding, were to prove an overwhelming emotional experience for Amélie, symbolic of survival – of 'the whole odyssey of my parents' saga from the moment they were married to this day'.

It is doubtful, however, that the hungry child, crammed into the refugee train, anticipated such events. Her mind was firmly on more practical matters. Mme Munk had taken with her whatever money she happened to have and had sewn it into a pocket in her underwear for safe keeping. In each of her children's cases there was some silver cutlery, the food which she had already cooked, a change of underwear, one change of dress, plus one or two silver baskets. She had put in the silver in case it might be needed for sale. But of course the food went bad by the time they came to eat it and it had to be thrown out of the window. They, like the other passengers, had to rely on the Scouts and Brownies who handed food in through the window, even though it was not kosher. Their faith would not permit them to eat meat that was not kosher, even though, Amélie later reflects, to save life Jewish law permits some relaxation of its Orthodox code. The Munk family, not conceding that their present difficulties constituted such an emergency, ate the bread of their affliction in the sandwiches they received and handed the meat to whoever happened to be standing nearby. It was naturally received with gusto. The volunteer organisations masterminded a massive feeding operation on that train which conveyed thousands of people to the South of France over a period of five days. Another miracle was that, as far as Amélie can ascertain, nobody died on it.

The Munk family got off the train at Albi, a small industrial town north-east of Toulouse, famous for its sixteenth-century Italianate cathedral and its most illustrious son, the French Impressionist, Toulouse-Lautrec. However, art and cathedrals were not uppermost in the Munks' minds as they left the train. They were still far from the Pyrenees border, but Mme Munk suddenly remembered that her last letter from her husband had been post-marked Albi, so she decided the family must get off there.

All the refugees from north and central France were taken in by the different southern cities and accommodated in schools, universities, and community centres. The accommodation consisted of rows of camp beds, one next to the other. The Munks were placed in a gymnasium which held some 1,000 beds. To reach her bed Amélie had to scramble over everyone else's, and, as there was so little space, she had to keep her suitcase underneath the bed. Despite the austere conditions Amélie was relieved to be in the city where her father had written his last letter. As he was a French-born father of four children, he was exempt from being sent to the frontier. Instead, he was employed as a blue-collar worker in a Foreign Legion boot camp.

So Fanny Munk settled her young family down for the night and the next morning told Amélie to find herself a bicycle and go in search of her father.

3   Searching for Father

IN COMMON with many of her contemporaries, Amélie looked older than her twelve years – a burgeoning maturity forged through sudden and unexpected responsibility. Despite her youth, the friendships she made at this stage of her life were deeper and her life goals were perceptibly higher than they had been during the time of freedom.

But Amélie wore these responsibilities lightly, so that when her mother asked her to find her father in a totally strange town, it was simply another adventure to her. Amélie borrowed a bike from one of the caretakers and cycled off to the military compound where her father was stationed, a two-hour ride away. 'I went off feeling for the first time in over a week like a free bird allowed to fly freely without any fear of arrest or bombs,' she says. 'It was an exhilarating sensation and I was only sorry that my mother and my brother and sisters, as well as the other thousands in that compound, could not enjoy it. I was totally devoid of any fear.'

She finally reached the military compound and asked for her father. The soldiers on reception duty confirmed that a Rabbi Munk was registered there and promised to tell him that she was waiting for him outside the barbed wire. Suddenly Amélie saw her father coming out of a hut about 300 feet away. He was dressed in the French military outfit of the blue-collar worker and was given permission to walk over to the barbed wire to talk to her. Rabbi Munk was totally overcome with emotion at seeing his eldest child for the first time in months.

'There was a big smile and immediately, as always, a blessing of gratitude to the Almighty for having brought us back,' Amélie recalls. Face to face with his daughter, both of them in tears, Amélie realised that her father had only vaguely understood the dangers his family had faced. He had not known whether they had remained in Paris, or had been forced to flee, or even whether they could afford the journey. Neither had he realised the extent of the German threat against the Jews. 'He was aware that France was being bombed, but knew nothing of the evacuation of the population from Paris, although only a few thousand in fact ran away.'

As his daughter explained the circumstances of their escape, Rabbi Munk's face flickered with many contrasting emotions. He gazed deeply at her. It became clear from her discourse how fortunate the family had been. Amélie told him about the shortage of trains and their great luck in managing to get on the last one. It was only then that Rabbi Munk understood the gravity of the dangers his family had faced. Not that he betrayed this anxiety in his demeanour. Amélie recalls her father being very positive at that moment, full of smiles and gratitude. She could not wait to get home to tell her mother about the meeting.

It took Amélie another two hours to ride home and she realised that she had no idea what day of the week it was. 'When I asked, I just knew that the answer would be Saturday. Somehow or another we Orthodox Jews seemed to find ourselves frequently in difficult circumstances often on our Sabbath. I prayed that the severity of the situation in which we found ourselves would mitigate in G-d's eyes against any possible wrongdoing.'

The next day she and her mother decided to leave the younger children with their grandmother in the refugee compound and to take a taxi to the military barracks to see her father and discuss plans for the immediate future. This was an important decision because they had very little money, but it somehow gave them the false sense that they were in control of their own destiny. However, when they arrived they were told by the guards on duty at the gate that there was no way they would be allowed to see or speak to Rabbi Munk because that morning they were expecting a contingent of German prisoners, and security precautions were very strict. Fanny Munk could only glimpse her husband at a distance of some 300 feet away before being told to leave.

By now Mme Munk's nerves were completely shattered. The events of the past week had exhausted the entire family, but on top of this she was responsible for a tiny baby and her own mother. By nature she had an exuberant personality, which she passed on to her eldest daughter, but she was also inclined to become tense and anxious without the support of her husband. Mme Munk's nervous condition was also possibly exacerbated by post-natal depression following the recent birth of Françoise, not something which was generally understood at the time.

Mother and daughter drove back to the refugee compound with heavy hearts. Two or three blocks before they arrived, Fanny suddenly insisted on stopping the car and getting out. 'She said, "Amélie, I really have no wish to live any more. I will just allow the next car which will come around the corner to run over me."' Watching her mother stand squarely in the middle of the road, refusing to move, Amélie managed to remain calm, yet summon complete self-control as she pushed her on to the pavement and out of the path of a lorry which was just rounding the corner. Had she not done so, her mother would certainly have been killed. Amélie could see that the shock of the past few weeks had completely overwhelmed her mother, shattering her nerves. Even at such a young age she grasped the sombre thought that this burden was not being borne by her mother alone, but by everybody in her family, and elsewhere, where people were desperately worrying about their closest relatives. Fortunately, Mme Munk was shaken but not seriously hurt. With the help of a passer-by Amélie picked her up and brought her back to the huge room where the rest of the family were waiting. The shock gave Fanny Munk the jolt she needed to carry on.

Life in the compound was not too terrible. A cook served meals three times a day. Each meal had a rota of three sittings. It was all paid for by the government. The Munks were served eggs cooked in a 'kosher' frying pan – a new pan which had not been used for anything else. On the Sunday afternoon of their futile attempt to see Rabbi Munk, they returned to find the entire compound being emptied. The refugees were taken on fifty huge trucks to different villages around Albi, where they were relocated. This had to be done every few days to enable more refugees from the north of France to be given initial hospitality in the compound. The Munk family was taken to Milhras, which had between fifty and sixty inhabitants. 'We arrived at about 6 p.m. and were disgorged from the truck on to the main square,' says Amélie. 'I remember clearly that in the middle of the square was a fountain, on my left was the local school, on my right a shopping parade, behind me was a very pretty little church and in front, the *Mairie*, or town hall.'

The inhabitants were mainly farmers who each had an attractive Gothic farmhouse and many acres of farmland. Each villager was expected to take in a refugee family and, as the evening progressed, the Mayor of Milhras assigned the refugees to their particular host family in the village. However, as 10 p.m. approached and the Munk family had not yet been placed in a home, Mme Munk once again grew agitated. She told her eldest daughter, 'You see, another anti-Semite! He places everybody in somebody's home and we will be the last ones left here and G-d only knows what will happen to us.'

Amélie tried her best to cheer her mother up. 'I kept on telling her, "You wait; because you are so charming and so lovely, the Mayor is going to keep us all for his own home." Maman didn't want to believe me; she was very tense because she had not been able to speak to Papa.' Amélie saw that her mother's faith which had imbued her own spirit seemed temporarily crushed, but, sure enough, the young girl's words proved prophetic. By 10 p.m., when they were alone in the square, the Mayor closed the main door of the town hall and turned to them. 'Well, Madame Munk,' he said, 'you and your family are coming home with me.'

Amélie was both relieved and touched to see how the Mayor took a particular liking to her mother and grandmother and the younger children, as he introduced them to his farmhouse, and recollects the event with considerable nostalgia: 'His wife turned out to be a very delightful woman; they had two children. By this time it was getting dark and he took us into this huge main room, which every French farmhouse has. There was a wonderful fire and a chimney and food on the table and then there was, of course, the question of *kashrut*, but for that particular evening there was no problem because we were served with eggs and potatoes and vegetables and fruit from the farm's trees.'

The couple even lent them their own bedroom, and gave them an antique washbowl and jug plus genuine farmhouse soap with fresh towels. The only problem was the toilet arrangements, which were virtually non-existent. They were obliged to go outside – 'anywhere in the grounds of the farmhouse' – and since Mme Munk was terrified of animals, eventually she had no choice but to ask Amélie to accompany her. 'First all the chickens came, then the cocks, and finally the little cats. It was ghastly,' recalls Amélie with some amusement. The next 'hurdle' was the extremely comfortable bed, a typically French antique with fresh linen and a huge eiderdown with wonderful feather pillows. 'It was really paradise on earth, but it was not made for anyone not really sporty. You had to climb into it by mounting a stool with two steps. Maman fell right into the bed and said, "I'll never get out of it again." I said, "Well, we'll worry about that tomorrow morning." I'll never forget this going in and out of bed. It was something wonderful to behold.'

The next day was very relaxed, away from any danger of Germans and bombs. The village was surrounded by huge cornfields. It was the first time that Amélie had ever seen artichokes – long fields of the high-stalked flowering vegetable – plus lettuces, tomatoes, green beans, runner beans and peas. Amélie surveyed the pastoral sight gleaming with its fruits of the land and felt this was the closest she had been to paradise.

In the few weeks of their stay, her nine-year-old sister, Ruth, developed a friendship with the farmer's son, who dared her to undertake all kinds of sports – climbing trees, playing football – that these city children had never experienced before. One day Ruth climbed the cherry tree, ate pounds of cherries which made her thirsty, drank a pint of water and soon developed a very high temperature. 'It was believed in those days that to drink water immediately after eating fresh fruit was dangerous. She was treated accordingly by the doctor, who was called in, and of course she recovered, but from then on I never gave my children water to drink after they had had fruit, even though this may be a bit of an old wives' tale.'

These idyllic weeks soon passed, however, and the edict came that the refugees would have to move on to the next village in order to make way for the next contingent of refugees. Thus the cycle of movement – from flight to refuge, refuge to flight – overtook them once again. Except that in the Munks' case it seemed that the Mayor had grown particularly attached to the family and did not move them out of the village, but merely requisitioned a very attractive cottage – 'a jewel of a house surrounded by fields', as Amélie recalls – owned by a woman who lived alone and bitterly resented being asked to leave her home and live with another family. The cottage was beautifully furnished and decorated, but lacked basic amenities. There was no oven, or even a kitchen, just a bathroom sink. Every morning Amélie had to get up and make a fire outside, using coal, charcoal and bellows, for cooking purposes; she also heated up a small pot of water for their early morning drink, and milk for the younger children.

'This was probably the closest that I ever got to live in a 'Fiddler on the Roof' type village, because just across the square from our little house was the bakery. So whenever my mother wanted to bake something, I would get the flour and the yeast from the shopping parade, and then I would take the dough into the bakery and fetch it again half an hour later. The bakers were very kind to me and often took our food into the oven to cook it for us.'

Every second day Amélie had to wash her baby sister's nappies, which had been improvised from odd bits of material scavenged by her mother. Washing them was no easy matter without sufficient water supply. She would kneel on the stones beside the river, using hard soap, grateful that this was summertime and grimly imagining what it must be like to have to do it in the winter.

They could pump water from the outside well and wash in the little sink, but there was never enough water to do the washing or to take baths. A bath was a luxury, as it was almost impossible to heat the water for a family of six. Unfortunately, baby Françoise developed a very bad nappy rash and the doctor at Milhras prescribed an ointment which was only available at a pharmacy some ten kilometres away. So once again Amélie had to cycle to the next town, which she visited every couple of weeks to renew the prescription.

Amélie has very fond memories of the months in Milhras in which she and her family became very close friends with the village people. It is really as though she has some atavistic yearning for the simple village life. She recalls only too vividly the chicken coup just behind their house and all the rabbits. 'You know, French people love rabbit meat, and I remember how we played with them. The only lady in the whole village who didn't like us was the one who was asked by the Mayor to move out of her home for us. She really wasn't very happy, but can you blame her?'

One afternoon when she and Ruth were hanging out the washing, Amélie suddenly saw her father appear in the middle of the chicken coup with the rabbits running around on the other side. 'I wish I had the words to describe our feelings of excitement when we saw Papa appearing out of nowhere, without any warning. He told us that he had tried to find us before. With the help of another soldier he had walked away from the camp only to be quickly recaptured.'

One week later, the rabbi had decided to do things properly and asked for official permission to leave the barracks and search for his family. France had lost the war in thirty-eight days and after the Armistice his services were no longer required. Rabbi Munk had anticipated a long journey from village to village in his quest for his family, but in fact Milhras was the first place he had reached. Discovering his family there owed more to divine guidance, in Amélie's view, than to chance or human inspiration.

They remained in Milhras until the approach of the Jewish High Holy Days in early October 1940, when Rabbi Munk decided that they should move on in search of a Jewish community, or at least an urban Jewish presence. Their destination was Toulouse, where the Jewish community officers eventually found them a third-floor apartment in town. The flat was light and modern with a balcony offering splendid city views, but it was devoid of furniture. It had two large rooms, one of which they divided into two. Grandmother Goldberger slept on a broken-down bed and the rest of the family slept on straw, which was renewed each Friday when Amélie and her brother, Jacki, brought fresh supplies from a local farmhouse.

While the family slept on straw, their parents went out to buy a double bed – a 'luxury beyond belief', as Amélie puts it. It was not intended for themselves, however, but was placed in the front room and rented out to other refugees in search of a temporary home. The rental enabled the Munks to buy food for the family. Within a week two tenants well-known to Rabbi Munk's family in Germany appeared: Dr Levy, a dentist, and Dr Joshua Breuer.

Amélie still retains a child-like and rather whimsical memory: 'I remember exactly what Dr Breuer looked like. He used to wear a French cap and a cape like Sherlock Holmes.'

The owner of the bistro downstairs loaned the Munk family a table and six chairs, which added a certain panache to the place – certainly more than most refugee homes possessed at the time.

In Toulouse Amélie shared the shopping and domestic chores with her mother, and rented a bicycle from neighbours on which to comb the local farmhouses around the city in search of food. Most of these responsibilities fell to her as the eldest child, and when she had no money left to rent a bicycle, she borrowed one instead. 'It was always an adventure to me. I was only upset when Maman, who had a heart of gold, used to give away the food in the evening to friends who came to visit. I would come home with a potato-sackful of food, and she felt she could not possibly say goodbye to her friends without offering a couple of potatoes or eggs, a cauliflower or tomatoes. Maman made a wonderful soup with the vegetables which she kept back, usually a cabbage, a couple of potatoes, onions and carrots, and then she would dilute the rest for the next day. That's how we lived and I used to get so upset about it.' Deep down Amélie admired her mother's selflessness. 'I knew she was doing the right thing, but emotionally I could not help saying, "Oh, we could have had such a wonderful meal!"'

Meanwhile, life as a refugee had played havoc with Amélie's education. At least in Toulouse, despite being busy with domestic chores during the daytime, she was able to attend school in the evening. She seems to have regarded her brother's more privileged educational opportunities with equanimity, and did not find it galling when ten-year-old Jacki, who could attend school, chose to play truant at the cinema with his friend instead. Rabbi Munk, acting on a tip-off from the school principal, elicited a confession at first through the use of gentle pressure and then with a slap around his son's face – again one of the rare times that Amélie saw her father use corporal punishment on any of his children.

The family stayed in Toulouse until just before the Jewish New Year of 1941. Elie Munk had heard rumours that Jews were about to be arrested all over France and taken to Germany. News filtered through that those arrested would be transported in cattle trucks. The rabbi, whose leadership qualities had already attracted an unofficial community around him, had the foresight to urge his fellow Jews to leave and hide in small villages around the city, which they did, some turning east and others west. It was time, too, for the itinerant Munk family to be on the move once again.

4 Escape from the Killing Fields

AMÉLIE AND her family headed west on foot towards Marseilles. They stopped at a small town, where they were accommodated in an old factory with other refugees. The following scene in the factory must have seemed as surreal as a Salvador Dali painting. In the huge hall filled with the sparsest of camp beds, a chicken was desperately darting around the foot of Rabbi Munk's bed, where it had been tethered with a long piece of string. Rabbi Munk had managed to buy the chicken somewhere between Toulouse and this forlorn little township. He wanted it for the ceremony of *Kapparah*, in which just before the Day of Atonement Jews spin a chicken around the head of every member of the family. The ritual, like that of the biblical scapegoat sent out into the desert and toppled over the edge of the rock, places man's sins on the head of the animal as a form of both penance and absolution. However Rabbi Munk had a phobia about touching any animal, so he would ask his wife to hold the bird's legs, then he would grasp her wrists and together they would turn the bird over the children's heads in fulfilment of this ancient ritual.

The rabbi's squeamishness had proved something of a problem in the past when women, concerned about some defect in the chicken they were about to cook, would bring it to his home before koshering it to enquire whether its particular imperfection – a broken bone, for instance – rendered it unkosher. As Amélie explains, 'There is a Jewish school of thought which holds that to eat blemished food could affect our individual character and our approach to life as well. Papa's job was to examine the chicken and decide whether, for instance, the broken bone was an old injury, whether the white stains on the intestines were mere pigmentation or something worse. It was part of his training to know exactly what constitutes a non-kosher and kosher animal.' However, because of his phobia, if the animal needed to be touched, he used to call in his wife. 'Maman didn't have to know much about it but, of course, she had so much experience that she knew as well as he did. But there is an important rule that rabbis' wives do not answer the question even if they know the answer, but merely offer to pass it on to their husbands.' So now Rabbi Munk glanced at the chicken running around his bed and could only hope that he would find a ritual slaughterer who could kill it quickly and humanely, according to Jewish ritual, so that it would feel no pain.

Cringe as he might at the thought of touching an animal himself, the rabbi was clearly no vegetarian; far from it. In fact, he would have had a spiritual answer to the ethical vegetarians and ecological puritans of today. In his book, *Ascent to Harmony*, he explains that for the first 1,656 years of creation, mankind had been restricted to a vegetarian diet, which, far from rendering him purer, had allowed him to become cruel, selfish and perverted. While the divine plan was for holiness to radiate down to the earth, the corruption of the animal world that occurred in Noah's generation blocked the path of this radiation. However, he adds, a new moral era came into being after the Flood. Quoting Rabbi Moses Ben Jacob Cordovero,* he explains that each element of creation continues to rise step by step:

> Rain falls on the earth and helps the seed to germinate and take root. The seed absorbs matter from the earth and transforms it into vegetable material as it grows into a plant. The plant is eaten by an animal thereby bringing it to a level of existence at which it can be

*The outstanding sixteenth-century kabbalist was a disciple of Joseph Caro and Solomon Alkabez and a teacher of Isaac Luria. He completed his first major systematic work, *Pardes Rimmonim*, by the age of twenty-seven and his doctrine is an attempt to construct a speculative kabbalistic system, bridging the mediaeval philosophies of thinkers like Maimonides with the transcendence of God. In his view, the world of divine emanation develops through a dual process: direct light emanating downward and the light reflected upward, the latter containing the origin of judgement (*din*). Cordovero taught that the transition from the world of emanation to the lower world is a continuous process.

converted to the animal life force, the physical soul. Ultimately, man eats the flesh of the animal. In becoming part of man's body, the animal is brought closer to the source of Light contained in man's spiritual soul. In this way the permission to eat meat is part of the universal uplifting of the elements of nature to the spiritual world.

For someone so dedicated to the integration of man's higher nature with the rhythms of spiritual life, the Nazi era must have seemed a particularly tragic waste of the potential for human growth. The fulfilment of Jewish custom and ritual, despite ever-increasing difficulties, was the way in which the rabbi and his family chose to meet this life-challenge.

The family remained in the factory compound for two or three days until after the Jewish High Holy Days. Their plan was to make for Marseilles, which had a Jewish community now boosted by the large numbers of refugees from all over Europe. Most of them hoped to remain in Marseilles for the remainder of the war; others intended to catch a boat, regardless of its destination, to America, Australia, or just out of Europe.

On arrival at Marseilles, swollen as it was with so many frightened people on the run, the Munk family did not feel particularly welcome. Fortunately, Rabbi Munk found the money to travel from Marseilles to Nice in the spring of 1941, where, once again, he had good friends who helped the family to rent an empty apartment at 6, Rue Lamartine, just off Boulevard de Boucharge. It was around the corner from a residence which the few Jewish families in Nice managed to rent as a modest community centre. They gathered there every morning and evening for prayers and lectures, and for small get-togethers.

Amélie recollects the cosiness and homeliness of this apartment – an oasis of friendship in the middle of the desert of war. With hindsight she believes that everywhere they stayed had this cosy feeling because of her parents' 'positive approach to life, whatever the circumstances'. Again it was a third-floor apartment with a dining-room on the right, which had two couches against the walls and which doubled as a bedroom. There was a table with chairs and, on the left, a modest sideboard in which Amélie's parents stored their underwear and anything they wanted to hide from the children. For instance, Mme Munk hid the goods she'd bought on the black market, such as sugar, but to no avail as she would frequently find them missing, or at least depleted, and would scold the children for taking them without her permission. It was only very much later that she discovered that the culprit had been her husband, who had failed to admit it, allowing the children to be reprimanded in his place. A telling account, perhaps, of the vicissitudes of great men, but certainly Amélie and the others seemed to have borne him no grudge for it and found it rather amusing.

The apartment was very cramped. For example, her parents and Jacki slept in a second-hand double bed in one room and baby Françoise slept in one of the two cribs left in another room, while Ruth and Amélie were together in the third room. At this point the family was joined by Mme Munk's sister, Etta Guggenheim, with her husband and their three children, Ruth, Hannah and Ralph, who had escaped from Holland and travelled throughout France down to Nice, where they had located the Munk family through the synagogue.

While all these events were taking place, Amélie's parents had been very busy trying to secure a US visa for Matthilda Goldberger, Amélie's maternal grandmother. Mrs Goldberger had already received an invitation from her elder daughter, Malie, and her husband, Alfred Grunberger, to join them in the United States. Finally the permit arrived, and a few months after the family settled in Nice, she caught a boat from Marseilles and crossed the Atlantic to join her children in Brooklyn, New York. A few weeks after that the Guggenheims, who were somewhat given to luxury, managed to rent an elegant apartment in a much more refined area of Nice, surrounded by a beautiful, miniature forest. It was in this apartment that Jacki was destined to celebrate his Barmitzvah reception in 1942.

While in Nice, Rabbi Munk was much occupied with giving private lectures, tutoring, organising religious seminars, and teaching individuals and groups. The seminars took place in the apartment because it was now against the law to hold large gatherings.

Amélie also remembers having to hunt for chickens several weeks before her brother's impending Barmitzvah. Her mother watched over them with great anxiety to make sure they would not be used for anything else. 'They were very precious, they were like gold,' says Amélie. 'I collected them over a number of weeks from different farmhouses around Nice and then I would bring them home. My father would take them to a ritual slaughterer and then Maman would cook them. They were very carefully stored on the windowsills in those days before fridges. Luckily it was December and relatively cold, although it never gets really cold along the Côte d'Azur.'

Although times were difficult, the South of France represented a certain lacuna in the fortunes of war for the Jews. France having surrendered to the Nazis, the South found itself divided up between Germany and Italy. Under Italian jurisdiction, the Jews were comparatively free there since the Italians had given no sign of any incipient anti-Semitism in France. It was only later, in 1943, when Mussolini capitulated, that the Germans occupied the whole of France and life for the Jews changed drastically.

5 Sun, Bread and Sawdust

UNDER ITALIAN control, the war for the Munk family meant a resurgence of social activity: many people had converged onto the South of France from all parts of Europe. Amélie, who had found it difficult to meet people of her own age, now rediscovered a small nucleus of friends from the Rue Cadet community in Paris with whom she began to work on behalf of other refugee children in Nice. This gave her the scope to develop her innate talent for leadership and organisation.

Although Hitler and Mussolini were working hand in glove, it did not take the Germans long to realise that the Italian administration of the South was a benign one. By the end of 1941 Vichy had made a deal with Nazi Germany to export at least seventy-five per cent of farm produce to Germany, so food restrictions were in place and ration cards appeared early in 1942. It fell to Amélie, as the eldest child, to join the food queues at 3 a.m., waiting up to six hours a day for something as simple yet as rare as egg powder – a great luxury at the time because of the shortage of eggs. The powder, which was made from the yolks, could then be used for ersatz omelettes or cakes.

As a family with four children the Munks were allocated extra ration cards, enabling them to sell some of their unneeded food on the black market every month. Friends would pay handsomely for the white mushrooms that were a favourite with Mme Munk, procured by Amélie after long hours of queuing, and the money would buy the family potatoes or bread and perhaps even the occasional cut of kosher meat. When Amélie visited the bakery, she discovered that the 'bread's' ingredients were sawdust and water, but the family subsisted on it over the next few months by a diet largely boosted by the Vitamin D which they derived from the sun's rays and the sea water. 'There wasn't a day when we didn't go swimming, the Côte d'Azur having absolute sunshine ten months out of the year', Amélie recalls. 'It was very important because it was the only recreation that we had.'

Amélie's description of these days contains the bitter-sweet sense of a dying era recollected in tranquillity as the dark clouds gathered. She describes the 'jolly days, the lack of parental supervision, the stony beaches of Nice – your feet got so hardened on these stones that they didn't really matter any more.' And perhaps this, too, is a child's metaphor for the violently changing times she was experiencing and to which she was becoming inured. Certainly something of the child adventurer remains in Amélie when she speaks of this period – lingering on the memories of the swimming, the fun of the make-believe, the beautiful gardens where she played for hours – until once again the Nazis took over and the terrible notices forbidding Jewish children and dogs returned to haunt her like a recurring bad dream, as they had done in Ansbach.

Still, those days lay ahead. Meanwhile, among the influx of young people to the South of France was a young girl called Lily Feiner. Lily had escaped from Belgium over the Pyrenees and both girls recognised in each other a similar sense of fun and adventure. They used to go out to collect things from the market or the dustbins, and then they would beg or borrow a bike on which to ride twice a week to any village between 15 and 30 kilometres from Nice. Sometimes they came back with a couple of cabbages and maybe a few precious potatoes. One incident which occurred on a farm, however, and is imprinted on Amélie's memory, was when she was chased and pushed to the ground by geese, which proceeded to walk all over her and bite her. 'I can still see myself falling on the floor and all the geese walking over me. I felt a terrible fear and I never thought I would come out alive. To this day I'm petrified of big birds.'

With their meagre pocket-money, the girls managed to buy what Amélie recalls as 'the most delicious ice-cream'. It did not take Lily long to recognise that Amélie seemed particularly immune to danger. This was reflected in the open life-style of the Munk family generally, who, Lily discovered, led a freer existence than anyone else.

Lily Feiner, now Borgenicht, who survived the war and now lives in north-west London, quickly saw that although Amélie was only a year older, she was the more sophisticated about life and relationships: 'Her mother really confided in her a lot more than other parents about personal issues which would have been absolutely unheard of in my family.'

As an only child, Lily's life was very different from Amélie's. Her mother was particularly house-proud and sometimes cringed at the mess made in her home by the Munks' younger children, although she could not help feeling great affection for the family. Lily also recalls how Amélie always looked after her siblings in a completely natural way, without making a chore of it. Rabbi Munk taught both the girls their Jewish studies in his own eclectic manner – a mixture of conversation and formality. He continued to do so even after Mussolini had capitulated and the whole country was under the Nazis' grip. The Jews went into hiding then, but not the Munk family, whom Lily remembers meeting in the street eating ice-cream. The ice-cream seems symbolic of their insouciance, their sang-froid, in the presence of real danger – or was it an unconscious belief that they were in some way protected? Elie Munk would probably shrug this off with a self-deprecating smile. But perhaps the answer has something to do with his robust approach to Judaism, in which the physical world, with all its joys and its hazards, is sublimated into a deeper awareness of intellectual, spiritual and aspirational values.

'Judaism', he was later to write, 'stimulates courage through its lesson of survival despite the suffering of countless hardships.' This attitude filtered into the fabric of the family itself. Lily noticed a very good relationship between Amélie's parents. 'The mother brought all the little spices and the priorities were right. When we ate, there was a big chicken on the table and everybody took a wing or something. We didn't waste time with formalities.'

When Mme Munk became pregnant again, she was so large that Amélie teased her, 'Maman, wouldn't it be funny if you had twins?', earning herself a slap. Her mother lamented, 'We haven't enough food as it is, and now that's all we need, to have twins!' Yet her daughter's jocular prophecy came to pass, and on 28 April 1942 Mme Munk went to hospital in a rickshaw and gave birth to the twins, Max and Miriam, that day. Miriam was so-named because, as she was born first, 'she was called the protector of her brother, just like Moses' sister who hid him in the bullrushes'. While others might have panicked at such a time, Lily remembers only the joy triggered by the twins' birth and Rabbi Munk's gratitude. 'G-d has given me a gift,' he said aloud in German.

It was while queuing for bread and mushrooms in the small hours of the morning that Amélie decided that she wanted to become an opera singer. She would belt out an aria from *Manon Lescaut* with total lack of inhibition. This boisterous aspect of her character enchanted her friend, Lily, even though she had reservations about the quality of Amélie's vocal gifts. 'I think it was wonderful that she wanted to be a diva, an entertainer, although I don't know whether she meant it seriously. Her voice was okay, yes, nothing special. A nice voice. I remember the pop songs, she remembers the opera. She used to sit on the windowsill singing a pop song about the Eiffel Tower. She might have fancied herself a diva, but she's not a prima donna.'

Amélie's parents did not crush her operatic hopes. Unlike other Orthodox families who might have stifled the desire at birth, they understood that Amélie would come to realise that a girl from her background could not expect a career in the Paris Opéra or New York's Metropolitan Opera House. Besides, the bare necessities of life at the time seemed to them far more urgent than the grandiose fantasies of an imaginative young girl. While the fantasies may have sustained her in difficult times, the children were generally immune to the fears that gripped their parents. While few of Amélie's friends would have been troubled by thoughts of imminent death, or even to have felt seriously threatened by the war, Lily found the Munk children to be even less aware of the danger because their family never went into hiding when the Nazis took over. When that happened, the Germans could not identify the Jews from the rest of the population because Southerners shared the same dark, Mediterranean appearance. Only the French themselves knew the difference, and collaborators were highly paid to disclose the whereabouts of French Jews in hiding. Many Jews, when arrested, went free if they gave in the names of five other Jews, Lily explains. This sowed tremendous suspicion and ferment within the community. However, it was not only the Jews who were arrested, but French Resistance fighters and other French nationals, too. The war had turned the French against themselves, often blurring the distinctions, confusing their sense of identity, as it had done for many Jews at the beginning of the war. Lily offers this sad paradox of their times: 'We were proud in ourselves to be Jewish but we were also ashamed of it. I went to school maybe more than Amélie did – she was busy with the family – but I would never admit I was Jewish. It was not the thing to be Jewish, even under the Italians, when things were good. Later on, we couldn't go to school anyway, because we were hidden.'

Because the Munk family were not in hiding, and perhaps also because of the particular power of their belief system, Amélie did not suffer this terrible psychological dilemma that so disturbed her friend. The Nazi race laws forced people to look deep into themselves for their own Jewish lineage since Hitler assessed them from up to three generations back.

When the Nazi law was passed forcing the Jews to wear the yellow star, very few actually did because it would have meant instant arrest. However, Jewish ownership of shops was banned: they passed to the hands of collaborators, forcing upon many people an awareness, often for the first time, that they were Jewish in Nazi eyes.

Although the French Resistance believed that the Allies would win, power remained in the hands of the collaborators. Stories, both bizarre and incredible, circulated among the members of the Resistance. In one newspaper kiosk a German stood over the collaborator who now managed it, watching him subtly identify Jews by the way in which he gave customers their change – the left side, say, for Jews, and the right for non-Jews – enabling many Jewish arrests to be made. The Resistance were told and they shot the collaborator the next day.

Thus the gradual decline towards the deportations and the death camps began. Back in 1940, people had already become reluctantly aware that Jews were being sent away to camps in

France and Germany, but could not cope with the ultimate truth. Stories about the building of gas chambers were ridiculed and their perpetrators derided. 'That was our downfall. We never really believed that it was happening,' said Lily.

Amélie had not yet experienced the side-effects of war: the betrayals, the ugliness, the weakness that surfaced in people under stress. But these were all happening in a France robbed of its national integrity and drowning in a sea of Fascism. And whether she was conscious of them or not, they contributed to an inner knowledge of life and its chances that a girl from her protected background might otherwise have never understood.

However, there were also stories of heroism and romance. When Lily's family were in hiding, they were brought food by the beautiful blonde mistress of a wealthy, older Jewish businessman. The girl was kind-hearted but somewhat jealous. Lily recalls her going through his pockets, certain that he had another lover, and finding a letter which she handed to the family. The letter was addressed to the Gestapo advising the Nazis to go to a place where they were certain to find Jews. Lily was sent by her father to warn the people in the house of the danger they faced, thereby saving fifteen or twenty people from the gas chambers, despite the obvious risk to her. Sadly the young girl whose jealousy had saved these Jewish lives became ill and died not long after. Lily's family, who had been hiding with a group of Jewish members of the Resistance, were arrested on 1 August 1944 and later liberated.

Sudden arrests, shootings, the constant fear of transports to the unknown – this was the climate in France which robbed people of their ability to create a personal happiness for themselves long after the war was over. Happiness to Lily, for example, is a collective one, such as the tumultuous joy of Liberation Day. Amélie, on the other hand, retains a grittier and more personal optimism.

Although Amélie's education during this period remained rudimentary, she studied French and maths with a non-Jewish friend, Raymonde, and the Bible, the Prophets and Jewish law with her father. Rabbi Munk was broadminded about the education of women and was happy to teach his daughters subjects that were generally regarded as the exclusive preserve of Orthodox males.

So Amélie did her chores and looked after the younger children, gleaning her education at the hands of her father as the biblical Ruth gleaned in the cornfields of Boaz. Rabbi Munk's rare wisdom and insight were already being noted by the younger people who visited the family. Jacqueline Lebrecht, *née* Klein, a friend of Amélie's younger sister, Ruth, remembers the rabbi as 'a very intelligent man. You could feel the intellectual within, but their home was a very wonderful and warm place.' The Munk family did not adopt the credo of the day: that children should be seen and not heard. 'They were so proud of their children and showed each one that he or she was special in their own way and their own personality.'

Rabbi Munk would fill his days reading, writing and teaching at home. 'He always had to apologise for having to be paid for teaching people,' says Amélie. 'This wasn't his way of doing things, but there was no choice because it was the only income he could have. You were not allowed a work permit even though you were French.' In addition to his teaching, he undertook the supervision of kosher food, which was, of course, by now an ever-diminishing commodity, and very difficult to import from other parts of France. Amélie was often taken for a young mother in the food queues, especially when she brought her toddler sister, Françoise, with her. To save embarrassing questions in the *haute bourgeois* culture of France at this time, Mme Munk bought her a curtain ring to wear on her wedding finger when she joined the queues. With her vivacious, upturned face and prismatic blue eyes, Amélie was beginning to develop a certain sophistication, a particular charm. People had started to notice her and flirt with her – 'a cleaner and more innocent form of flirting than we have today' – because, as we have noted, responsibilities had lent her a maturity beyond her years, although some of it she attributes to the high-wedged, wooden-soled shoes of the time.

Towards the end of 1942, Paul Klein, one of the main youth leaders of the new Yeshurun movement which had grown out of the younger nucleus of the Rue Cadet community, sent Amélie a postcard requesting permission to come to Nice to speak to her father on behalf of a young man who wanted to marry her. Amélie declined to meet him, arguing that she was only fourteen and that, if he put his request to her father, she would never be allowed to go to Yeshurun again. Klein ignored her protests, however, and asked her to meet him at the station on the day of his arrival. Amélie picked him up, but staunchly refused to bring him to her father, although she told him herself much later. Rabbi Munk was shocked that such a thing could even occur to the leadership of the youth movement, but very proud that Amélie had turned him down.

The emotional climate of these times was so strained and life itself seemed so precarious that it was not unusual for parents and youth leaders to encourage such young marriages when they believed that the couple concerned loved each other very much and wanted them to be able to live together, according to Jewish law. One very touching such 'Romeo and Juliet' story involving a marriage between Amélie's close friend, Edith, and her boyfriend, Jacob remains a powerful war metaphor in Amélie's mind. Both were aged fifteen and one week after their wedding they were arrested. Edith never saw her young husband again. She was sent to Auschwitz and nine months later gave birth to a baby boy, delivered in a forlorn stone corner of a tiny room by a midwife who had risked her life countless times to help pregnant women give birth in hiding. It was a very long and difficult labour, which utterly exhausted Edith. Moments before the child was born, the midwife asked her, 'Edith, just tell me what I should do with the baby after it is born. You know that if I let the baby live, there is every chance that once the Germans see you walking around with the baby, they will take you both into the crematorium. If, however, I do what I think I ought to do with the baby, then you might just have a chance to survive.'

The shock of these words proved too much for the young girl, who promptly fainted and thus avoided the agonising decision of whether to allow the nurse to give her child a lethal injection. When she revived, two SS men were standing in front of her with the baby in their hands. They taunted her: 'Look at this child, woman, it's a little baby boy, he's very healthy but this is the first and last time that you are going to see him.' They then held him upside down and smothered him. Edith survived and not long after that miraculously escaped from Auschwitz. She was able to rebuild her life, marry and start a new family. However, her terrible, yet significant, story was to haunt Amélie throughout her adult life.

6 Compassion and Collaboration

AS CHILDREN, living with danger did not dampen the young peoples' zest for life and adventure. Even when some of them were in hiding, they used to bake *matzos* on Passover and have a good time. They grew up with a clear awareness of fear, but without a political understanding. This meant that while the threat of sudden arrest and deportation was tangible, their child-like perception of events was rooted in the present. As Lily explains it, 'Today is Monday and we are alive, and tomorrow is Tuesday. When everybody is under the same circumstances, life goes on in a different way.'

After the Germans took over, the small Jewish community in Nice bribed the French police to give them prior warning of any forthcoming harassment. On 15 July 1942 Elie Munk was told that the first mass arrest of Jews – 800 people – would take place the following night. However, he was assured that any French-born French citizen would be protected. While others scurried to cellars and forests and even to beach cubicles, or were taken in by courageous neighbours, the Munk family stayed gamely in their home. Rabbi Munk was French-born with three French-born children – Françoise and the twins. What did they have to fear? Unfortunately, his confidence was ill-founded.

At 2 a.m. the following morning there was a knock at their door, and five menacing Nazis and one obvious collaborator in a French uniform came in to arrest the entire family. However, the French soldier saw Mme Munk with the twins, then aged between two and three months, and took pity on her. He begged the Nazi soldiers to allow him to find a telephone booth in the street in order

44

to ask his lieutenant at the police station whether he should take the mother and her babies and three-year-old Françoise, as well. Eventually, they were given permission to remain at home. Jacki was away at a youth camp in the Alps, but Rabbi Munk, Ruth and Amélie were all arrested.

Amélie recalls that 'the most poignant emotion was the terrible fear of what would happen to Mother and the children if she were alone without us. How could she possibly cope, we wondered. The pain and that fear were so deep that my father and I didn't talk about it, we just looked at each other and squeezed hands.' Amélie was also silently concerned about all the other Jews who were in hiding, wondering whether they, too, would be arrested. 'As we walked along at about 2 a.m., Ruth on one side of my father and I on the other, there was an eclipse of the moon, and all my father could do was to explain to us the wonders of the Almighty's nature and the colossal impact on the world of an eclipse – that was our first lesson in astronomy. That was all he spoke about, the wonders of G-d's nature and His creation. He was absolutely calm.'

The other lesson that Amélie learned on the way to the police station was about the vagaries of the human spirit. The French collaborator who accompanied them revealed that he had never phoned his senior officer at the police station; he had only pretended to do so in order to save Mme Munk and the babies, whom he could not bear to arrest. Amélie remembers his compassion on this bizarre journey and also the way he flirted with her. Her curiosity was aroused: here was a man who, despite being a collaborator and under orders, was willing to save lives and take risks in doing so, possibly many times even that very night. Amélie longed to see him again simply to thank him, but at the moment they arrived at the place where the 800 other Jews were held, he disappeared. Amélie was left with the uncomfortable speculation that he had joined his colleagues in making more arrests.

The Jews were herded into lorries and driven to a huge shoe factory outside Nice which the Nazis had requisitioned for the purpose of arresting as many Jews as they could get their hands on. It was a scorching hot day and all 800 people were assembled in the courtyard and called into the office alphabetically. So, it took until nearly 3 p.m. before the name Munk was called, during which time they had had absolutely nothing to eat or drink, despite the intense heat. They walked through a door into a small alley, turned left and were faced with a long table behind which five Nazi officers were sitting, requesting identification papers. Amélie notes that, 'As far as I was concerned, it was the very first time that I was made to feel a nobody, that some other person looked upon me as a moron, but I can't remember that I realised that it was because I was born Jewish. I did not really comprehend the enormity of the situation.'

It was not long before she did, however. After taking down every detail of her siblings, her address in Paris and her father's name, it was nine-year-old Ruth's turn. She was asked slightly different questions because they realised that she could not give all the answers they wanted. However, Elie Munk was subjected to a very long interrogation, which amounted to a psychological assault on a human being, 'designed to make him feel as if he were not a member of a family, a citizen of a country, [nor the] very proud link in the chain of the Jewish people'.

At the end of the interrogation, Rabbi Munk was told to say goodbye to his children, who were then free to go. Amélie made a terrible scene, screaming, crying, shouting and stamping her feet in a frenzy of protest. She adamantly refused to leave the building without her father. After a few moments, Rabbi Munk came towards her, took her in his arms and then, holding both his daughters' hands, walked to a corner of the police interrogation centre and stared long and hard into Amélie's eyes. 'Listen, Amélie,' he said. 'I want you to be very sensible. I want you to be very courageous. I want you to go home to Maman and tell her that I am fine and that I will be back within a matter of a day or so. I want to give you and Ruth a blessing and I am sure everything will be fine. So please, please listen to me and go as a good, quiet little daughter.'

Amélie didn't understand, but she knew that deep, penetrating look of her father and had no choice but to obey. It took three hours for the two young girls to walk home, accompanied by a social worker recruited in a rare mood of moral fastidiousness on the part of the Nazis.

Delighted as Mme Munk was to see the girls, her mind was obviously not at rest without her husband. She urged Amélie to visit all the hidden places she knew of in order to inform their friends – those who were lucky enough not to have been dis-covered – of the day's events. Amélie visited all the secret addresses she could find between 10 p.m. that night and 1 o'clock the follow-ing morning. She returned home physically and emotionally drained. She was just about to say her night prayers and go to bed when she sat up suddenly, absolutely certain that she had heard her father call her mother's name downstairs. She got up and told her mother, who, strained and tense from the day's experiences, urged her to go back to sleep and not disturb her. Amélie put the covers back over her, but within a few minutes she was sure that she had heard him again. This time Mme Munk herself had heard her name being called. They ran down three flights of stairs in their nightdresses to find Elie Munk standing outside in the street.

Rabbi Munk had a habit of never telling anyone of his recent experiences until a few weeks, months or often several years had passed. But within a couple of days he did tell his story to his family. It transpired that after their ordeal standing all day in the scorching courtyard and then facing interrogation, the Jews were herded into cages filled with straw for the night. Then a rumour was passed around that if anyone had a French connection, for instance an uncle or cousin or grandmother, they should write a little note to that effect with their own name on it. Rabbi Munk felt he had nothing to lose, so he wrote his note containing a prayer and his name: Elie Munk, born Paris 1900, cité de Trevise, Paris, father of three French-born children. He folded it and saw it taken along with all the 800 other notes to the Nazi officers. Rabbi Munk, who tried to relate this story with his utter conviction that he accepted everything the Almighty had sent him as a trial, a test of character, then lay down on his straw 'mattress', said his night prayer and fell asleep. Suddenly the light went on in his cage and he heard his name called out loudly, roughly.

Elie Munk's first drowsy thought after such a terrible day was, why did this man have to wake him up when he was so tired? Could he not have waited until the next morning? He was taken into the main hall, where, to his shock, he witnessed an orgy of drunkenness among the Nazi officers, who clearly felt that they had earned their pleasures after having triumphantly captured 800

Jews on the first night of the arrests. So while the Jews lay caged like animals for the night, the Nazis indulged in their excesses, impervious to the French national principle that it was not the done thing to get drunk during the war, even if the French could afford it in the first place.

In the midst of this Bacchanalian revelry sat the Nazi commander, grim-faced, jack-booted legs on the desk, a bottle of wine and a glass in his hands, and beside him, stuffed into a giant waste-paper basket, were hundreds of notes from the imprisoned Jews. The fatalist surrealism of the scene was not lost on the rabbi as he was brought before the Nazi to be told: 'Munk, you didn't have to have *three* French-born children, one would have been enough. Just go away, you dirty Jew, right now before I say one more word and change my mind.'

So Rabbi Munk left the compound and walked back home to his family. Apart from the Munks and two family friends, none of the other 800 Jews arrested that night was ever seen again.

One Monday morning a few months after this incident, the rabbi went to the synagogue around the corner from their apartment and met a young Jewish student, who told him that he had been arrested and taken to the SS headquarters the previous afternoon. He had been warned that if he continued to give religious seminars in his home, he would be reported by neighbours and sent to Germany. During the interrogation, the student noticed a file on the officer's desk bearing the name Munk. The officer left the room for a moment and the student, knowing he was risking his life, found the courage to open the file, which read that Rabbi and Madame Munk were to be deported on Wednesday morning to a camp in Germany.

That night Elie Munk again went out to the synagogue and did not return. Fanny felt convinced that the Germans had taken him away, as they had done so many others, and had a severe panic attack. She became extremely irritable and impatient with everyone around her and could not bear to be kissed or touched by anyone. 'I could see on her face how desperately she was tortured by her conviction that Papa had been arrested and would never come back,' says Amélie. At about 10 o'clock the next morning, the doorbell rang and little Françoise, then four years old, opened the door and came into the kitchen to tell her mother that there was a gentleman at the door. Fanny went out and immediately recognised the stranger as her husband.

Much later, when Rabbi Munk recounted the full story of what had happened to him, he remembered crying because his own daughter had not recognised him. '*Oh, ce que tu es moche!* [How ugly you are!]' the child had exclaimed. Amélie was deeply moved by his tears because it was the first time she had ever seen the father she so loved and respected cry, which proved to her that tears were not a sign of weakness but could denote strength of soul. What – the family wondered – had made the Nazis change their minds and open a file on the Munks after so recently releasing them? It transpired that they had been betrayed by the rather unpleasant woman who lived just beneath them and who used to knock on her ceiling at night with a broom when she was disturbed by the twins' cries. Relatively affable when the South was under Italian occupation, she turned nasty once the Germans took over and publicly offered the then princely sum of 5,000 francs to any family willing to give them the name of a Jewish family. She threatened to do just that if she suffered any more disturbed nights from baby Miriam, the more restless of the twins. Now she had proved to be as good as her word. She had betrayed her neighbours for 5,000 francs.

As a result of this news, Rabbi Munk had gone to the underground movement, the Maquis, who had given him a total change of appearance to render him virtually unrecognisable. It had cost him a great deal of money to be transformed into a street-sweeper whose face was scratched and bleeding, with torn trousers, a patched-up jacket with holes at the elbows, a typical French beret and filthy fingernails. One shoe was brown and the other black. Most significant of all, they had shaved off his beard. The metamorphosis from dignified rabbi to the poorest street-sweeper of them all was complete.

Elie Munk then sat down with his family and told them that the family's ration cards had been taken away by the Maquis and replaced with new ones bearing the name Martin instead of Munk. They had also taken away all passports and given him false identification papers, plus a certain sum of money to negotiate the trip from Nice to Geneva over the Swiss border. Rabbi Munk now handed his family their passports with the name Martin and gave instructions regarding their impending escape.

They pored over the map given to Elie by the Maquis and were shown the little farm near the Swiss border where they were to meet on Thursday night, 14 September 1943, having travelled separately by train from Nice to Geneva at 10 a.m. on the following day, Wednesday. Amélie was to take her sister, Ruth, and brother, Jacki. Rabbi Munk was to bring Françoise, and his wife and the twins. They left separately the next morning with almost no luggage, praying that their neighbour would not notice their departure.

The family reached the station and caught the train, but were immediately separated by the sheer volume of people who crowded on to it. Amélie was left to look after her brother and sister, who were eighteen months apart in age. The journey itself was a nightmare for Amélie – each incident more horrible than the one before. At one point a German who came in with a French Nazi officer asked Jacki to take off his trousers so that he could see whether he was circumcised. The poor child was far too young to desist and was about to comply when the German was called away to some other business, and the French soldier, who remained with them in the carriage, said, 'It's okay; forget about it.' It was an incident reminiscent of the goodwill shown by the other French collaborator who had earlier spared Fanny Munk and the twins from arrest.

In another incident, a Nazi officer took such a long time scrutinising their passports and ration cards bearing the surname Martin that the suspense became unbearable. Amélie knew this officer was playing a game of cat and mouse with them. Would he detain them or let them go? But then he glanced at Amélie, gave her a flirtatious wink and left the carriage. Amélie, fearing for her younger siblings, understood that she looked much older than her fifteen years and could easily attract men. 'I managed to cope with their flirtatious behaviour so long as they didn't touch me. I responded to that flirtation, which I always knew was for the best, as it ensured my survival.'

All this time the family remained apart. Their plan was to

pretend not to know each other if they met accidentally because there was nothing as dangerous as a full Jewish family together on a train. Elie Munk could not disguise the quintessential Jewish quality about him, even without his beard.

Amélie reached the farmhouse, where she met the others at about 11.15 p.m. There was nobody else there. Rabbi Munk could not believe that the Maquis had let them down. They waited until past midnight, but he did not feel confident enough to find the border with Switzerland without their help. This would have meant perilous hours spent in the forest trying to guess where it was. There seemed nothing else to do but to spend the night in the empty farmhouse praying that they would not be discovered. The next morning, Friday, they hitch-hiked separately to nearby Aix les Bains, a two-hour drive away, where they hoped to spend the Sabbath.

Elie Munk, to whom even at such times of danger the Sabbath was of paramount importance, suggested, as did all refugees during the war hoping to locate each other in strange places, 'We will meet in the main square of the city.' When they did so, Elie registered in the first hotel he could see – a place called Hôtel de la Paix. Immediately afterwards he took his son, Jacki, out for a walk in the hope of meeting a fellow Jew who would take them to a Friday night service. Amélie recalls here the enormous faith of her father – less of ritual commitment than of almost irrational belief in destiny – which would lead a man in such times to take his young son out into the dangerous streets in search of another Jew.

Rabbi Munk did indeed meet a close friend and member of his own Paris community. His faith acted as a magnetic field. But when he approached him with the question, 'Are you not Mr Klein from Paris?', the man ran away in terror. He clearly did not recognise the beardless rabbi and took him for a Frenchman or even a German with evil intent. Immediately Munk sent Jacki after him to reassure him of his identity, after which Klein turned around in tears, mortified that he had not recognized his own rabbi. 'Of course, you didn't recognise me,' was Elie's riposte. 'I am not meant to be recognised. But I *am* Rabbi Munk.' Klein stared at him and acknowledged the truth. He took them both to a friend's basement, where they celebrated the Sabbath eve. After the service everyone gathered around to ask where the rabbi and his family were staying. When he told them the Hôtel de la Paix, they turned white. The hotel, they said, was the Nazis' headquarters. Munk smiled at them and said calmly, 'Well, surely then this is the only place where the Nazis will not look out for a Jewish family!'

His wisdom was well-founded. Under their assumed name of Martin, nobody asked any questions at the hotel. The Nazi presence, however, was very high profile. Whatever kosher food the Munks had, they ate in their room. Meanwhile the tiny community found them another Maquis cell and again the Munk family had to pay, after which they were told to meet on the Sunday at the same farmhouse.

The time for the meeting was fixed for 11.30 p.m. The family once more made their way separately. Rabbi Munk told Amélie that an orphanage or children's home was located very near the farmhouse. She hitched a lift on a huge hay truck with Jacki and Ruth, and for a few moments the children were free to be what they were – children again with nothing more on their minds than climbing up the hay along the strings which secured it, and then sinking with great excitement down into the hay from the top. But when Amélie told the driver that her destination was the orphanage, he winked at her as if to say, 'Aha. I know better than that!' Amélie was petrified that he realised they were on the run and might betray them to the Nazis, but soon the driver resumed his cheerful flirtatious manner. In fact, he drove them not to the orphanage but straight to the farmhouse. He was clearly either a member of the Maquis or a sympathetic Frenchman, of whom, Amélie says gratefully, there were many who were unwilling to give up little children to their deaths.

When the family reunited once more, it was the day before Rosh Hashanah, the Jewish New Year of 1943. Every move during that day as they tried to reach Switzerland and safety felt like an eternity. Amélie could tell there was something not right just by looking at her father's face. Would they be let down again as they had been a few days earlier? After what was probably no longer than ten minutes after their time of rendezvous, the Maquis actually turned up. There were two huge men, known in Resistance parlance as *passeurs*, with a revolver each, and they instructed the family to follow them through the forest but without making a sound. If they turned round, it would be to tell them to lie down flat because they had heard a suspicious noise.

The burly Resistance men took the twins on their shoulders while the rabbi carried Françoise. Ruth walked with her mother just ahead of Amélie, who remembers every emotion she felt at that time. She describes the very crackle of the autumn leaves and the overwhelming smell of pine which arose from the forest – so redolent of her childhood in Ansbach. She walked on the right of her father with Jacki on his left. It was 11.45 p.m. Elie Munk held a little book of Psalms in his hand and they very quietly read them out aloud together.

This spiritual moment in the midst of danger was to prove for Amélie another link in a mystical chain binding Jews together over time. Many years later, she learned that a near-identical tiny black leather-bound book of Psalms lay in the breast pocket of Natan Sharansky in his moment of liberation as he walked from Soviet power in Siberia to the freedom of the West during the last days of captivity for Jewish refuseniks* in Russia. Responsive since her earliest days to a sense of mysticism shaping lives, Amélie came to believe that nothing could ever break the Jewish people because of the powerful links of this divine chain.

These ideas were still subliminal within the mind of the young girl conscious only of the tensions of escape. Many times on that journey into the forest, the family had to lie down flat on the ground because of suspicious noises. Suddenly the men from the Maquis put the twins down and told the family to remain where they were for a few moments. They were going to run on ahead to cut a hole in some barbed wire and then return.

'The times were such that you didn't trust anyone, you didn't even trust yourself. You were so frightened that you might say something wrong, or that you might make a gesture which could be misinterpreted by anyone who saw or heard you, that would

---

*Collective name popularised in the 1970s and 1980s for the Soviet-Jewish dissidents, many of them high-ranking intellectuals, who applied for exit visas to Israel. Most were unsuccessful and spent years in penury under the threat of constant danger, since persecutions, from job dismissal to labour camp sentences, followed their courageous expression of Jewish belief.

put you or anyone with you in danger. So when the men said they would return in a few moments, we didn't think we would ever see them again.' But the men were as good as their word. When they returned, they told them where the hole was which they had cut in the barbed wire. They then said, 'You will have to negotiate the hole one by one, and then you must roll or walk down a hill. When you come to the bottom of that hill, you will be free and out of danger. Switzerland and the Swiss citizens will take care of you.'

They then made the family search their pockets for any cash or valuables which they could take away: ration books, passports, even Mme Munk's wedding ring. 'I remember them asking my parents to open their mouths to see whether they had a gold filling. Had they had one, they would have tried to take it out. They took away whatever was portable. At that point each of us was wearing whatever we owned, one dress and then a layer of sweater and skirt and a couple of pairs of underwear. Then they also took away something which, a few moments later, would have turned out to be the most precious possession my parents would have owned, and that was a small matchbox. Finally they said, 'Okay, you're on your own, we're leaving you. You'll be safe in a few minutes.'

So alone once more the family found the hole that had been cut in the barbed wire. One after the other, the children squeezed their way through, tearing their clothes, of course, and getting scratched in the process, but not caring for anything except getting into Switzerland. Some of them rolled down the hill, some walked, but when they reached the bottom they found something which the men from the Maquis had failed to mention: a river.

Without the desperately needed matches, and despite the light from the moon, it was simply too dark for them to gauge the width and depth of the river. How would they possibly negotiate it? Neither Mme Munk nor the twins could swim. Fanny grew philosophical, putting her trust in the words of the Maquis. 'There's nothing to worry about,' she declared. Hadn't the men said that at the bottom of the hill they would be free? So whether there was a river there or not was irrelevant. Geographical issues did not concern her. She was quite convinced that they were free.

'My mother was a very wonderful, spur-of-the-moment person', says Amélie. 'A poet, in fact. She composed a poem in German and made up her own tune to it. It was full of the images of freedom, safety and the wonderful scent of flowers.' However, baby Max, normally the more placid of the thirteen-month-old twins, did not seem to take to the song because he began crying inconsolably. His mother tried to breastfeed him – which she was still doing because there was little enough to eat at the time – but Max would have none of it. They each took it in turns to walk him up and down, but the child continued screaming.

Amélie recalls that she looked at her father and suddenly she understood that they were experiencing the most dangerous moment of their lives. 'I saw him looking up the hill and then he lay down on the grass and I lay next to him. I always had this wonderful relationship with my father where we could under-stand each other without speaking.

'Now I lay in his arms and I felt that this was possibly the last moment of our lives. I suddenly saw a light some distance away and began to point this out to him when he put his hand over my mouth so that I shouldn't make any noise – as if that mattered at this point when Max was crying so desperately. The light went off and a moment later it went on again, and I could have sworn that the light was closer than before. It went on and off again, coming closer and closer. We had no idea what was happening. Maman didn't notice it and my father and I were petrified. I was petrified because just lying in his arms conveyed his fear to me.

'Then something very heavy fell on to us and a torchlight illuminated a uniform. A voice spoke to us: "I am a Swiss soldier. I heard that baby crying. I want you all to follow me." He picked up little Max and then, seeing his twin sister, put them both on to his shoulders. We all got up. We had no luggage. We had nothing to carry any more so it was easy. We followed him across the river, which turned out not to be so deep and wide as we thought, and then we found ourselves on the main road. None of us will ever forget the moment he turned to my father and said, "I am the father of seven children. I couldn't bear to hear the baby cry on the other side of the river, which is no-man's-land and where the Nazis come with their dogs on the dot of midnight. Had that baby not cried, I would not have asked permission from my Commander-in-Chief, a few hundred yards from here, to cross the river and, at the risk of my own life, pick up that baby who was crying so desperately. I had no idea that there was a whole family with that child. Never forget that you owe your lives to that little baby boy's crying. Had I not heard him, had I not had permission, had I not had the courage, as a father of a large family, to come over and pick up the baby, the Germans would have come at midnight with their dogs, which is now, and they would have found you all. So never forget that it is this child who saved your lives."'

Twelve years later, on the day of Max's Barmitzvah, any member of Elie Munk's synagogue in Rue Cadet in Paris before the outbreak of war would have understood the poignant message contained in the rabbi's address to his son from the pulpit – a rare Barmitzvah homage paid by a father to the child who had unwittingly saved his family's life. 'I am going to say thank you, Max, in the midst of those of us who have returned by the grace of G-d – and to thank Him for your having saved our lives that night at the Swiss border. Had it not been for you, neither your mother nor I, nor your brother and sisters would be here. But I want you to know, Max, that you didn't only save your parents' and your brother's and sisters' lives, you saved entire generations yet to come who will ensure the survival of the Jewish people and so many hundreds of children who have been born there in the heart of our families, and that's how we have been able – through one member of our family – to contribute to the survival of our people.'

As they accompanied the Swiss officer who led them into neutral territory, Amélie grew pensive, chewing over what he had said about baby Max. She turned to her father and asked him what she could do to commemorate their rescue for the rest of her life as a personal act of thanksgiving. Rabbi Munk suggested that, in accordance with custom upheld by some Jews, she might like to begin fasting on the day before Rosh Hashanah.

They walked on with their Swiss saviour for another one and a half hours into one of the reception camps designed and built by the Swiss all around their frontier lines in order to accommodate refugees from the war zone. At this camp, known as Val Fleuris, they were offered manna from heaven in the shape of croissants and hot cocoa, served by Swiss soldiers. Yet Amélie, who had not eaten for some thirty hours, had just made a promise to herself, her father and to G-d that she would fast for the rest of her life on the day preceding Rosh Hashanah.

The Swiss soldiers, however, did not take kindly to this rejection of their food and in their fury they began beating Amélie and her father. 'I remember one of them shouting at me, "Who do you think you are? You are only a refugee in my land and you will behave as long as you are here as we want you to behave. There is no such thing as not eating in our reception camps. After all, we received you out of the kindness of our hearts. We give you food and you refuse to eat it. That's just not on." I remember how he beat me and so I pretended. I just nibbled very slowly at the croissant and sipped the cocoa.' Mme Munk and the other children did, of course, partake of the croissants and cocoa, for only Amélie and her father had taken the oath.

After this they were taken to a larger reception camp just outside Geneva, one of several which had been prepared all around the Swiss borders with Italy, France, Germany, Austria and Romania. This one was called the Centre de la Croix.

7   *The Swiss Role*

AMÉLIE WAS soon to discover that although she and her family were safely in Swiss hands and no longer in physical danger, the attitude of the guards at the first reception camp revealed something of the true behaviour of the Swiss during the war. Despite her gratitude to the Swiss soldier, in the first few days of their life in Switzerland she felt that there was little to choose between the German and Swiss mentalities. Both she considered to be harsh and inhuman. 'It is well known that the Swiss work very hard to make money which is never spent. It is carefully collected, hidden under the mattress, but not spent. That is my view of the Swiss mentality.'

With hindsight of course, Amélie's jaundiced view of her saviours anticipated the bitter truth about Switzerland's role in laundering Nazi wealth and embezzling Jewish money during the Second World War. The discoveries of Nazi gold hordes, stolen from Jewish victims – gold rings and gold teeth ripped from the living as well as the dead – and melted down into gold bars later deposited in Swiss banks, calls into question the country's much vaunted neutrality during the war. Although some Nazi survivors set the figure being hoarded by Swiss banks as high as $7 billion in unclaimed assets, the Swiss Government at first dug its heels in and refused to pay compensation, which prompted the campaign more than fifty years after the war for the stolen gold and other financial assets to be returned to Jewish survivors or their families.

But years before the gold scandal broke, Amélie found disturbing evidence which already fuelled doubts as to Switzerland's neutral wartime status. On a visit to Grindelwald in Switzerland a few years ago, she saw a documentary film made during the war proving that the Swiss had already begun to build some concentration camps on their frontiers in compliance with requests from Nazi Germany. The film, she explains, makes quite clear that had the war continued, the Swiss would have responded to the Germans' demand to bring in Jews to be burned in Swiss crematoria. It has been admitted now that the Nazi death trains* passed through Swiss territory on the way to concentration camps and, at the dead of night, the Zurich Jewish community were asked to bring soup to the Jewish prisoners. The Swiss later rationalised that if they hadn't allowed the trains through, the passengers might have suffered more. But Amélie asserts that, in regard to such conduct, 'There is not much to choose between the cruelty of the Swiss persons involved and the cruelty of the Germans.'

Perhaps it is as well that the Munk family had no inkling of these facts at a time when they regarded the Swiss as their saviours. The Centre de la Croix – clearly one of those camps which would have been adapted to a Nazi regime in the event of a German invasion – proved extremely unpleasant. Grateful that their lives were not at risk, the family nevertheless found the treatment dished out not just to Jews, but to any refugee who had entered Switzerland illegally, punitive. Some, it is now known, were even returned to Nazi Germany at the frontiers.

Again, more than fifty years later, these grim facts have been acknowledged by Swiss President Arnold Koller, who admitted national culpability when he announced a £3 billion foundation for victims of catastrophes, including the Holocaust. 'People who stood at our frontiers in extreme need were faintheartedly sent to a certain death,' he said. Certainly many Jews escaping from the clutch of Nazism between 1938 and 1942 were less fortunate than the Munk family. The Swiss had asked the Germans to stamp the letter 'J' in Jewish passports to facilitate their recognition and deportation back to Nazi territory. While the Swiss accepted 17,000 Jews, some 40,000 from Germany and Austria were turned back at the border. The Swiss have confessed to 30,000 turned back as the war progressed.

*Despite recent documentary material testifying to the fact that these trains passed through Swiss territory on the way to Nazi death camps, Dr Rolf Bloch, president of the Swiss Humanitarian Fund for Holocaust Victims, claimed at a London conference on Nazi gold in 1997 that no evidence existed.

As Amélie says, 'It is on record that many people who escaped into Switzerland were treated so badly and became so low-spirited after what they had already suffered in the previous few years that they committed suicide, mostly by pushing their wrists through a pane of glass or scratching themselves long enough on the barbed wire until they bled to death.' Medical facilities at the Centre de la Croix and other camps were appalling, with a total lack of nursing staff.

The refugees' living quarters were huge rooms with straw on the floor on which some 100 men, women and children were compressed like sardines. The rooms were locked at night, which made going out to the toilet something of an ordeal. One night Amélie knocked at the door to be let out, but as she walked back the light in the hallway was suddenly switched off. In total darkness she found herself in the arms of a huge Swiss soldier, who seemed intent on raping her. In terror, Amélie managed to bite his left arm. The man yelled and let go of her, and she returned safely to her own 'bed' on the straw.

One day Rabbi Munk was suddenly taken away and the family kept in ignorance as to his whereabouts. Another family came in over the frontier from France to join them in their living quarters and were found to be full of head lice. A few soldiers thought it a brilliant idea to punish both sets of families by shaving their heads completely. The person most affected by this was, of course, the eldest daughter, Amélie herself. The others were either too young or lacking in sufficient vanity to care, and Mme Munk, more concerned about her husband's safety and whereabouts than her looks, could at least console herself with her *sheitel*,* but Amélie, at the delicate age of fifteen, struggled against the edict and tried vainly to prevent one last lock of hair from falling to the cruel scissors of the woman assigned to shave her tresses. Totally traumatised by her baldness, each day Amélie pestered a different girl in the camp to allow her to cut off some hair which lay under the back of her neck and would not be missed. Amélie tried to fasten this hair lock – one day it was blonde, another, brunette – to

*A wig worn in public by very Orthodox women, who do not wish to show their natural hair in deference to the Jewish customs relating to female modesty.

a piece of material, which she wound into a turban around her head. Unfortunately, however, the hair did not stick and kept falling into her soup, which, although barely edible and consisting of only potato peel and fish bones, was certainly better than starvation. These rations, plus a piece of bread just bigger than the fare dished out to concentration camp inmates, was their staple diet for breakfast, lunch and supper. Occasionally, a small amount of jam was put on the table. Hungry, angry at the violence done to her hair, desperately missing her father, Amélie tried to fight her unhappiness by recalling his profound advice, which was always to find a positive moment during life's downers.

'There's no such thing', Rabbi Munk used to tell her, 'as an entirely grim twenty-four hours. There is always a moment of cheer, of sunshine, and it is up to you never to go to sleep without first recalling the experiences of the last twenty waking hours you have had. You will invariably find during those hours, one moment at least when you didn't feel tearful, where you saw something positive, a ray of sunshine, even if it lasted only a split second. If you can capture that before you go to sleep, you will find your night easier and the next day easier to cope with.' The depth and love in those words had never had such meaning until now.

Meanwhile, the family's fears for Elie, of whom nothing had been heard for two days, increased. Their main concern was that he had been sent back into France as a punishment for having crossed illegally into Switzerland. Fortunately, he had been sent to another camp and was reunited with his family after two days.

Some three weeks later the Swiss authorities announced a deal with the American Joint Distribution Committee (referred to as 'The Joint') to finance Jewish families willing to take in a refugee child, by paying for upkeep and other expenses. Sadly, here Amélie discovered that her somewhat negative view of the Swiss people equally encompassed the Jewish community. Most volunteer families would only accept girls between the ages of eleven and fourteen, who were immediately consigned to work as maids and rarely permitted to eat with the family, even on Friday nights. This condescending pattern of behaviour occurred in families of every religious persuasion, from Orthodox to secular, as far as Amélie could ascertain from the experiences of nearly all the friends she had met at the camp. Here were very young girls separated from their families, made to do heavy, unpaid housework and left to eat alone in a strange kitchen on Friday night. And these were Jewish families! Very few of their host families even dreamed of slightly supplementing the income they received from the Joint to enable the girls to go to night school. Neither did the Joint suggest that these children should be used as unpaid labour

Amélie could not believe that Swiss Jews, and the religious community in particular, could show such little interest in the physical, spiritual and moral welfare of their own people in distress. She found Zurich Jews particularly intolerant. Yet here again Amélie herself was fortunate. The family who accepted her, Akiva and Salmi Krauz, a young couple with a baby who lived in Baden, near Zurich, were not only prepared to share their home with her as an equal, but on their first Friday night dinner together they surprised her with the gift of a pair of nylons which they had placed beneath her napkin. In return for her place in their home, paid for by the Joint, Amélie was expected to keep the house spotless and take care of the baby, although the heavy housework was done by a cleaner. Amélie was also allowed to go to evening classes to study maths, sewing, German, French and Italian. She was also lucky to live in beautiful surroundings: 'Baden is a small village like all these Swiss villages are – extremely clean, you could eat off the floor – very countrified. I remember wonderful gardens, greenery and, in the winter, snow all around the mountains in which Baden is so comfortably couched. I was taught to ski by the rabbi of Baden, whose classes I used to attend with other local Jewish teenagers.' Amélie noticed that the rabbi was extremely Orthodox and never shook hands with women, and it amused her to pretend to fall down while skiing just to see whether he would actually pick her up or not. 'He was a very lovely man and of course he helped anybody who fell whether they pretended to fall or not!'

While Mme Munk was nursing her twins, she discovered that she was pregnant again. The new baby girl, whom they named Judy, was born in a comfortable clinic in Chenes Bougeries, a Geneva suburb, on 8 May 1944. When the family visited her, they were given strawberries and cream – a luxury that was in total contrast to everything that had happened before. The Joint paid for Mme

Munk and the twins to be removed from the reception camp and sent to a home for mothers and young children, called La Pouponière. They also accommodated Jacki, now nearly fourteen, in a Montreux yeshiva (a centre of Torah learning) and Ruth in a children's home, while Françoise remained for a while with Rabbi Munk in the camp.

Thanks to the intervention of a very well-connected member of the Rue Cadet Synagogue in Paris, Maître Mathieu Muller, who had fled to Switzerland much earlier, Rabbi Munk was offered a position as chaplain to the thousands who crammed the refugee camps all around Geneva. For this he was paid a small salary – not by the Swiss authorities, but by the Joint – and given an apartment at 55, Route du Lausannes, where he was joined by his wife and the rest of the family. His duties consisted of visiting the camps every day in order to bring material and spiritual succour to the inmates until they, in their turn, were taken out by other institutions or families. Those unlucky enough to remain in the reception camps until the end of the war had a hard time, with minimal food and poor housing. The weather, too, was bitterly cold, and there was no heating and very little water. But those who were accepted by other organisations or families had a chance to travel to different cities in Switzerland and also once a year to visit a centre where they could pick a set of nearly new clothes for themselves and their families. The goods were sent to Switzerland by Jews in Britain, America and Australia through the Central British Fund (the British equivalent of the American Joint).

Once a week refugees had to present their residents' permits to their local police station and the day chosen for this was Saturday, which, naturally, caused problems for Orthodox Jews. Rabbi Munk would go to synagogue on Saturday morning and then, after lunch, put the permits into the lining of his hat, while his wife would do the same, or even conceal them under her wig, in order not to break the Sabbath injunction against carrying. Thus they would report to the police station as required.

Life in Geneva was pleasant enough. Rabbi Munk was able to give his evening classes in Jewish studies, which were very well attended. Amélie found a job as assistant nurse to a paediatric dentist a short walk away from home, and the children were at school. Although they had little money, Amélie and her friends spent their free time window shopping amid the beautiful and well-maintained shops of Geneva. She was now sixteen years old.

Among the refugees in Geneva was the Satmar Rebbe, who had lost his wife and many children in Auschwitz and had been rescued by an underground Zionist movement and hidden for many days in a baking oven. Having survived these experiences he came to live in Geneva at the same time as the Munk family and remarried a young woman, who was very clothes-conscious and could speak neither French nor Swiss-German, but only Yiddish. She often requested Amélie to join her at the shops in order to buy dresses. The Rebbe was helped in these material matters by a coterie of other Chassidim, who kept few rituals but devoted their lives to catering to all his physical needs. One of these benefactors was a very well-groomed Hungarian-Jewish refugee, with an elegant bearing and meticulously cut and polished nails.

This wealthy man, who similarly kept few of the Jewish laws but enjoyed taking care of the temporal needs of others who did, met Rabbi Munk at the home of the Chassidic Rebbe, took a liking to him and decided to extend his generosity to the Munk family. He sent them two chickens a week for the Sabbath as well as fish, chopped liver, *challot*,* soup and dessert. These provisions would arrive at their home on Thursday or Friday afternoon, given, as Amélie appreciates, in the best charitable nature of all, that of subtlety, because the elegant donor himself always kept a low profile and was rarely seen in their home.

Although it was accepted practice in Europe for rabbis to receive gifts of food from their congregants, for Amélie it was quite a new experience to find such generosity of spirit coming from a Jew who appeared all but assimilated. It opened her eyes. 'I accepted it easily because he was a benefactor and so well-received by the Rebbe, who was, of course, in my eyes a very great man, a very gentle and natural person with great warmth and care for people around him despite his extreme suffering during the war.'

*Plaited loaves served on the eve of the Sabbath.

8   *The Return*

WITH HITLER'S defeat at the hands of the Allies and the signing of the Armistice, the Munk family was at last able to go back to Paris. Having left the French capital in 1940 with four children, they now returned with seven. The festival of Rosh Hashanah, which had dawned on their great escape to Switzerland, now loomed again – a spiritual landmark of change and resurrection, which seemed to pursue them at the most significant moments of their lives.

After the devastation of the war, the Munk family returned to the city on 27 August 1945 accompanied by a straggle of survivors. 'It is very difficult to imagine the sensation of coming back to the home you had left a few years ago, after having gone through the most ghastly experiences,' says Amélie. Even the poor weather conditions seemed to reflect the general mood. For Rabbi Munk, the journey home was possibly the first opportunity he had to truly digest the full facts of his personal tragedy. A postcard from an inmate of Theresienstadt had reached him in 1942 informing him of the precise date of his father's death, enabling him and his brother, Felix, to say memorial prayers and light a *yartzheit* candle* for him on each anniversary. Of his stepmother's fate, nothing was ever known. However, God had once again smiled on the Family Munk as they found their apartment at No. 18, Rue Nôtre Dame de Lorette, totally intact – although not, alas, vacant. Ensconced in it was the Metzger family, refugees from Strasbourg, who had been given the apartment by the community elders on the Munks' departure. Although they had been forced to wear the yellow star, as did all French Jews from 1942 onwards, M. Metzger's job with

*A memorial candle lit on the anniversary of the death of a close family member.

the French Railway organisation had miraculously protected the family during the war. They were themselves strictly Orthodox and took great care of the apartment on the question of *kashrut*, but the question of cleanliness was another matter. Mrs Metzger was so anxious not to disturb any item the Munks had left behind that Mme Munk found the sock that she had been darning just before they had left home, with the needle and thread exactly as she had left it! Amélie recalls that, 'When we touched the drapes to close the curtains on the first floor, they collapsed because Mrs Metzger had been too worried to wash them in all the years since we had left. So the apartment, out of Mrs Metzger's fastidious respect, was in fact totally neglected.'

However, far worse than that was the Metzgers' refusal to vacate the apartment when the Munk family returned. This resulted in acrimonious scenes between the two families which were only resolved when M. Levy, the president of the community, offered his own home to the Munks for a few days, to give the Metzgers time to find another apartment. On the Munks' final return, the place was found to be crawling with huge beetles and – with the hideous irony of the times – an extermination firm had to be called in to gas the creatures.

As to the relationship between the Munks and the Metzgers, from such bitter beginnings a true friendship was born. After a new home was found, the two families instantly made peace, and there was hardly a Sabbath when the Metzgers did not visit. Amélie has remained good friends with two of their daughters to this day. As she points out, 'It was natural that after the terrible tensions of just trying to survive, situations arose in the immediate aftermath of the war that you couldn't handle. It took years for people to rediscover their natural understanding and tolerance for anybody else.' Even those who had remained in France during the war bore psychological and emotional scars since 'anybody who was walk-ing the streets with a yellow star was never one hundred per cent sure they were going to survive [from one day to another]'.

For Amélie and her siblings, the excitement and relief at return-ing home was overshadowed by fears that they would not be seeing most of their friends again. But this terrible fact had to be confronted. There was a gradual dawning on the community consciousness of the great Jewish devastation that Hitler had wrought. It involved a rehabilitation process that Amélie compares with the recuperation period after a serious operation: 'At first you are on a high because you have come out of it alive, but it is a totally natural thing for a human being to fall into an emotional depression after that high because the realities of rehabilitation are fraught with lots of pain, whether physical or emotional.'

Mme Munk, exhausted and particularly sensitive after having just given birth again, took things hardest. Her husband, despite the loss of his father and stepmother, was the calmer and more philosophical of the couple. 'She was a very much more excitable person than my father,' Amélie declares.

The aftermath of war was brought home very acutely, however, by a very likeable house-guest, a woman who had survived both Auschwitz and Birkenau. Unable to express the horrors she had seen in words, her ordeal came through most vividly at night, when she would scream endlessly with the agony of her unquenchable nightmares. As she slept in Amélie's room, it was Amélie herself who bore the worst brunt of this. 'She screamed in a language which I never quite understood, and I concluded that the words were made-up in her imagination. Yet I knew she was depicting the images and atrocities she had witnessed in the concentration camps. She wasn't always asleep. Often she was wide awake, sitting up in bed and screaming out all kind of things that she never remembered the next morning.' After a few weeks the woman obtained a visa in response to an invitation from her family in America, but, as Amélie was to discover, her nocturnal torment continued for the remaining forty years of her life.

These were the realities of survival. They had their inevitable influence on the character of an impressionable young girl with a burgeoning idealism. Soon afterwards the teenage Amélie joined a group of other young people who formed themselves into the Yeshurun youth movement, an equivalent of Ezra, the well-known Orthodox youth movement in Germany before the war. The group consisted of thirty-three boys and girls dedicated to the task of rehabilitating Holocaust survivors.

Every morning they would assemble at the various railway stations in Paris into which the trains were disgorging refugees from the concentration camps of Europe. Working alongside these young people were the Jewish Scouts movement and the Joint, whose work had so benefited the Munk family in Switzerland. With financial aid from the Joint, the Yeshurun would welcome those ingathered exiles from Nazi persecution who would arrive often so devastated that they could barely speak. The aid workers would then 'adopt' one, two or even three families each, and in a bizarre reversal of Nazi policy in France under Vichy, they would requisition the same reception centres into which arrested Jews had been flung by the Nazis and turn them into places of warmth and hospitality, offering the bewildered refugees shelter, food and clothing.

For Amélie, who had been involved in both processes, this was a poignant experience. 'Until this day it remains for me one of those amazing volte-faces of human nature, the fact that people can be so utterly cold on the one hand and, on the other, so wonderful and kind under totally different circumstances.'

After taking care of the refugees' immediate physical needs, Amélie and her young compatriots would then sit down with them and try to piece together their future. 'Many, of course, were so confused that we had to allow them a few days to ponder and reflect.' The next grim task was to try and establish whether or not there were any surviving relatives. 'In most cases, of course, we didn't find any, but we had to go through the motions of trying for their sake and also for our own, in the sense that we desperately needed to feel we could be of real emotional help to each other. This was an unbelievably painful experience, but at least you were doing something, so you could deal with the pain by helping them find their loved ones, or to get the necessary papers, passports, finance and travel documents once they had decided where they wanted to go.'

Through this catharsis, the young aid workers were able to deflect their trauma, but it was only a temporary measure. The shared pain of this ultimate misery of the Nazi legacy returned, as Amélie describes, much later when the work was over and there was more time to reflect. According to her friend Lily Borgenicht, many young refugees refused to trust the aid workers and went out at night to steal bread. 'They were the children of parents who never came back as well as those taken in by Catholics and baptised, some of whom were permanently lost to us. We asked them what they would do once they got to Palestine, and they all replied, "We're going to shoot, we're going to fight." They didn't know anything else.'

There was a particular poignancy in the involvement of young people like Amélie and Lily in the rehabilitation of this torn remnant of European Jewry. Amélie and her fellow Yeshurun members proved to be mature enough for this task because they had all gone through experiences during the war which equipped them emotionally to deal with it. 'Now that we were called upon to do very intensive practical work for the other survivors, we found we had learned things we would never have learned on a school bench. If you did survive you came out with capabilities that young people, at the ages of eleven to sixteen, or whatever, would not develop in normal ways.'

They were thus very aggressive in obtaining the refugees' requirements, whether it was lodgings, money for food, or documents and air tickets. The Joint supplied the finance, aided by the new French Government under General de Gaulle. It took some three years for German reparations money to come through for the survivors, negotiated with President Adenauer by the late Nahum Goldmann, the fiery and tenacious founder-president of the World Jewish Congress.

Amélie alludes to the false historical perspective in which the reparations deal has sometimes been seen, raising the issue of a questionable morality which may never be adequately resolved. 'I remember how, in discussions on this deal, which was a stroke of genius on the part of Nahum Goldmann, it was felt by some people that paying out enormous sums to the survivors gave Germany an opportunity to rehabilitate itself in the eyes of the world, which it did not really deserve to do. On the other hand, it would be fair to say that we, the Jewish people, could not have been able to raise that kind of money ourselves, and it has been a wonderful thing for the survivors to continue to receive, fifty years later, a monthly pension from Germany. Not that we have to say thank you for this because that was money owed to us, which the Germans had confiscated before and during the war years.' At a deeper and more philosophical level, it has been argued that the war reparations helped the Jews rehabilitate the Germans more than they helped the Germans rehabilitate the Jews. As the architect and broker of the reparations deal, Nahum Goldmann's skill and acumen on behalf of his people was, Amélie has always felt, 'nothing short of incredible'. She regards him as a leader of foresight and ability, who may have had his share of criticism but whose willingness to help his people she has always admired.

As to the attitude of the French Government towards the survivors, Amélie's cynicism is based on bitter memories of the Nazi puppet regime under Vichy, which so swiftly capitulated to Hitler. However, a contrite new government under de Gaulle proved itself anxious to make amends for the cruelty inflicted not only on the Jews, but on humanity itself by being caught up in the hypnotic dragnet of German Fascism. A new element entered the psyche of the returning Jews. Conflicting emotions sometimes made it difficult to look a Frenchman in the face. On the other hand, while disgust for the past was almost tangible, there was sheer joy in being able to resume normal contact with fellow citizens free of mortal fears. Amélie found that the French could not do enough for them and she recalls their kindness. 'There was nothing as exciting as speaking to non-Jewish people at that time, whether it was the concierge of the building in which you lived, or a woman you had just met at the market.'

In fact, Mme Munk would deliberately keep the household a bit short of food so that she had an excuse to go out and meet the stallholders. 'Of course, the French market traders are highly cultured in comparison to – dare I say so – the English or Americans, and they love discussing the latest play or opera production with you,' Amélie says, adding, 'I also enjoyed getting to know non-Jewish French people as I had not remembered them before the war.'

Not everybody, of course, shared this generous perception. Many Jews laid the responsibility for their fate squarely at the door of the French themselves. France deported 75,000 Jews to Nazi concentration camps during the war, and a pervasive bitterness defines the attitude of many French Jews today. One survivor, Sarah Yalibez, who campaigned for fifty-two years for permission to commemorate her murdered family with a marble plaque in the Marais district of Paris, makes a telling point: 'I never saw a single German uniform when they took us away on 1 May 1944.' According to the *Guardian* newspaper of 18 February 1997, the reluctant agreement after so many years to allow Mrs Yalibez her memorial – the only one of its kind in France – 'marks an unprecedented admission of guilt by the French authorities'. The guilt of collusion – or capitulation – is something which can be sensed in France to this very day and remains palpable, like a grim shadow, upon the city of Paris.

The spirit of adventure which had helped the child Amélie to cope with the reign of terror in France was now tempered by the needs of the refugee problems around her. The teenage Amélie involved in the hard struggle for rehabilitation was already beginning to sense a future role of service to the Jewish people. Yet there was a residual sadness. Amélie's war had spared her life and those of most of her family, but taken away her educational opportunities. *The Lord hath given and taken away*, she might have reasoned, but it was difficult for her to accept the denial of a further education to which she felt her quick natural intelligence and perspicacity would have entitled her.

Meanwhile, the Jewish community led by Rabbi Munk resumed something of its old vitality. The intellectual fervour and warmth that characterised Munk's spiritual leadership drew many to the Rue Cadet Synagogue, and in some way compensated for Amélie's educational needs. Jacqueline Lebrecht recalls the atmosphere in their home as particularly united: 'There was always amicable debate, but they never let things become an argument. Rabbi Munk was a diplomat *par excellence*. If he was worried about something, Fanny would light up the atmosphere with a joke, and vice versa. He had a marvellous sense of humour. I really learned to laugh there. They saw a joke in every situation.'

Friends recognised that Rabbi Munk's Orthodoxy was of the enlightened kind. He was neither stern nor rigid. Because his actions were informed by wisdom and intelligence, the children did not feel restricted in any way. They were encouraged to behave normally and integrate socially with Parisians of all backgrounds. There was a general feeling among those who knew them best that they had been saved for a special reason and that they should never forget it. Thus, although times were hard for the family and they were not very well paid and certainly lacked luxuries, they were considered warm, generous and welcoming. Friends were all part of the community and felt included in the family.

The traumatic birth of the Jewish state in 1948 caused something of a Moses syndrome for Amélie: she glimpsed the Promised Land but did not reach it herself. Family responsibilities as the eldest child always prevented her from taking the next boat out there to join her friends. She was the odd one out, since thirty-two of the thirty-three Yeshurun members married each other and emigrated to Israel. She describes herself as having married out – at least out of the group; she was the only one who went west instead of east. Nearly twenty years would pass before she saw the Promised Land just after the Six Day War of 1967. Yet images of Israel continued to flow through her consciousness in her romantic view of the state as the central base, the heart of the Jewish people.

9 *The Paris Match*

FIXATED ON her father who had groomed her for the life of a rabbi's daughter, Amélie had decided from the age of ten that she wanted to marry either a rabbi or a doctor. The yearning for education inspired her quest for someone who could lend her life a depth beyond marital fulfilment alone.

Although her father did not actually teach her rabbinics, she imbibed from him the practice and philosophy of domestic religious responsibility. This had to be balanced with her own view of herself as a romantic – something which could never be developed, she says, because of her deeply religious background. Thus she learned to dispense her emotions with care. 'I found that I could achieve a synthesis between feelings and their expression within the spirit of Jewish law. My siblings and I were allowed out because our parents felt that we were all deeply devout Jews and would always behave with morality. The emotions might have been stronger, but they never passed that threshold of anything physical.'

When speaking of love, Amélie repeatedly uses the term 'intellectually attracted'. This is what she says she experienced with one of her co-leaders of the Yeshurun movement, with whom she conducted summer or winter school in the Pyrenees. Once the younger members of the group were asleep, the two of them would stay up much of the night preparing their programme for the next day. And apart from the work itself, she admits, 'There was a spark, yes.' Within this collegiate environment the *coup de foudre* of real, passionate love eluded her, however. 'Although I had this warm intellectual relationship with a number of people, there was always something wonderful, and yet not quite right.'

In early 1948 Mme Munk flew to New York to visit her now ailing mother, who had left Nice six years before and caught the

73

last boat from Marseilles to join her other children in America. Among the many social engagements Fanny accepted from ex-members of the Rue Cadet community was a dinner invitation from the parents of a close childhood friend from before the war. Over dinner they described an outstanding young German-born rabbi currently in London, named Immanuel Jakobovits. The twenty-seven-year-old had already been appointed rabbi of London's Great Synagogue in Duke's Place, the leading British synagogue of the day and traditional seat of the Chief Rabbi, which had a history dating back to the eighteenth century. Destroyed by the Blitz of London in 1941, its communities decimated, it still retained a powerful aura of past glory which illuminated the reputation of its young spiritual leader. There was talk of his being made Chief Rabbi of Ireland.

The family mentioned his name in conjunction with the Munks' daughter, Ruth. They recalled her as a very pretty girl, but it was Amélie whose name now stirred in her mother's mind. On Fanny's return to Paris, she discussed the matter with her husband and they both proceeded to make enquiries in London. Rabbi Munk asked his first cousin and namesake, Rabbi Eli Munk, founding father of the Munk Synagogue in London's Golders Green, what he thought of the idea of inviting the young man over to Paris to meet Amélie. Uncle Eli, as Amélie knew him, had no children of his own and considerable affection for his cousin's family. It transpired that he had had the simultaneous thought and had intended to phone Elie in Paris suggesting that his cousin might like to invite the young rabbi over.

At the time Amélie was in Switzerland visiting her foster family, Mr and Mrs Krausz, who had rescued her from the reception camp and had now moved to Basel. Amélie had planned to stay on another few days in Switzerland to meet other friends. Meanwhile, Amélie's parents had secretly invited the young rabbi to Paris and phoned her with a request to cut short her visit and return home. Her father wisely avoided telling her why he wanted her back because he knew that, had he done so, she might have declined. The reason for this, as her father knew, was that while in Geneva Amélie had met a cousin of Immanuel's who had not particularly impressed her.

On her return, her father's weak excuse for asking her to come home early was that he thought she should be back in time for work the next day. Amélie grew suspicious. Rabbi Munk finally dropped his bombshell that he had brought Immanuel Jakobovits back from the synagogue and wanted her to show him the sights of Paris before he had to catch his train for Switzerland.

Amélie remained suspicious, but then she realised that she could bribe her father. She needed a handbag which she could not afford, and she thought to herself, 'If Papa comes forward with the money, then I'll show the sights of Paris to this young man. If he says no, then that settles it. I won't.' But to her great surprise, her father handed her the money. 'I thought, oh well, that's it; he's won, and then I saw Immanuel Jakobovits through a mirror. I hid myself behind a curtain. He wore a long fur coat belonging to his father and a big rabbinic hat. It wasn't quite my scene, but I had promised my father I would go and so I did.'

Despite Amélie's coy excuse about the handbag, her curiosity was aroused. This was pure gamesmanship. But a deeper truth persisted: Orthodox Jewish life implied that an arranged marriage was at least on the cards. The rest – all the fun and frivolity of youth – was just vanity. It could not disguise the fact that her choice in the question of marriage was limited. Was she actually happy to defer that choice to the father she so adored and respected? These were some of the questions in Amélie's mind as she sat down with the tall, awkward young man over breakfast. She had to balance her own desires with what she admits to have been 'blind confidence in my parents' judgement and particularly my father's instinct'.

Much later her father confided in her his own thoughts about Immanuel's suitability for her. He had felt from the beginning that Immanuel was the kind of person intellectually, and in spiritual and moral terms, whom he would want for his daughter. She, for her part, had always been attracted to people with great intellect, despite her own rather disarming confession that: 'It was audacity on my part because I had so little conventional education. But I had always preferred intellect – or life intelligence – to physical beauty alone.'

That first meeting of the young pair could not have taken place in a more romantic setting as they traversed the Champs Elysées and the majestic avenues of Paris. She tried to initiate him in the beauties of her city, but the language problem proved almost insurmountable: his mother tongue was German and hers, French. She relates the encounter with some confusion and a touch of coquettishness: 'I was somewhat in awe of trying to communicate without language, about how to behave with a man of twenty-seven who was about to become Chief Rabbi of a country. He was so young for this position, and on the other hand, of course, in comparison to my nineteen years he was a very mature man.' Yet there was a contradiction. Amélie was not 'attracted to him intellectually', as she explains, but admits to being 'overawed by his enormous, unique intellect'.

'He was way above the kind of person I had ever met or spoken to before on a one-to-one basis. So I concentrated very much on what I knew of Paris rather than on worrying about whether he understood my French or not. I had to make a choice. Was I going to make a fool of myself and pretend to reach his level of intellect and intelligence, which would have put me under very great pressure, or was I going to be myself?' She decided on the latter tactic. 'After all, I was the hostess, I was showing him my wonderful, beautiful Paris, my capital city, and therefore I was going to describe it in French.'

Amélie remembers one or two odd, 'rather cheeky' questions that he asked her in broken French and a little German. As they were crossing the bridge over the Seine, he offered her a cigarette and enquired whether she was a smoker. She declined, but wondered why a rabbi would offer a cigarette to a rabbi's daughter. Later, in reference to a law in the *Shulchan Aruch*,* which demands that things be done slightly differently on Shabbat, he asked whether she used a comb or a brush. He was clearly teasing her because Amélie well knew that the teaching insists that a comb should not be used because of the danger of pulling out one's hair. Amélie was somewhat annoyed by his line of questioning and his entire manner. 'Do I really have to answer that?' she said brusquely.

---

*Compiled by Joseph Caro *c.*1500, it literally means 'The Prepared Table' and is Caro's more comprehensible interpretation of Halacha, or Jewish law.

It was December and bitterly cold, but she took him up to the top of the Eiffel Tower, where very few ventured in such weather. What seemed to seal the young rabbi's fate was that as they gazed down on the turreted, French metropolis, Amélie overheard two teenagers remark on Immanuel's resemblance to Christ. 'I said to myself, oh no, that's it. Let me get him back to the station and get it over with!'

Immanuel's view of their first meeting is more chivalrous, tinged with the emotional restraint of his German-Jewish up-bringing: 'There was a great congruity of spirit. I felt a fascination meeting a girl of such evident qualities, and her personal charm and attraction made me think that maybe this is the sort of person that I envisaged. I found her very vivacious and youthful. She charmed me.' He also admits that 'The first thing that attracted me was the name – Amélie.'

The following Tuesday Amélie came down with the flu and went to bed with a very high fever. The next day her father entered her room and told her that her dear friend, Arlette Levy, had just got engaged to a 'very lovely young man'. Amélie didn't even bother asking who this man was. 'I simply said to my father, "You see, I told you Jakobovits didn't come to Paris to see your daughter. He came to get himself engaged to Arlette." I knew that Arlette had been an au-pair girl for a few weeks in the Jakobovits' household in London. I wasn't thinking straight because of the high fever I had and because of a small but very strong pinch of pain in my heart when I heard that Jakobovits had got engaged to another girl. I don't know whether it was jealousy or pride, but it did hurt. So on Wednesday I had a fever and the flu and a heartache and on Thursday I had a high temperature and the flu and the heartache. I was so sorry for myself that when anybody asked me how I felt, I said lousy, absolutely lousy, and while I was only referring to the flu, the truth of the matter was that I suddenly realised that Jakobovits did something to me after all. Maybe it was the overwhelming feeling that someone of that particular calibre, who had achieved so much at such a young age, had taken notice of me. Yes, I had to admit in spite of myself that Jakobovits had a tremendous attraction for me, and a spark of that realisation came to me when my father, who was also a brilliant psychologist, put me through this test.'

By Friday lunchtime, when she felt a little better, her father said to her: 'By the way, you didn't ask me who Arlette is engaged to.'

'No, because I know it's Rabbi Jakobovits,' Amélie replied.

'No, not at all,' said Rabbi Munk. 'It's another member of our community she's engaged to, nothing whatever to do with Rabbi Jakobovits.' The two looked at each other and Elie read his daughter's face. Her relief was tangible. Neither raised the issue again.

A week later Amélie received a postcard from Immanuel in Switzerland, asking whether he could visit her again on the way back to London. 'I can't tell you how much my heart jumped for joy and I just looked at my parents and said, "Would you believe it?" They knew by then what was going on with my emotions.'

Immanuel then phoned the Munks directly and told them that he was returning to London via Paris again, but this time with his sister, Lotti, and her husband, Fabian Schonfeld. So exactly two weeks after his first visit, at the end of December 1948, the Munks invited the three for a light supper on Sunday night. Amélie can remember Lotti staring at her all evening.

'The whole scene was really very funny. Papa was very nervous and kept excusing himself and going out to telephone someone every few minutes. Maman was stuttering from pure nerves. I mean this was the eldest daughter and this was the first time something serious was really happening. I didn't open my mouth because I was uncomfortable seeing that Lotti was staring at me all the time, and I was just taken aback myself, having had no intention, ten days ago, of giving the whole event any credibility whatsoever.'

The family left after a rather tense couple of hours, and the Munks could not resist peeping through the window to the large courtyard in order to see the reactions of their departing guests. Lotti's husband was looking at Immanuel with a huge smile on his face.

Within a few days Amélie's parents received a phone call from Rabbi Jakobovits' mother in London, thanking them for the hospitality they had extended to her son, and later her daughter and son-in-law. The next letter Amélie was to receive from Immanuel had an Irish stamp on it. He had now been appointed

Chief Rabbi-elect of Ireland. Thus began his steady courtship-by-correspondence with her. They wrote to each other in a polyglot of German and Hebrew, and what could best be described as the stilted argot of tentative love.

In February 1949 Immanuel took up office as Chief Rabbi of Ireland and invited Amélie to come over as his guest at the induction ceremony, which was to be a very impressive, regal affair. This was the first such Irish appointment for thirteen years since Chief Rabbi Isaac Herzog retired from that position in order to take up his new appointment as Chief Rabbi of Palestine. However, thirteen years had elapsed between his retirement from the one post and his taking up of the other. Amélie recalls with amusement how she and her father pored over the map to try and locate the Emerald Isle which, Rabbi Munk pondered, must be a tiny gem 'somewhere behind England'. They had both barely heard of the place and it took a while to find it.

Yet Amélie received the invitation with mixed feelings. If she attended the induction ceremony, in what role would she be seen? Immanuel had not proposed to her, so she could not be introduced as his fiancée. Nor did she wish to be simply the cousin from Paris, so who would she be? She decided to decline the invitation and, with hindsight, realised that it was the wisest move she could make.

10   The Mother-in-Law Elect

ALTHOUGH AMÉLIE did not attend Jakobovits' 1949 induction in Dublin, the correspondence between them continued. She was visiting her ailing maternal aunt, Ruth Kohn, wife of the principal of the famous Gateshead Seminary for Girls,* where her younger sister was studying. The Kohns and their young family lived in Cambridge Terrace across a typically English village park accessible to the locals by a key. While she stayed with the family, Amélie crossed the park three times a week to study English with a little old lady who lived in a house with dozens of cats. Although Amélie found it difficult to get used to this early manifestation of the British obsession with animals, the study of English was to prove timely.

Suddenly Jakobovits' mother decided to come over and visit her younger son, Solomon, a student at Gateshead Yeshiva, from her new abode in Dublin, where she was making a home for her bachelor son. Now that Aunt Ruth was on the road to recovery, the Kohns organised a lunch party for her. The planning of this event had all the mannered drama of a Jane Austen novel. Expensive and interminable telephone calls blocked the airwaves between Gateshead and Paris because Adolf Kohn refused to make any move without the Munks' consent. Everything was discussed

---

*The Gateshead Seminary for Girls was founded in 1945 by Ruth and Adolf Kohn. It began with one pupil and swelled to 400 over the next five decades, during which time Kohn and his partners on the faculty bought up five houses on Bewick Road, Gateshead, which now comprises the campus. It has a transitional community of some 40–50 families, who move on to Israel and other parts of Britain and the West, largely to teach.

and decided between them: what Amélie should wear, what her hair should look like, what the meal should consist of. Amélie found these protracted negotiations quite incredible and highly amusing.

She wore her favourite navy-and-white dress and had her long brown hair trimmed and drawn off her face with a hair-band. Food was still rationed and Mrs Kohn wanted to serve eggs, so young Ruth, Amélie's sister, was sent out to buy them, but in her excitement she dropped them all on the floor. Mrs Kohn became very nervous and tense and spent hours just walking around the kitchen table followed by Amélie.

Before they sat down, Kohn decided to have a private meeting with Mrs Jakobovits to assure her that if anything developed positively between Amélie and her son, she would be a very lucky woman indeed.

'I remember my aunt coming out of the kitchen and listening through the keyhole of the room where her husband was conferring with Mrs Jakobovits. She ran back and to the kitchen and said, "Do you know what she asked him? She asked whether you can play an instrument. Do you play the piano, Amélie?"

'"Oh yes," I pretended. "Of course I play the piano." "Oh good," my aunt replied, "because he told her not only do you play the piano, but you're an excellent pianist. What about her son? But she didn't answer that question!"'

Amélie's first impression of Mrs Jakobovits was of a distinguished lady with an air of the *châtelaine*. 'She wore a little black hat and a tight black coat with an old-fashioned rabbit fur collar hanging down. It wasn't fashionable, although nothing was really fashionable after the war, you just wore what you had salvaged. She certainly wasn't a lady who would go by fashion anyway. She was very formal and quite lady-like with an elegant carriage. She was very German, highly cultured, thin, pale and impeccable. She spoke to my aunt and uncle in German.'

They all sat down to a comparatively lavish lunch by the standards of the day, but Amélie had already been warned by her uncle not to ask for a second helping because it would make a very bad impression. So every time more food was passed around the table, Amélie and the younger people pinched each others' knees under the table to make sure they wouldn't burst out laughing. Amélie, determined to puncture the high ceremony of the occasion, teased her uncle by asking for a second helping of soup, despite the severity of his gaze.

The conversation around the table concerned the post-war situation, the growth of the Jewish community in Gateshead-on-Tyne and particularly in Dublin, and the excitement Immanuel's mother felt at her son's appointment as Ireland's Chief Rabbi. Throughout the meal Amélie felt Mrs Jakobovits' eyes assessing her as she attempted to engage her in conversation. Amélie understood more German than she could speak and was astute enough to realise that Immanuel's mother was testing her out as far as she could, given the girl's faltering speech.

Although Amélie's mischievous spirit loved a discreet dig at people who took themselves too seriously, she perceived something in the gaunt, frail lady which aroused her compassion. She could sense the suffering she had endured both in Germany and during her long widowhood, when she had had to bear the responsibility for raising her family alone. She was also prepared to like her.

Yet, as Chaim Bermant observes in his authorised biography, *Lord Jakobovits*, Mrs Jakobovits' first impression of Amélie was that she 'seemed a bit too lively and unrestrained for the wife of a rabbi and especially a Chief Rabbi'. As they became better acquainted, this view was confirmed. Bermant enlarges on Mrs Jakobovits' perspective: 'She [Amélie] showed her feelings. If gloomy, she looked glum; if upset, she could be tearful; and if happy or amused – as she often was – she could be convulsed, and would convulse others, with laughter. When she talked, she spoke rapidly and with great animation.'

In a letter written by Mrs Jakobovits to her sister, Erna, shortly after her first meeting with Amélie, she wrote: 'I have met Amélie Munk, in whom Immanuel seems to be more than interested. She seems to be a very nice person, but she'll never make a lady.'

After lunch Amélie dutifully saw Mrs Jakobovits off to the station at Newcastle, from where she took a train to London to visit her other children. After her departure Amélie went back by bus to Gateshead with a smile of relief, hoping that she had behaved in accordance with her uncle's wishes. She shrugged off the incident as another 'lovely little chapter in my life's saga'. But later that evening the whole family expressed their relief that everything had gone according to plan and had a good giggle when they compared their rather relaxed way of life with the rectitude of Mrs Jakobovits.

'She brought in an atmosphere of strict propriety, correctness, heavy social behaviour, and we, on the other hand, were all so very light-hearted,' Amélie observes. 'She didn't appear to have much sense of humour either, in contrast to my own mother, who felt that the most important thing in life was to have *joie de vivre* and always see the positive side in everything.'

11 Under the Veil

AMÉLIE'S ENGLISH was improving through her lessons with the cat-lady, which helped in her correspondence with Immanuel. Their relationship tentatively unfolded through these letters, still conducted mostly in Hebrew and now some basic English, which revealed their views on subjects such as Jewish ritual and their personal philosophies gleaned through the war. Although he lacked her traumatic and vivid war history, he had his own tale to tell: he had been interned with his father and brothers on the Isle of Man as an enemy alien in June 1940, just after the fall of France. He had narrowly missed being killed one Saturday morning by a huge bomb which destroyed Woolworth's close to the New Cross Synagogue, of which he was rabbi.

He also disclosed his feelings through descriptions of his personal history. Jakobovits had come to Britain from Germany in 1936 at the age of sixteen and was joined two years later by the rest of the family just after *Kristallnacht*. Immanuel, like Amélie, was the eldest of seven children and had started life in Britain as a pupil of a famous school for refugee children run by the late Dr Judy Grunfeld before accepting his first position as reverend of the Brondesbury Synagogue at the age of twenty. From then on, despite what was often regarded as his somewhat stilted, old-young personality, his star was on the ascendant.

In their letters, in which they formally addressed each other as Rabbi Jakobovits and Miss Munk, they disclosed their emotions on having to leave their cities: the Paris of her early adoption, the Berlin of his birth. He also discussed his early dreams concerning his new position in the near 6,000-strong community in Ireland, and the challenges that lay ahead.

Amélie was to discover later that the condition of acceptance to his new post was that he had to get married as soon as possible. She continued to be gratified by his attentions and his phone calls twice a month, but despite the flutterings of delirium during her attack of the flu, she now brushed aside any early thoughts of marriage. It was as though she had not yet made the intellectual distinction between being awe-struck and love-sick, but was prepared to enjoy the dilemma anyway.

One innocent phrase is quite revealing of her state of mind: 'I remember well – although I was sure that I was not emotionally involved – my heart missing a beat because the Chief Rabbi of Ireland telephoned me.' He, for his part, had decided after their second meeting that she was the woman for him.

The following March he told her that he planned a trip to Manchester for the induction of Dayan Weiss as head of the Manchester Beth Din, and she accepted his offer to meet him there, accompanied by her ever-present uncle, who refused to allow her to travel from Gateshead alone. They were due to stay in the South Manchester home of Amélie's distant relatives, Rabbi Felix Carlebach and his wife, Babette. Amélie set out calmly enough, pleased that for the first time in months her adventurous spirit was about to be gratified with some action. In her mind, as she mulled over the forthcoming meeting, was her father's affectionate description of her as a *femme à sensation*. Life had recently run a fairly predictable course and was very different from the drama of the war years. Now a hint of excitement was in the air.

In an echo of his sartorial interest on the eve of Mrs Jakobovits' visit, Mr Kohn re-introduced the subject of what his niece would wear, as they sat down to breakfast on the morning of their departure. Far from being offended, or feeling invaded, Amélie found it all highly entertaining. She loved the way her rather charismatic uncle took control of everything, perhaps because it reinforced the sense of detached anticipation with which she had decided to view the whole enterprise of her formal meeting with Ireland's Chief Rabbi. Again he chose the outfit. He selected a navy dress with a white border and, of course, the obligatory long sleeves. He then decided that she must wear a hat. It had never occurred to Amélie before to wear a hat, but Kohn insisted that his wife take her to nearby Newcastle and buy one. Amélie lightheartedly accepted: 'I was having such fun I wasn't going to argue with him. Suddenly, for the first time in my life, I was going to buy a hat when I couldn't even afford one. I didn't even ask who was going to pay for the hat!'

They bought her a very fashionable navy beret with a jaunty feather, and on their return Kohn demanded a dress rehearsal. So, with the practised eye of a provincial Karl Lagerfeld, Kohn studied her carefully from all angles. Something was missing, he decided. The hat wasn't good enough. It needed a veil. So his long-suffering wife was sent back to Newcastle via two buses in the intense cold of a northern British winter to buy a veil, which Amélie was prepared to attach to the hat herself. But no, her fastidious uncle did not trust her to sew it on correctly. So back to the shop again went Aunt Ruth with the hat and the veil and a request to the shop's sales' staff to sew it on.

Amélie was fascinated by the fact that her uncle, the head of a girls' seminary and dedicated to their spiritual and mental development, should also be such a connoisseur of beauty and elegance. Kohn himself always looked immaculate as though he had just stepped out of a fashion magazine. He was very concerned that the girls, whether his children, his nieces or his students, always looked their best. If one of the girls had a stain on her dress, Kohn had been known to call her into the office and discreetly inform her. Amélie recalls him as a gentle, generous person blessed with a great understanding of people and a rare insight into a woman's mind. Kohn clearly liked the idea of nurturing the outer as well as the inner person and was as punctilious about perfection in the home as he was about personal grooming. He was often found tidying the house or straightening a picture on the wall.

Conversely, his wife Ruth had enjoyed all the wealth and privilege of the Goldberger textile heritage in Nuremberg and yet had remained disinterested in material possessions or appearances. Thus Ruth was quite content to begin her married life in a tiny, terraced house from where the couple launched the Gateshead Seminary, attended by Amélie's four younger sisters.

Meanwhile, in Manchester Amélie was dressed immaculately in her navy dress and her chic, veiled hat with the feather, for tea with the Carlebachs, where Jakobovits was due to arrive. The Chief

Rabbi of Ireland turned up looking very elegant in a huge black hat, a long coat and a white scarf. Suddenly the Kohns and the Carlebachs excused themselves and left the young couple alone. Although it was pouring with rain, Jakobovits, armed with a large umbrella, invited Amélie to go for a walk. They walked in the park for two and a half hours. Amélie remembers saying nothing at all; he did not ask her anything, but spoke at length about how he viewed himself. 'He wanted me to understand that he was a man with enormous self-control, who never flinches, and he also discussed all the negative parts of himself he felt it important for me to know.'

Amélie, whose sharp mind and impatient spirit were not designed for tortuous confessionals, does not remember much more than 'this long walk, this monologue about himself and the terrible, terrible rain, with this huge black umbrella protecting us, and then eventually, thank G-d, we got back to the house and had a nice cup of coffee. I remember there was a huge piano – Rabbi Carlebach was a first-class pianist, who played regularly at the Hallé Concert Hall in Manchester – when suddenly Immanuel turned to me and said, "Now what do we do?"

'So I said to him in my very broken English, "Well, man proposes and I will dispose." I was so proud that I remembered that line so well. But he couldn't actually get himself to propose and he just said to me, "Well, should we call our parents to say *Mazeltov*?" I took some time over it and didn't answer right away and then I said, "I think I'll call *my* parents first." So I phoned them in Paris and said, "I think I'm going to marry Chief Rabbi Jakobovits," and he looked at me with very big eyes, clearly very delighted. This was as romantic as he could be at this point. I found nearly everything in him at that time, the only thing I didn't find was romance. However, romance did come later.'

They had met only three times.

If Amélie was disappointed in the lack of sentiment at the romantic pinnacle of her life, she was compensated by the overpowering sense of trust she felt given to her by someone whom she admired so intensely. She was also gratified by the knowledge that he had found in her someone he believed equal to himself and able to share the challenges of his future life. 'I think he had more confidence in me than I had in myself. I know that what attracted me most at that time was his wonderful bearing, his sincerity, his perceptive, striking blue eyes, analytical eyes.' Years later she would try to recapture her first physical impressions, which were somewhat more vague – studying his profile, 'trying to figure out what his chin was like under his beard', and deciding that she liked the beard because it 'lengthened his handsome face'.

Immanuel gave Amélie the feeling of immense security in himself and hence would be able, she believed, 'to take care of me and give me that rock of security and stability. I already felt then that he was a man of enormous courage.'

However, the lack of romance jarred. Amélie felt a little sorry for herself because, as a Frenchwoman in particular, she had imagined people only married for this reason. Yet as she considered the question more deeply she began to see a reflection of her situation in the Biblical story of Jacob and Rachel. Now Jacob's phrase, 'I took her and then loved her', had a new meaning for Amélie. The more Jacob knew Rachel, the more he developed his love for her. Jakobovits takes a similar Biblical analogy in describing his feelings for Amélie, but in his case he illustrates the story of the first Jewish marriage, that of Isaac and Rebecca, of whom it is said: 'He took her into his tent and he loved her.' Jakobovits quotes the Jewish philosopher, Avraham Hirsch, who describes love as the climax rather than the beginning of the relationship. 'The excitement or the climax of love grows every day,' he says. 'I always told my students that you cannot start with love, which might, of course, peter out. When a young man gets married and tells me this is the happiest day of his life, I always say, no, that's wrong. This is the beginning. It must get better.'

His decision to marry was based on similarity of background. Both families represented famous rabbinic dynasties, they were pure German-Jewish aristocracy. What was important to Jakobovits was that both their fathers had attended the same rabbinic seminary in Berlin. He had tested the chemistry and such a marriage was, he reflected, 'likely to gel'. He admits that in relationships he was driven by the mind rather than the heart. The family stock, the pedigree, were as important as the personality, 'although she, of course, charmed me. There was a vivaciousness in her which I found most attractive, womanly on the one hand, intensely Jewish on the other. She had never had a formal education since the war. She was completely self-made.'

Yet, he points out, it was her father, Rabbi Elie Munk, who was the constant, an influence on her life and a man with whom he had a deep chemistry shared by his own father. 'There were very few rabbis with whom I could communicate as well as with him. There was a great congruity of spirit which helped to cement the relationship. The family is of considerable importance. We were always concerned with that. The health of the family, their Jewish attitude, were very important factors. Yet before taking the plunge I spent a good many hours hearing and enquiring about her. I picked up more about her from third parties, who, I find, can be more helpful than what you find out for yourself. By listening to outsiders and third parties you may finally make a better decision. You see, it is important to see how she is regarded by her friends. The question of compatibility is grounded on individual assessment. We should complement and not duplicate each other.'

It is easy to see why a nineteen-year-old girl, hailing from an Orthodox patriarchy, would accept this rather clinical approach to her marriage, but Amélie had a strong will and more than a touch of vanity. She was French, good-looking, robust and hedonistic. She had been through the war. She craved love. She craved excitement. Here she was, about to get married to a man of whose intellect she stood in awe yet who seemed ascetic to the point of remoteness. Could she ever really get close to a man who seemed so other-worldly?

She responded to all these emotional conflicts by freezing them out. A numbness settled on her and remained there until quite a few months into her marriage. 'If anybody had put a needle into me, I wouldn't have felt it. I was so numb and overawed, and there was a sense of enormous achievement, in a way. There was I, a little French girl only caring for the joys of life, suddenly finding myself given, by the grace of G-d, the opportunity to share the rest of my life with a powerful personality in the making. The challenge was overwhelming.'

Amélie returned to Paris and then flew with her mother for the first time from Paris to Dublin in an Aer Lingus plane. Mrs

Jakobovits had invited all the religious and lay leaders of the community to an engagement reception to introduce her future daughter-in-law. Immanuel had not yet thought about the ring. He wondered whether Amélie would have preferred a fur coat or a piano. 'It was so funny. He gave me the choice. Being a woman, and a French one at that, it immediately occurred to me, let's have the ring first, then the rest can follow.' Immanuel, however, had not had the time to order one.

Mrs Jakobovits did not find this omission amusing, even if Amélie did. Her inherent rectitude would not have permitted Amélie to greet her guests as her son's fiancée without a ring on the third finger of her left hand, so Amélie's sister-in-law was asked to lend hers for the occasion. 'It was so amusing at that time. It remains one of those funny anecdotes of my life,' Amélie declares. 'Everybody admired my ring, which, of course, was not my ring. I played along with it because everything had to be correct.'

The marriage was booked for 5 July of that year in a hall in the Hôtel des Deux Mondes on Avenue de l'Opéra in Paris. French law insisted on a civil marriage at the *Mairie* before the religious ceremony, and many documents, even blood tests from the bride and groom, had to be submitted, involving a lengthy bureaucracy between Paris and Dublin.

At the civil ceremony itself Immanuel did not understand the mayor's question to him as to whether he had chosen Amélie Munk to be the partner of his life. The question was, of course, in French, and Amélie had to repeat 'Oui' twice, once for him and once for herself, which became an enduring joke between them.

Theirs was the first major wedding to take place within the religious Jewish community in France after the war and generated much excitement. Her dress was one of the first to come on to the market after the war; the flowers for her bouquet had to be made to appear as opulent as possible because, again, flowers were not widely available and were extremely expensive. The caterer chosen by Mme Munk had been hired to cook the first communal wedding dinner since the war.

So the wedding was a fanfare in itself, both for the young couple, and in its celebration of the post-war spirit in which everyone wanted to express joy and relief that the dark days were gone.

Although the extended family and wider community had been depleted during the war, many people, including refugees, came from all over the world to fill the synagogue to overflowing.

According to French custom, Amélie and Immanuel did not stand under the *chupah* (wedding canopy), but sat with their respective parents on either side. Amélie cannot remember a word of her father's speech as she could not stop her bouquet shaking. Afterwards she and Immanuel drove into the Bois de Boulogne and then returned to meet their respective families at the Hôtel des Deux Mondes for the elegant family dinner.

Although brides rarely remember the intricate details of their wedding day, which passes for most in a euphoric miasma, for Amélie the festivities were illuminated by a sense of post-war opulence – a return of small luxuries breaking through the gloom of past austerities. For instance, Amélie was enchanted by the white gloves worn by the waiters, a particular French conceit, but she was convinced that none of the guests had ever before been served by waiters wearing them. It was very exciting for war survivors, she considered. She remembers the menu chosen by her mother which resembled a royal feast in comparison to the days of the Holocaust. There were platters with entire salmons beautifully displayed and presented at a time when there were still food shortages. 'Many of our friends did not come back from the war, but those few who were there were invited for dessert and the dancing. It was a wonderful gesture, a custom which I think my mother started, to invite the friends of the bride and groom to the informal part of the celebrations.'

However, the wedding party was almost hijacked by a scantily dressed group of entertainers who mistakenly burst in on them before realising that the distinguished religious assembly could not possibly be their crowd. An embarrassed Rabbi Munk turned to Amélie and said with a rueful smile, 'It could only happen to my daughter.'

The guests duly dispersed and the bridal couple entered their hotel room, just a couple of blocks down the street. As they looked out of the window, they heard a commotion under the balcony and looked out to hear several of their guests discussing the wedding. One person praised Amélie's beauty, another felt it was the bridegroom's distinguished looks that had stolen the day. Amélie good-naturedly told her new husband that his mother would love that. 'We were in a very jolly mood, thank G-d, and we had a good laugh about it all. It gave us a little bit of romance together. And I found on my pillowcase a very beautiful little basket of marzipan with a little note from my mother saying, "I have already heard from my little finger on the right hand that your young husband loves marzipan. I went a long way to obtain it just outside Paris, so please let him enjoy it." That was so typical of my mother!'

There followed the customary seven nights of celebratory dinners, the *sheva brochot*.* Amélie found that first week of her marriage very taxing, both emotionally and intellectually. It occurred to her later that she had crossed a bridge from carefree youth to the responsibilities of marriage. The young couple now had to discover each other's different idiosyncrasies and character traits, to come to terms with them and learn to live with them.

'One of the issues we contemplated concerned the simple issue of living together. It was not that any one particular thing irritated me, it was just a whole new person that I had to accept in my way of life in every little step I took every day.' Like every newlywed, Amélie recalls how they had to get used to the way they each brushed their teeth, or combed their hair; his manner of shaving, her way of eating her breakfast. 'For instance, when I got up to wash and get dressed, and when I left the house, and when I ate and what I liked and what I didn't like. It is never easy for anyone.'

She speaks of her numbness as a Divine blessing, enabling her to take on board 'unconsciously' every detail of the human being with whom she hoped to share the rest of her life.

---

*A custom observed by Orthodox families in which the bride and groom are invited to a dinner party by family and friends on seven consecutive nights after their wedding. After each meal, ten men form a *minyan* and say seven blessings in their honour. Mosaic law itself only insists on one day of celebration, after the *chupah* and the wedding meal. The *sheva brochot* became a widely observed post-war custom. When the Jakobovits' second son, Shmuel, got married just after the Yom Kippur War in Israel in 1973, he insisted that he did not want the customary seven nights of celebration, but only three, as a token of sympathy with the Jewish people over the terrible losses sustained in that war.

12   Rite of Passage

THIS PROTECTIVE shell isolated Amélie from the fact that all the challenges of the war had not prepared her for the radical adjustment from girlhood to married life. She was about to leave her family in Paris for the Irish Republic, and for all its charm and blarney, a very different life awaited her there from the metropolitan buzz that had formed so much of her personality.

For a start, she had to master a strange language, English. She had a good knowledge of Hebrew, since it was the Jewish state she believed was her destiny, in company with her friends from Yeshurun, not the Emerald Isle. However, the final culture shock was that she was not moving into her own bridal home, but into the house of her mother-in-law, who was stern, austere, disciplined and totally different from her own mother, with her passionate, yet practical nature and inherent sense of humour. It must have seemed to her that, far from being in control of her own future as a married woman, she had merely exchanged one parental home for another.

Before these realities dawned, however, came the honeymoon: three weeks in Switzerland. Amélie takes a somewhat dismissive view of this social institution, 'which one lives by, but which is, I think in practical terms, not a very clever idea, because you go to a very beautiful place and yet you are so busy with each other that you cannot appreciate it'. They stayed at the well-known Jewish hotel, the Silberhorne in Grindelwald, where they were recognised by Jews from all over the world who flocked there. Everybody knew them, either as the Chief Rabbi of Ireland or the daughter of Rabbi Munk from Paris. The privacy they had sought on honeymoon totally eluded them.

However, after breakfast they went for very long walks and,

despite her denial, they did manage to admire the august beauty of the Jungfrau mountains. For the first time they began to discuss the serious issues of the recent past which had so shattered Jewish history. Amélie, of course, was in the Switzerland of her earlier refuge, and many memories came to mind. As Immanuel discussed their troubled histories and spoke with such commitment of the future he envisaged, a glimmer of recognition broke through Amélie's numbness, of what it would really mean to be the wife of a great rabbi. She confessed that she had not wanted marriage just for the sake of it, but to be able to share the calling of her husband, whether he was a rabbi or a doctor. It was years before she was to discover that her husband would become an authority on Jewish medical ethics.

By the second week of their honeymoon, some of this gravitas had dispersed. Amélie remembered that she was still a teenager and began to behave like one. It was during a long walk that a touch of jealousy, half in jest, took an unfortunate turn. She knew that there was a girl in London who had given Immanuel a beautiful silver cigarette holder. Pretending that she wanted a cigarette, she snatched the silver case from him and ran away. He gave chase and tried to retrieve the case but could not catch her. Then he decided not to speak to her, so they continued walking in total silence.

The young bride was filled with doubt and anxiety. Suddenly all she wanted to do was to go back home to her parents. So she returned to the hotel and started packing her bags in the hope that by the time her husband returned to the hotel, she would be at the station. She would go to Zurich first for the weekend and then back home.

She was already in the lobby with her bag packed when her young husband came in and said, 'I want to speak to you.' They went to have a cup of coffee together. Immanuel rose gallantly to the occasion and said, 'I have a gift for you.' It was a pair of candlesticks, beautifully carved in Swiss wood.

Today, Amélie half brushes the incident aside as a mere joke. Yet, in its rather infantile way the incident served as an ice-breaker. 'I wanted to give him that chance,' she says. 'All I had done really was to tease him, and I was having fun, just as I had always had fun before I was married. I'm a great teaser, although not so good at being teased myself.' It was incidents like these which prompted Immanuel's younger sister, Lotti, to congratulate Amélie, some years later, on having influenced her so serious brother 'to have some fun in life'.

After a few days Amélie felt unwell. Before moving to Ireland as man and wife, the couple had booked to go to Paris via Zurich, where they met some of her refugee friends from her days in Switzerland. Among them were the rabbi of Baden and his wife.

From her time as an au pair in Baden, Amélie remembered a Saturday afternoon lecture in the rabbi's house when he mildly asked for quiet because his wife was not feeling too well and was resting in the next room. Amélie saw the door open during the lecture and the rabbi's wife came in with a baby in her arms. 'It was an amazing phenomenon to see how this woman delivered while we were sitting next door, calmly got up carrying her baby into the lecture room, and said, "*Mazeltov*, I have a beautiful little boy." But to me the baby looked strange, and yet she said he was so beautiful. For many months her remark and my reaction to the baby went through my mind, and yet something held me back from asking any questions.' Much later Amélie discovered that the child was a Down's Syndrome baby, but the experience had left a deep impression on her. It was first the wonder of the woman apparently giving birth so easily, and second the discrepancy between the mother's view of the child and her own, plus the fact that some instinct told Amélie not to mention it to anybody. It was all part of growing up, Amélie reasoned.

They left Zurich for Paris, but Amélie still felt unwell with what she believed was a virus. To make matters worse she had also developed an unsightly boil on her chin. She told her mother that it must have been as a result of something she had eaten at the Silberhorne Hotel, but her mother gave her an old-fashioned look which Amélie did not understand.

Parting from her parents in July 1949 was a terrible wrench. She describes herself as 'still so insecure and, like any young bride, full of hope, of romantic imagination and yet terrible trepidation'. The train that was to bear the young couple away was already pulling out of the platform. And like that other train which, years before, had pulled them out of the Carthage that was wartime Paris and brought them to the safety of the South, Amélie literally jumped on to the train at the last minute because she could not bear to leave her parents and longed for the sound of their voices to continue.

'My father, very French, very romantic, gave me a little interpretation of that week's *sedra* [Torah reading] and then the traditional daughter's blessing in which you ask G-d to make her like the matriarchs, Sarah, Rebecca, Rachel and Leah. He kissed me and we both shared tears of sweetness and sadness, and then mother gave me her blessing and she – with her unique, instinctive and worldly intelligence – tapped me on the shoulder and looked me deep in the eyes: "Amélie," she said to me, "you'd better make a success of your marriage because I am not taking you back and there is nowhere else to go."'

Amélie stared blankly at her mother, too numb to take in what she had said. Mme Munk's valediction stung because of the closeness of mother and daughter. Amélie reflected how she had not taken up her sisters' opportunities to study at the Gateshead Seminary because she knew she was needed at home. Years would pass before she would come to understand the meaning of her mother's message to her and how hard it was then for her to give it. 'Had there been any severity in her face I might have collapsed. But she had this smile. She was telling me in her courageous and very practical way that any woman has to work on her marriage to make it a success.' Subliminally or not, Amélie accepted the challenge contained in her mother's words for the future of her marriage and came to see its relevance later in life when the divorce rate began to soar. 'I have used it in counselling my daughters and many others, because it is a true blessing for a mother to be able to say to her daughter, I am not taking you back.'

13   Of Wives and Mothers

AMÉLIE QUICKLY discovered that the 'food poisoning' on honeymoon and the boil on her chin were the first signs of pregnancy, as her mother's old-fashioned glance had hinted. She was pregnant in a strange land, with a husband who was still a virtual stranger, far away from her family. And although thirteen years had elapsed since the eminent Rabbi Isaac Herzog's departure and the time of Jakobovits assuming his office, the critical eyes of the community were upon her. Amélie, too, had a hard act to follow: the much lauded Sarah Herzog, with whose memory they seemed almost to chide her. Amélie recalls ruefully, 'I learned soon enough what the community expected of me and after a few months I became very tense just on hearing the name "Herzog" because people came to tell me all the things they had done. Sarah Herzog was indeed an epitome of what a rabbi's wife should be like. She was very kind, very intelligent, a tremendous help and support to her husband in all situations.' But even the great and the good had their problems, as Amélie reveals. 'Chief Rabbi Herzog was a great scholar and a sage, and not very aware of the realities of the practical situations in life.'

This was well illustrated by an incident brought to the Jakobovits' attention soon after taking office. In Dublin Rabbi Herzog had been besieged with requests for money largely from charity collectors from Israel, which he found himself unable to refuse. Consequently, he left debts to the bank totalling £300, a considerable sum in those days. After a few months in his new job, Jakobovits was called in by the bank manager and discreetly advised to take more stringent measures as far as charity or expenses were concerned in order not to fall into the same trap.

However, Amélie has a lighter anecdote of Rabbi Herzog's

ministry, again concerning charities. Before decimalisation, Irish coins bore the imprints of different animals: the halfpenny boasted the head of a pig. One man asked Rabbi Herzog whether it would be wrong to put such an 'unkosher' coin into a charity box, inviting the retort, 'Don't be a pig and give a full penny instead!'

But Dublin was not Paris. In fact, it was unlike any European metropolis. In 1949 there were 5,300 Jews in the South of Ireland. Most of them were vociferous enough to suggest that there were three times that number. The community was born late in the nineteenth century when Lithuanian Jews fled the pogroms by boat and disembarked on the Emerald Isle thinking that they were in America. It was a fantasy which lent the community a certain piquancy, the charm and magic of suspended reality.

If Ireland was not America, and Dublin was certainly not Paris, the place was hospitable and warm-hearted, and the countryside alluring. 'I have never heard of any Jew having difficulties in settling down successfully in the South of Ireland, or even the North, for that matter,' says Amélie. Another refreshing factor was that the country had no history of anti-semitism. 'We always believed that the Catholic and Protestant factions hated each other so much that they didn't have time for the Jews. There was also no tension in the Jewish community itself between the North and the South of Ireland. Even to this day Dublin helps and supports the tiny community in Belfast.'

Their time in Ireland was a pastoral lacuna: nearly thirty years after the Irish Troubles and over ten years before Bernadette Devlin and the civil rights movement in the North tragically triggered the violence of the 1960s that was to reverberate into the end of the century.

In contrast to the growing secularism of England, however, Ireland was a fervently religious country, and if any of this rubbed off on to the Jewish community, it was Zionism which mostly benefited. An intense interest in Israel spawned many Israeli-oriented organisations and youth groups.

Amélie refuted the widely-held belief that her husband was presiding over a dying community, an ethnic minority poised to emigrate to Israel. After several months of intensive English tuition, she managed to get the feel of the city and its Jews, and found them to be a very thriving group. 'From the Zionist point of view it was a very committed and active community. From the social point of view it was a very lovely community, with an old-age home which could serve as an example to many other communities.' It was, however, an ageing community and, as events were to prove, the majority of the young people who flocked to Bnai Akiva, Habonim and Maccabi and attended lectures and discussions at the Jakobovits home at 33, Bloomfield Avenue, were destined for Israel, a sizeable proportion choosing careers in Jewish education. There are today perhaps under 1,000 Jews left in Dublin.

Educationally the community was rather poor when the young couple arrived. It was to this that the country's new Chief Rabbi addressed himself. One of the first things he did was to launch the publication of a Jewish New Year book, which lists some twenty-six Zionist organisations and is still being published nearly forty years later. His commitment to the importance of the early years boosted the standards of Jewish primary schools – attended by nearly half the community's children in Dublin – and led to his opening of a Jewish high school, Stratford College. The lectures and discussion groups in his own home formed the bedrock of a Jewish awareness he felt moved to create among local youth groups.

Dublin at the time was the heart of Irish Jewry, with smaller arteries in Limerick, Waterford and Cork. Hazel Broch, a neighbour in her early teens when Amélie and Immanuel arrived as newly-weds, describes Dublin as a 'strong community because it was isolated from anywhere. Perhaps you could find one Jewish family living in Limerick and one in Galway.' Dublin had seven diverse Orthodox synagogues. Presiding over a community as diffuse as this did not make for an easy life. One of the first religious decisions the new Chief Rabbi had to make was to abolish the singing of the Israeli national anthem, the *Hatikvah*, at the end of the Sabbath service. Introduced when Israel was established a couple of years earlier, they had simply forgotten to withdraw it when the Jewish state was no longer a novelty. Judaism was formally recognised by the Irish Constitution as a minority faith and Chief Rabbi Jakobovits was expected to represent his community at state ceremonies. An era of civic and pastoral functions gradually smoothed away his social gaucheness and lent a new dignity to his personality.

The young intellectual who had wooed Amélie with such awkward courtliness was slowly being transformed into an ecclesiastical gentleman of refinement and composure. Or perhaps it would be more accurate to suggest that he was gaining the confidence to be more like himself. Certainly his Zionist involvement was augmented by the Dublin experience. In the absence of diplomatic relations between Ireland and the newly born State of Israel, he suddenly found himself the official spokesman not just on religious issues but also on Zionist politics.

At his installation dinner, Jakobovits notes proudly in his book, *If Only My People,* 'that the Irish Prime Minister announced Ireland's *de facto* recognition of the Jewish state'. Yet shortly after that the Chief Rabbi was hurled into the eye of an international Catholic storm over the safety of the Christian holy places in Israel. Following anti-Jewish demonstrations in Dublin, he sought equal assurances from Archbishop McQuaid, Primate of Ireland, for Jewish–Catholic relations in Ireland as he personally promised to secure from the Israeli Government the protection of Catholic rights and property in Israel.

These demonstrations had come as a great shock. With the war over, the young rabbi and his wife now tasted a new form of latent anti-Semitism. The Jewish community risked being held accountable for unpopular measures taken by Israel over which they had no control or influence. It was the beginning of anti-Zionism. 'It rendered rather hollow, in my view,' Jakobovits continues, 'the argument that Diaspora Jews had no right to express critical views on Israel since their fate was not at stake. Often it clearly was and continues to be.'

Amélie offers a graphic description of the encounter between her husband and Archbishop McQuaid: 'we had close relations with both the Archbishop and the Protestant leadership. Archbishop McQuaid was perhaps the person who brought us closest to some sense that there might be a certain amount of anti-Semitism in Ireland. I remember calling on Archbishop McQuaid with my husband and being told, "You might perhaps convey to the Government of Israel that I cannot predict the consequences if access to religious and holy places important to the Catholic church and other denominations is not made totally available and free of all possible unpleasantness. I cannot promise how the Church both in the Vatican and here in Ireland will react." It was said in an uncomfortable and unpleasant tone and it made me feel rather uneasy.'

Meanwhile the young couple were kept busy with a very active community, which no doubt honed the vivacious rebbetzin's interest in people and public affairs. Hardly a Sunday passed without three or more functions to attend, at least one of them a wedding. Amélie recalls the Irish years as among the happiest of their lives. Despite the acute differences in outlook between the synagogues, in her recollection there was harmony between them, even with the small Reform Jewish community, over which her husband had, of course, no jurisdiction.

This was the public face of Ireland's Chief Rabbinate. What was going on more privately in Amélie's mind? One of the first things she had to get used to was finding her place in the home so capably set up by her mother-in-law. Amélie already knew Mrs Jakobovits Senior to be a lady of great propriety and social correctness. The exactitude with which her mother-in-law conducted her life made Amélie feel, at least in her first year of marriage, that her goals and attitudes were quite different from those of her parents.

Sometimes Amélie became nervous because of this. In the first months of marriage, for instance, she broke a dish and her mother-in-law was quite devastated. 'In fact, after that, I think for the first year of my marriage there wasn't a day in which I didn't break something in the house, just out of sheer nervousness.' Mrs Jakobovits was very house-proud, and Amélie, whose own mother came from a wealthy home and had developed a certain nonchalance about material things, found it difficult to come to terms with such concerns. 'To my mother-in-law, every piece that she owned was very precious and when I did break something she was quite upset. In retrospect, of course, it was amusing, but at the time it wasn't funny at all.'

Amélie began to confide her troubles to her sister-in-law, Lotti, with whom she was developing a very close relationship. Lotti tried to console her over her unfortunate clumsiness, which peaked the night Amélie stood up in bed to reach for one of her novels. As she flopped down on the bed, she heard it crack. 'My poor mother-in-law went absolutely berserk, but somehow my reaction was to burst out laughing. I laughed because I felt that if I started crying I would be finished altogether.' Fortunately her husband shared her amusement, while delicately avoiding any criticism of his mother, as did Lotti, for whom the incident confirmed her original view of her sister-in-law as someone who would bring fun and lightness into Immanuel's life. 'I'm proud of you,' she said. 'He was a very serious young man when you married him.'

In her perfectionism, Mrs Jakobovits may have seemed like a dominatrix with little inclination to surrender her womanly power to the fiery French teenager, who was anything but a 'material girl'. Chaim Bermant succinctly sums up Amélie's mother-in-law as a 'traditional, stern German *hausfrau*, made sterner by heartache', having lost her husband and whose youngest son had been struck down by polio. Yet at the same time Amélie could empathise with the emotions of a widow who felt supplanted in her adored son's affections by his new young wife. 'It was a very natural period of pain, adjustment, transition for each of us. She certainly didn't mean to have any control over me; what she *did* mean was to try and teach me what it was like to be the wife of a Chief Rabbi, and the successor to this wonderful, perfect Rebbetzin Herzog.'

There is often a touch of blatant irony in Amélie 's vernacular, but here it is also tinged with wistfulness, as though she is asking, could I really ever emulate either of these two women? In time she came to appreciate in her husband's mother some of the qualities she felt she perhaps lacked. People loved her mother-in-law, she says, for her lady-like demeanour, her sincerity and the purity of her religious faith. 'Many things were kept not just according to the letter of the law, but also according to the spirit.' For all her authoritarian ways, Bermant regards Mrs Jakobovits as a quiet and subdued lady. Amélie, for all her good-naturedness and empathy, had a wild streak that served to humanise and humorise the rigid orthodoxy around her. She says that she regretted the differences between their backgrounds and 'only wished I could be the way she wanted'. However, Amélie did absorb a number of domestic arts from her mother-in-law, notably, embroidery, baking the Shabbat *challah*, thriftiness – her mother-in-law frowned on wasting the flour on the side of the bowl, which she taught her to scoop up – and the ability to feminise her home with flowers.

However, despsite wishful thinking about wanting to please, Amélie was her own woman. If at times it seemed like a power-struggle between the wife and the mother, 'Maman's advice would sustain me: "Never take yourself too seriously and you will see that married life will get better and better if you only give of your best." And that's exactly right. It wasn't easy,' says Amélie in that tender, slightly capricious way she has of speaking about herself as a young girl. 'Lack of language communication, for a start; a little girl from France who just wanted to enjoy herself, marrying a man who was already very mature, very grown up, rather serious and with a very sharp, dry sense of humour: on the whole, a very much more serious person than, of course, I am.'

Her mother's now remote but well-remembered philosophy helped her to cope in the early days of her marriage. She taught her that the younger generation should simply swallow any indignity passed down by their elders. 'So when my mother-in-law became cross with me, I just swallowed. I pulled my ear as I had seen Julie Andrews do in a film. So I pulled my ear ten times and remembered that I was the younger one and had to swallow.'

Her mother's advice was well-founded. Her own memories of early married life bordered on the surreal. Mme Munk's mother had been so irritated by her son-in-law's tic, a kind of whistling sound, that she convinced herself it was a secret language between him and his wife designed to exclude her. Finally her daughter was driven to collude in her mother's fantasy, even having to invent certain things Rabbi Munk had said just to appease her.

Mme Munk's second piece of advice was: 'In life there are no problems, only situations.' Thus over time her mother's innate wisdom helped Amélie 's relationship with her mother-in-law to grow in mutual friendship, love and respect. Although a married woman living far from home, Amélie still felt close to her parents and sustained by their confidence in her. They accepted her difficult childhood not as a burden but as a challenge which, they told her, would be reflected in the challenge of living with her husband and his mother as well.

Lily Borgenicht would certainly support this view of Amélie's instinctive behaviour, intelligence and personality developing through the tolerant wisdom shown by her parents. In her own words; 'She brought a lot from home and was always able to learn and to do the right thing at the right time.' But Amélie considers that 'everything we do has the extremes of weakness and strength. If you put them together, they will touch each other. Mrs J was, after all, my husband's mother, and in order not to hurt him too much, I did everything possible to make it more pleasant for her. But the main reason was that she had given birth to my husband, to my other half, and – it is up to me to say – my better half, and I thank G-d for it.'

If Jakobovits ever noticed his mother's influence on his wife, he never remarked on it, although Amélie regards him as not particularly given to deep observation of that kind. She considers that he avoids becoming too philosophical about situations or, more particularly, about people. 'He's very much a realist and very much a man of facts. He wouldn't allow himself to be disturbed by any comparison of this sort; he's a very crystal-clear thinker.'

However, he shared his mother's predilection for tidiness and later, when they became a family, Amélie sensed that he expected the room to be tidy when he came home at the end of the day. 'Oh, by all means have the children run around and so on, cry and laugh,' Amélie recalled him saying, 'but I do like a tidy room.' Amélie was therefore careful not to allow the house to become messy, although she considers it must have been part of her nature anyway, as she remembers her mother frequently asking her before she got married why she had to be so tidy. 'Do you think that if a robber comes in it makes any difference?'

Thus Amélie, soon to become a mother herself, learned fairly quickly to harness her more turbulent emotions in order to achieve a sometimes fragile domestic harmony. Her husband was very excited about the pregnancy and insisted that she took a two-hour rest every afternoon, although it was the rest, she wryly recalls, that brought on violent bouts of nausea every day. 'Immanuel had the brainwave of calling our expected baby, Immalie, a conjunction of both our names. He used to ask me again and again, "How is Immalie behaving?" Forty-three years later they were to name their London bungalow in Hendon, Immalie, in acknowledgement of that tender time between them.

Immalie, however, soon became Yoel, their first child, born at home in April 1950, in the presence of his father, a rare event in those days. The pregnancy undoubtedly softened the ascetic side of the young husband, drawing from him all the sentiments of future paternity. The new parents were fortunate in having selected a country which is famous for large families and, therefore, breeds gynaecologists at almost the same rate as babies. Amélie's favoured obstetrician, Dr Edwin Solomon, whom she assesses as 'one of the finest in the whole of Ireland', would have preferred a hospital birth, but bowed to his patient's wishes when he heard that the father-to-be wanted to be present.

Yoel weighed in at 5 lbs 4 ozs, after three days of labour. 'However quick I am at everything else,' says Amélie, 'I am not quick at delivering babies!' Yoel was in fact a dry birth. 'I remember being given a black gas mask, a kind of oxygen mask, into which I was told to breathe when the contractions started. This was just a few months after Queen Elizabeth had been one of the very first women in labour to have been given that support. It helped for the first few hours, but not for the last fifteen: the pain was great.' Through a miasma of agony she remembers her husband putting his *talit* (prayer shawl) over his head and walking up and down the room praying hard that everything would go well during the labour. It is a picture she retains to this day. He did not show his anxieties. 'He doesn't allow himself to get too worried about something which he himself cannot control. He was just very concerned, and it was enough for me to know that he was in the room working very hard with me to give birth to our child.'

At one point, after hours of intense pain, Amélie heard Dr Solomon suggest taking her to the famous Rotunda Hospital for a Caesarean section, 'if she doesn't deliver within the next half hour'. He hesitated to do so because he guessed the couple would want more than three children and in those days the medical profession held that after a Caesarean no woman could carry more than three pregnancies to term. Within half an hour, however, their baby boy deigned to make his appearance. Giving birth to him meant the sacrifice of Amélie's soprano voice, which she literally lost through ten hours of screaming with pain. The voice with its operatic promise never returned and was replaced by the husky tone which characterises Amélie to her contemporaries today, although there is still more than a ghost of its beauty when she is caught singing unawares.

The child was named Yoel for Immanuel's father. Thus, on 11 April 1950, the young couple became a family.

14 *Unto the Breach*

ACCORDING TO Amélie's neighbour, Hazel Broch, the Jakobovits home in Dublin was an ever-open door, and the lady of the house herself very welcoming, young and vivacious, even though her command of English was still somewhat limited. As the eldest child in her own family, she adapted easily to motherhood and living in her mother-in-law's home offered the distinct advantage of additional support where baby Yoel was concerned. However, in such a vibrant community there was no shortage of willing hands to help with babysitting, freeing Amélie to develop her social gifts as Jakobovits went about his pastoral duties.

Amélie first met Hazel Broch in Hazel's father's butcher shop in Clanbrassil Street, heart of Dublin's Jewish shopping area, when Hazel delivered meat parcels to the Jakobovits family. Hazel paints a picture of a community well in need of Jakobovits' ministrations: 'The Jakobovits' were very close-knit and had a very high standard of religious observance. In those days, traditional Judaism meant merely lighting the candles to most of the community. Theirs was a strict Talmudic Judaism.' The Jakobovits' clearly bred a much deeper Jewish awareness into their congregation largely through the children – and with more than a touch of ceremony.

Hazel recalls a Chanucah parade in which all the Jewish children participated, starting out from one of the main synagogues in Adelaide Road. Everyone, the children and the youth groups, marched with their flags under the banner of Jewish Guides, Scouts, Bnai Akiva and Habonim, and then they turned and acknowledged the Chief Rabbi. The image of Jewish provincial celebration remains vivid with Hazel, whose memory is of streets packed with children, and parents giving them a goodies bag and

Chanucah *gelt** – maybe twopence or threepence and a packet of Smarties. 'The Jakobovits home would be open at Purim for the youth groups. We would turn up in fancy dress. I remember little Yoel would come in dressed up in one of Amélie's *sheitels*. He had the most gorgeous blue eyes.' Hazel, then in her early teens, describes the family as being 'very instrumental for our particular age group. They made a very great impression on us and we accepted their love of Judaism.'

Working through children and young people clearly paid off. Both Amélie and Immanuel were the eldest of seven; and she had cared for the war refugees while he was by now utterly committed to Jewish education, seeing this as the way forward in creating a cohesive Jewish identity. Influenced by the large number of weddings within the community, they developed a custom of their own which had an instant and enduring appeal: they would invite every bride and groom to their Friday night table. When Hazel was engaged at nineteen, it was at their table that she first tasted tongue that had not been pickled. As it had become an accepted tradition that each wedding would be solemnised by the Chief Rabbi himself, Jakobovits preferred to address a couple under the wedding canopy if they already knew him and would therefore pay more attention to what he had to say. The Friday night custom also gave the young couples – particularly those who did not come from a religious background – a taste of Shabbat.

This custom particularly appealed to Hazel Broch as one of the ways in which the family projected Judaism and encouraged teenagers. Hazel admired Amélie's gift of empathy and maintained their friendship after leaving Dublin in 1955. 'She never forgot us although she must have met so many people in her life. There was something very special about her Irish girls, as she called us.'

Soon after the birth of Yoel, Amélie was pregnant again. 'I discovered that the widely held belief that a mother who breast-feeds her child and thus has no monthly periods cannot become pregnant is a complete fallacy,' Amélie dryly observes.

Towards the end of the eighth month of her pregnancy, in May

---

*Yiddish for money. Chanucah *gelt* is the Yiddish expression for the gift of money traditionally given to children at this Jewish festival.

1951, Immanuel was invited by the then British Chief Rabbi, Israel Brodie, to give a paper at a London conference on Family Unity. He was due to leave on Monday and, although he had accompanied his wife to her ante-natal check-up at Dr Solomon's surgery the previous Thursday, Amélie suddenly panicked. 'If you go to England on Monday, I'm going to have that baby while you are away,' she predicted. Immanuel calmly reassured her by suggesting a further visit to Dr Solomon on Monday morning. 'If he feels that you are perfectly okay, will you let me go?'

She agreed, and the gynaecologist confirmed after an examination that her baby could not be born for the next two or three weeks. Relieved, Amélie saw her husband off to the airport and returned home. She and her mother-in-law spent the evening listening to classical music and doing Irish embroidery. Finally, Amélie went upstairs at about 11.30 p.m. taking with her one of her very first English novels, Charlotte Bronte's *Jane Eyre*. At nearly midnight she thought she was having her first labour pain, a contraction which was repeated ten minutes later and from then on every ten minutes until, very nervous by now, she had no choice but to waken her mother-in-law, who called a taxi to take her to the clinic. Amélie's plan to have her second baby at home had to be abandoned that night because the maternity nurse could not come before another three and a half weeks. At 11 a.m. the following morning, on 15 May 1951, just thirteen months after the birth of Yoel, Shmuel entered the world weighing in at 7 lbs 3 ozs.

Mrs Jakobovits Senior telephoned her daughter-in-law, Cessie, wife of her second son in London, and asked her to call the British Chief Rabbi's office in Woburn House and tell Jakobovits the good news. However, a few minutes before this phone call, Chief Rabbi Brodie, irritated by a spate of calls to the dozen or so assembled rabbis, had given orders that nobody was to be disturbed again at this conference. So when Cessie insisted on being put through and wished her brother-in-law *Mazeltov* on the birth of his new baby son, an embarrassed and somewhat testy Immanuel refused to believe her. 'I have no time for such jokes,' he retorted and put the receiver down. Poor Cessie tried again two hours later. As Jakobovits came to take the second call, he was so angry at the interruption that he tripped over the telephone wire. Again she repeated her good news and again he admonished her for disturbing him and told her not to phone again. Cessie now had no choice but to call her mother-in-law in Dublin and ask her to do the job herself. 'Anyone who knew Mrs Jakobovits would have known that she was not the type of person to make such jokes,' smiles Amélie, with a touch of irony.

Ireland's now contrite Chief Rabbi did indeed believe his own mother and flew back to Dublin the following morning accompanied by Sesi. He returned to London on the Thursday to deliver his paper.

The couple were blessed with three more children during their stay in Ireland: Esther, on 6 January 1953, Shoshana on 15 March 1956 – born in panic as Immanuel was suffering a raging attack of the flu and could not find a taxi to take her to hospital until the last moment – and then Aviva on 21 April 1958.

The birth of her first five children not only crowned her marriage, but drew Amélie closer to the husband who had seemed at first so self-contained, enabling her to visualise a clearer role for their future together. A powerful synthesis was already at work here, as her life-long friend, Lily Borgenicht, suggests: 'She was able to influence him because, although he did all the thinking and took the intellectual part in the marriage, she voiced her opinions, too; she did not just accept everything. Her personality contributed to the happiness of the marriage, because we know they are a very close couple. They say that opposites attract each other. I think they completed or complemented each other.'

Lily's perception of Jakobovits was fairly acute: he did not enjoy social activities, but he valued his wife's efforts at them. These activities were not, of course, merely social but an extension of his pastoral work. Amélie herself was beginning to nourish the taste for care and community work that had been born in the post-war refugee trains of Europe.

One contemporary who taught in a Zionist school across the road from their Bloomfield Avenue home, and who had been hidden by a non-Jewish family during the war in Holland before being reunited with her parents, tells a story reminiscent of the Biblical Hannah praying for the birth of her son, Samuel. She had been praying very hard to have a child and Amélie was indirectly active in helping her through an adoption process, even though it was not considered 100 per cent legal at the time. 'I taught Amélie's three older children to write Hebrew before I went to Gateshead, and I would often eat or have a drink in their home after school.'

Amélie, she explains, was like an aunt to her. 'She even carries a photograph of our daughter in her bag. She is very aware of society around her and is always eager to help towards any needs. She did an exquisite job as a help to her husband during those Dublin years,' she says, adding a coy and romantic touch to her story: 'As a young girl I had a crush on Immanuel Jakobovits, and I remember running along the beach with him and his sister-in-law. We sat there watching the sea hitting the rocks, and once a huge wave soaked him from top to toe!'

15   Baby Blues

ONE SUNDAY evening when Shoshana was about nine months old, she developed a temperature for which she was prescribed antibiotics by their GP, Dr Robinson. However, her condition deteriorated, and when Amélie called the doctor again, he prescribed another type of antibiotic. By the following day she was no better and, on Thursday, Dr Robinson again changed the antibiotic. Her condition failed to improve and on Friday night Amélie and Immanuel agonised over whether to call him out again or let the drugs take effect. However, the child soon became desperately ill; her head had fallen to the side, and she had become so dehydrated that her eyes could not close and her rectum could not hold the thermometer. The doctor reassured them with offers of further antibiotics, which he was convinced would prove effective.

But Amélie was sceptical and insisted on seeing a specialist. The GP did not take too kindly to this suggestion and left, somewhat miffed, assuring them that he knew best. The family then tried to contact Professor Stein, who was considered the leading paediatrician in the country. On being told by his housekeeper that the doctor was at a party at Trinity College and could not be called out, Immanuel went there on strict instructions from Amélie not to come back without him. The young father's persistence paid off and the Professor's colleagues went to fetch him. Professor Stein, who, despite his name, was not Jewish, emerged from his revels completely inebriated, and it took two students to help Immanuel get him into the car and to bring him home. There, an anxious Amélie, who had been praying hard for her child's recovery, was faced with the bizarre sight of Immanuel supporting the drunken doctor up the steps of the house. Anxiety at his state of inebriation gave way to terror, but then something incredible happened. 'He took one look at our baby, who was lying virtually motionless on the bed, and he sobered up within a matter of seconds. His personality completely changed and he was in total control of the situation. He didn't even examine the baby, he just wrapped her gently in two blankets, took her into his arms and said, "I'll call you the minute I have something hopefully good to tell you, but don't be impatient; it won't be tonight. I am sure it will take a few hours. Just pray to the Almighty to help us." With that he left the house with our baby, and Immanuel drove him to the hospital.'

The next morning the Rabbi took his eldest son, four-year-old Yoel, to synagogue with him, and when Yoel returned he said, 'Mummy, Daddy cried. Why?' Amélie gently told him that his father had cried because Shoshana was very ill, but that she had just heard from Professor Stein that at last the baby had turned the corner and had managed to keep down some water. In a few hours, the doctor said, they could come and see her.

Soon the young couple were gazing at their daughter through a window into an isolated ward. She lay in a tiny crib – there were no incubators in those days – and beneath her mattress were two 100 watt light bulbs. The baby's eyes were closed and she was totally naked, warmed only by the light bulbs and the stable temperature of the room. She was clearly more comfortable than the previous night, when she could not close her eyes due to dehydration caused by gastroenteritis.

'What Professor Stein had done was to stay with her all night and keep a bottle of water in her mouth. As the water was taken in through her mouth, it came right through her little body until at last the weight of what came out was not equal to her intake, indicating that she was on the way to a slow recovery.' From that moment, baby Shoshana improved hourly and her parents' hearts began to lighten.

Shortly afterwards the Chief Rabbi began the first in what would become a series of regular lecture tours to the USA, and he wanted Amélie and Shoshana to accompany him. The doctors gave permission for the baby to travel as long as she remained under careful supervision and her feeding was regulated. The child eventually made a full recovery and is regarded by her mother to this day as their twice-born child because they so nearly lost her.

Amélie learned from that experience not to suppress her own natural maternal instincts and urges women to have the courage to supersede medical advice, if necessary, in order to seek a second opinion. As for Dr Robinson, he was not happy with Amélie's decision at first, but as time passed she believes he made peace with himself. 'He was a special man,' she says generously.

This was not the last of the couple's serious problems with childhood illness. Another incident occurred with their second baby, Shmuel, who had been left in his father's care one night while Amélie attended a meeting. The baby had been well fed that night and was asleep. 'Although Father went up from time to time to look at the children, he didn't check as frequently as I might have done, and in any case they were quiet,' says Amélie. However, on her return that night she discovered to her horror that the baby had turned blue and his mouth was dangling open. She could still hear his heartbeat and began to scream for her husband. The good Dr Robinson appeared in a matter of minutes. The doctor examined the child and discovered he had eaten something which did not agree with him. He prescribed a sedative to enable him to sleep for at least twelve hours. The baby slept calmly in his parents' bed that night as they watched over him and saw the colour gradually return to his face. Next morning, Amélie discovered that the baby's cot sheets had a huge yellow stain from the egg she had given him the previous afternoon on which he had choked and lost his breath. 'Thank G-d I found him just in time and his little life was saved.'

When Shmuel was three, he became particularly attached to the family pet, a blue canary called Zippy, the Hebrew short-form of Zipporah, for bird. Amélie used to let the bird out of his cage to fly around the bathroom when she bathed the baby, much to the excitement of all the children. One Friday afternoon, after the baby was wheeled out into the garden in her pram, the bird zoomed overhead and flew away. Poor Shmuel was so upset that he sat in the garden the whole afternoon howling for his pet. As Shabbat came in, the child became lethargic and developed a temperature, refusing to eat or drink. On Sunday morning the doctor was called, who said it was a slight cold and prescribed antibiotics.

At 10.30 a.m. the following morning an advertisement in the local newspaper's Lost and Found Pet Corner matched Zippy's description. With the sickly Shmuel still pining for his lost pet, Amélie and her husband hurried to the address to be told by the woman who opened the door, 'You are the twelfth couple to call today claiming to be the bird's owner. How do I know it is your bird? What will you do to identify it? Convince me that you are Zippy's rightful owner.' Not expecting to be thus challenged on their proprietorial rights, Immanuel and Amélie looked at each other and wondered what trial by ordeal she had put the other eleven couples through. Then Immanuel said, 'I will stand in the far corner of the room. Open the door of the cage and I shall call Zippy. If it comes and stands on my right shoulder, it belongs to us. If it doesn't come anywhere near me or sits on my head or my left shoulder, it's not our bird.' So – like a character in some dark fairy-tale – the woman opened the cage and Immanuel whistled and called out, 'Zippy!' On hearing his master's voice, the obliging bird immediately flew over and landed on the rabbi's right shoulder. The woman relinquished the bird with relief that she had at last found its rightful owner. They gave her a generous donation and brought the bird back home to find that Shmuel soon recovered.

One of the worst childhood accidents the family experienced occurred one night just after Amélie had poured hot water into a thermos flask for baby Esther's bottle. Amélie put the flask on the table, but her eldest son, Yoel, was too quick for her. He managed to reach the table from the stool and crawled over to the flask, which opened and emptied its contents over him, badly burning the right side of his face. Amélie rushed him upstairs to her husband: 'I was always nervous when something happened and needed his moral support.' However, the child would not stop crying, and his desperate parents could not appease him. 'He loved going in cars after his father had passed his driving test – 'disgustingly easy, all you needed was to pay £1 for a licence and you were on the road.' Yoel cried for twenty-four hours, calling out non-stop, 'Daddy, Daddy, car, car.' They gave him all the toy cars in the house in the hope that they would pacify him, but nothing eased his pain.

When their nanny arrived, she told Amélie that had she removed the child's cardigan immediately and treated him with cold water, he would not have suffered such serious burns. In paying attention to his face, Amélie had been completely unaware that the child had suffered second degree burns to his arm. They rushed him to the emergency hospital, where his arm was bandaged and he was given morphine for the pain. He now bears a five-inch scar on his right arm, like a dark pigmentation, as a cruel testimony to the accident. Amélie too bears a scar of her own – the memory of her son's screaming which continued for three days and nights, and which she claims she can still hear to this day in her head.

Amélie considers herself to have been 'very much spoiled' in Ireland, where there was no lack of help, and she had the benefit of a maternity nurse who would stay for four weeks after each birth. During this time she never experienced a sleepless night, as the nurse would give the baby the night feed from milk Amélie had earlier expressed. Yet, each time the nurse left her she felt sad and nervous, somewhat sorry for herself, fearful that she would not be able to cope with nobody to help her.

Immanuel's mother, apparently 'a typical European woman of her day', did not approve of the man in the household undertaking domestic duties. Amélie remembers an incident at the breakfast table early in their marriage when she dropped a knife and asked Immanuel to pick it up. He did so and left the room soon after. His mother instantly took the opportunity to admonish her for her action. 'In our way of life, in our social background, men do not do anything like that, not even picking up a knife,' she said. Although the bile rose to Amélie's throat, she remembered her mother's advice to swallow her rebellious feelings. At the same time she was mortified to think that she might have offended her husband and took the first opportunity to ask him. Her young husband reassured her that it really did not matter.

Certainly Mrs Jakobovits Senior imposed her rules and values on the household rigorously. Strict times had to be observed for rising, eating and retiring. The day was sliced like a cake into equal parts – not a crumb more or less was allowed to disturb its shape, no matter what happened.

In the evening, as the two women did their embroidery,

Immanuel worked on his thesis on Jewish medical ethics, and Amélie was told to be absolutely silent. 'Let's not talk,' said Immanuel, 'let's just listen to music.' So the three of them sat in the study listening to classical music and *Chazanut,** a particular passion with Immanuel. Amélie says that her musical education came from those months and years in the cosy study upstairs at 33, Bloomfield Avenue, although she has probably forgotten her days of singing *Manon Lescaut* in the bread queues of wartime Nice.

Mrs Jakobovits Senior had brought beautiful furniture with her from Germany to England and now to Ireland. The bedroom furniture was highly polished post-Victorian rosewood with bedside tables almost reaching to the ceiling. There were drawers at the bottom and the top cornices were embossed with inlaid mother-of-pearl. She had handed over this bedroom to the young couple when they came to live in Bloomfield Avenue, and Amélie has often reflected on the strange fact that her husband's family had still managed to ship this furniture out from Germany in the late 1930s.

As time went on and her family grew out of the hazards of early childhood, life began to change for Amélie. She was no longer treading on eggshells with regard to pleasing her mother-in-law. In fact, after the first three years of their marriage, Mrs Jakobovits Senior left them to make a home in Liverpool for her third son Joseph, a medical student. In those first years Amélie had missed her mother deeply, but refused to admit the fact because such acknowledgement would have been simply 'another burden' to carry. Nor could she have expected any support from her mother in dealing with Mrs Jakobovits Senior, because the diplomatic Mme Munk would have shrunk from doing anything that might be construed as interference. Amélie reconciled herself to the view that it was futile to 'talk yourself into something you cannot have. My time was concentrated instead on building my marriage and my relationship with the one I had chosen to share my life with. I wanted that to be as beautiful as possible with no conflicting emotions coming into it.'

*Liturgical music sung by the cantor in the synagogue.

Soon the children began to develop their own individual personalities and she became aware of the differences in her relationship with each of them: ' Each of our children has qualities which appeal much to me and I love them each in a different way. Attractions are not always rational.'

Like many parents she sometimes experienced the pendulum swing of more 'attraction' for one of her children than another. She explores these emotions with pragmatic insight. She never gave voice to them, she says, despite her concern if they intensified or endured too long. In every case she discovered that eventually the sentiment subsided or reversed itself and the emotional balance of the family was restored.

16   *The Jewish World –*
and Beyond

WHILE THE Irish Jewish community was small, it had a disproportionate impact on Irish culture, science and business. 'People contributed enormously in every sphere of Irish life, whether it was the sciences, medicine, business, theatre, cinema, music or law,' states Amélie. 'We often asked our non-Jewish friends how many Jews they believed were in Ireland, and the answer invariably was between 25,000 and 30,000. The reality was, of course, nearer the 5,000 mark. That's how much the Jewish input was perceived in the general national life.'

One Irish Jew who was able to contribute this particular indigenous flavour was Robert Briscoe,* the Mayor of Dublin, first Jewish member of the Irish Dail (parliament) and first Jewish Lord Mayor of Dublin. At an inter-parliamentary conference which took place in the Dail in 1950, not long after the establishment of the State of Israel, the honour of welcoming the first ever Israeli delegation fell to him. During the lunch break a waiter discreetly approached Briscoe and murmured politely, 'I think your friends from Israel do not understand English because they actually ordered pork.' Briscoe had the prophetic wit to retort, 'These are

---

*1894–1969, Irish politician and communal leader who was involved in the struggle for Irish independence. He served in the Irish Republican Army from 1917 to 1924 and was envoy to the USA seeking financial and moral aid from Irish Americans. He represented De Valera's Fianna Fail Party in the Dail from 1927 to 1965 and served two terms as Mayor of Dublin in 1956–7 and 1961–2. He supported the Revisionist movement and the Irgun Zvei L'eumi and was an executive member of the New Zionist Organisation. He was president of the Dublin Board of Shechita. Retiring from politics in 1965, he was succeeded by his son, Benjamin, in the Irish Parliament. His autobiography, *For the Life of Me*, was published in 1959.

not Jews, these are Israelis!' Amélie offers this as both a comment on Briscoe's diplomacy and as a sad parable of the times. 'It saved embarrassment on all sides as it avoided showing non-Jewish people the divisions between or the weakness of many of our people in not keeping our religious dietary laws.'

For Briscoe to be elected Mayor of Dublin, she observes shrewdly, 'was like having a Catholic as the Mayor of Tel Aviv. But he was very popular and no one will ever forget his tremendous impact on New York City when he led the Irish parade on St Patrick's Day. He was a strictly observant Jew in public life because this is part of being a successful politician in Ireland. Religion is of great importance in Ireland and you must be seen to keep your religion.'

If the still idealised reputation of Sarah Herzog – 'who took great care to be wherever she was needed in times of pain' – influenced the way Amélie had begun to see her role in Ireland, she was herself growing in confidence and becoming increasingly aware of the strength of the rabbinic background into which she had been born and bred. Amélie had the example of her own mother, whose demeanour as the wife of a distinguished and widely involved rabbi in Paris had deeply affected her own. However, there must have been something in the Irish air to boost so many of its rabbinic incumbents or their offspring to high office. The Herzog sons both rose to fame: Chaim to the presidency of the State of Israel, and Ya'acov,* an outstanding Hebrew scholar, to the world of international diplomacy. Both were born in Ireland, one of them at 33, Bloomfield Avenue. Amélie can remember Ya'acov Herzog's brief return to Dublin when he came to visit them and asked Amélie to take him down the memory lane of his old home. His surprise at seeing his bedroom converted into a girl's room – there were no girls in his family – flashed into Amélie's mind when some years later Rabbi Ya'acov Herzog returned to Dublin for a United Jewish Appeal dinner. There she heard her husband compare the Herzog boys with Jacob and Esau, the sons of their father's Biblical

---

* An ordained rabbi, Ya'acov Herzog became Ambassador to Canada in the early 1960s, but the top diplomatic job in Washington eluded him. Later he was invited to succeed British Chief Rabbi Israel Brodie, but contracted a virulent blood disease which forced him to resign shortly afterwards. He died in 1973.

namesake, Isaac. Chaim, he declared, was a man of the field, a man of battle, and Ya'acov was a man of spiritual leadership. Amélie endorses these words with the reflection that Ya'acov was, in her opinion, the only truly great visionary with which the modern State of Israel was blessed, but who sadly died young, depriving the nation of his unfulfilled potential mission. 'He had the ability and the courage to assess current events in Israel and place them in the context of an extra dimension and predict their possible consequences. He was a deeper thinker than his brother, Chaim.'

Forged in anxiety and self-deprecation, Amélie's friendship with the Herzog family was also to deepen over time. After Israel's Six Day War in 1967 – the date of her first visit there – Amélie would renew her friendship with Rabbanit Sarah Herzog in Jerusalem. 'She called me the daughter she had never had. We grew very close and she came back into my life again and again.' For her part, Sarah's daughter-in-law, Penina, reciprocates these emotions with warm descriptions of Amélie's charm and unmitigated love of humanity. Amélie would say that she had good mentors in Sarah Herzog and her own mother, from whose examples she 'slowly learned, or rather shaped' her own role. 'I have tried to stick very carefully to my priorities and these are my love and my duties, my attention to the well-being of my husband, followed very closely to those of my children, and after this the love and affection and well-being of the community.'

As her own children grew old enough to be involved, the Friday night with the engaged couples took on even greater symbolism. From the age of four the children were encouraged to take part in the family meal. A loving ritual would be observed in which the children would sit next to their father, with the guests forming a circle in which each member was as important as the other.

The Irish community in those days was extremely pro-active in every aspect of Jewish and Zionist life. Their vitality drew Amélie into many of their activities, from the Women's International Zionist Organisation (WIZO) to the Scouts movement. However, she resisted taking an executive role in their affairs which might have compromised her own position within the community and impeded the development of true friendships. The other reason she refused to accept office is because she felt such action would deprive a lay person of the opportunity of an organisational role.

During her time in Ireland, Amélie became acquainted with many outstanding Jews including the fiery cleric, Isaac Bernstein, who became minister at London's Finchley Synagogue until his recent untimely death. He, too, began his religious life in the Jakobovits' study in Bloomfield Avenue, achieving prominence and the slightly Shavian insouciance that was to characterise his ministry.

Both Amélie and the Chief Rabbi regard their Irish years as being close to perfection. The latter's early ambition to boost Jewish education proved successful, with the Zionist schools which he founded growing in secular and religious scope over the years, and increasing their student population. During his tenure, Amélie claims the community became both more consolidated and more tolerant, although her view that anti-Semitism, if it existed at all, was very low key, is not shared by all. One London Jewish industrialist who established a factory in Dublin in the 1950s encountered extreme hostility, which culminated in his factory being burned down. Jewish Ireland gave Jakobovits, however, the opportunity to learn how to relate to all the different factions which make up a community, whether in Ireland, Britain, Europe, America or Israel. It also taught him to communicate with the non-Jewish world.

The Jakobovits' developed close ties with Irish President, John O'Kelly, whom they met at functions and who frequently consulted the Chief Rabbi on diplomatic issues and other developments that arose between the State of Israel and Ireland. Perhaps even more crucial was the relationship between Jakobovits and the Catholic leadership, notably Archbishop McQuaid, which had reached such a delicate stage over the issues of Christian rights in Jerusalem, described in an earlier chapter. 'McQuaid made us feel that we were certainly a member of a minority, although he also believed we numbered some 25,000, an inflated figure which betrayed his view of our tremendously beneficial influence in all walks of life in Ireland,' Amélie recalls.

Dealing with the politics of the non-Jewish world was one thing. Developing a coherent modus vivendi with the Jewish Progressive movement, however, was something else. Amélie says that its leader, Rabbi Leo Baeck,* had had friendly relations with her late father-in-law. 'It was due to his visit to my husband in Ireland in the early 1950s that Immanuel understood better how to deal both communally and in personal relationships with the members of Ireland's Progressive community. It stood him in very good stead for all the coming years of his leadership in the rabbinical world and in the Jewish community generally.'

Baeck's visit also helped Amélie herself to develop a more tolerant attitude towards Progressive Jews, including the Masorti element, known in America as the Conservative movement.** Nourished since early childhood in the security of her total belief in the teachings of the Torah,§ Amélie has long voiced a desire to set an example by her own behaviour to encourage others to respect, tolerate and understand the spirit of the Orthodox Judaism she represents. It is a desire which stops short of missionary fervour, yet is expressed with all the passion of a zealot: 'If I couldn't convince everyone that the only way of Jewish life is a *religious* Jewish life, I wanted with all my heart and all my soul to create that respect. I hope that – although to a great extent this kind of work is never finished – I have been able to do so.'

It is clear from this statement that Leo Baeck's teachings and influence served merely to reinforce the Jakobovits' own Ortho-dox values and perhaps to help them present their case not more flexibly – in order to accommodate the beliefs of others – but with greater subtlety. This subtlety and certainty were to come into play nearly four decades later when the death of the British Reform Movement's most magnetic communicator, Rabbi Hugo Gryn, exposed serious religious schisms within Anglo-Jewry.

In 1957 Immanuel was co-founder with British Chief Rabbi

---

* A German-born scholar who developed his ideas for Progressive Judaism during the Second World War, largely while interned in Theresienstadt in 1943, settled in London in July 1945, and became chairman of the World Union of Progressive Judaism. He is known as the Father of the Progressive or Reform Movement.
** The American movement born in London in the mid-1960s which, while adhering to most of the tenets of Orthodoxy, differs from it in one basic respect: it accepts, according to its controversial British proponent, Rabbi Dr Louis Jacobs, the Five Books of Moses as having been divinely inspired, rather than divinely given to Moses at Mount Sinai.
§ The Five Books of Moses brought down by the Patriarch from Mount Sinai.

Israel Brodie of the Conference of European Rabbis, an organisation which predated the European Union and had the declared aim of preventing the outbreak of any serious anti-Semitic incident on the continent. Not long after its inception, Jakobovits was asked, because of his association with the Catholic leadership in Europe, to meet the papal astronomer, an Irishman, in Rome. The international community was considering radical proposals for calendar reform, whereby every 1 January would fall on a Sunday, thus fixing permanently every other date too. But since the year has 365 rather than 364 days (which can be divided into seven), the suggestion was to call the 365th day a 'Nark Day', so that there would be one eight-day week every year. For Jews, who cannot adjust the weekly Sabbath, it would have meant introducing a 'wandering Sabbath' every Saturday in the last year of the old count, followed by every Friday in the following year, and every Thursday the year after. Jews were not alone in their concern to prevent this change, which would have caused upheaval in the Jewish world, and Jakobovits was asked to prevail on the Catholic Church not to undertake the calendar conversion. His efforts proved effective and the proposals were not adopted.

Another call was on the horizon for the young couple, and it came suddenly from the New World. Neither of them could have imagined that by the Jewish New Year of 1958, Rabbi Jakobovits would be officiating at the new Fifth Avenue Synagogue in New York formed by a clutch of influential Americans who had wanted to create a community more consistent with their Orthodox beliefs. They now sought the right rabbi to lead it. For the Jakobovits', accepting the call meant being thrust into an environment completely alien to the old, familiar European soil that had nurtured them.

Joining the founding fathers of this vibrant New York synagogue was indeed a far cry from the rural comforts of Dublin. As she pondered the move, Amélie realised that they would be in transition again, hardly a novelty for her. But she had grown fond of Ireland; it had the sentimental flavour of the country where she had become a mother. It was difficult simply to look back on Ireland as a place in time.

To Amélie, the Irish experience had offered an opportunity to join her husband in working as a team on behalf of the Jewish community, whether on the religious or quasi-political front. Amélie – ever seeking mental stimulus – recalls the vibrancy of the intellectual relationships they shared with many young people, regardless of background. The Irish period also offered a chance to contribute with her husband a deeper dimension of Jewish teachings, ethics and philosophy, while at the same time enabling them to achieve excellent relationships with the presidents of Ireland as well as the archbishops and cardinals.

While the Jakobovits' Emerald Isle connections remain strong to this day, backed by memories of close and important relationships, Amélie now accepts that she is looking back on a community which has been in decline for the last twenty or thirty years. Many had their hearts elsewhere, seeking transition to Israel, America or Britain. A majority of the young people she had known subsequently made *aliyah* (emigration to Israel), enriching the Jewish state in their respective fields mainly of medicine, the media and education.

Irish Jews were not alone in their cosmopolitan urge to join larger Jewish organisations and work in the fields of education. Untouched by the troubles that loomed just over the border except by their desire, still manifest today, to support the tiny and precarious Belfast community, the Jews of Southern Ireland simply saw no need to replicate themselves or strengthen their roots at home. Disturbingly, Amélie notes that the birth rate for Ireland's Jews has slumped and intermarriage has been on the increase over the past fifteen years. The present Jewish population of Ireland is barely 1,000, consisting mainly of the elderly, for whom moving to a more vibrant or larger metropolis is no longer an option.

There is no question in Amélie's mind that the Golden Age of Irish Jewry was launched during the decades under the leadership of Chief Rabbi Herzog, followed by the Jakobovits' themselves, and Jakobovits' successor, Rabbi Dr Isaac Cohen, whose previous posting had been Edinburgh and whose incumbency he secured on Jakobovits' departure in 1958. Relations between the Chief Rabbinate and the Irish Government continued to prosper after Dr Cohen was succeeded by the charismatic Rabbi David Rosen.

When years later Rabbi Jakobovits received his honorary

doctorate from the University of Cardiff, of which HRH the Prince of Wales is Chancellor, he shared the honour with the then Irish President, Mary Robinson, who was subsequently appointed United Nations High Commissioner of Human Rights. The sight of her husband on the platform beside Mrs Robinson evoked a moment of pure nostalgia for Amélie.

17 Jakobovits Joins the Founding Fathers

IF DUBLIN was a transitory community perceived to be too diluted by Zionism for its own growth, no such identity problems affected America, as the Jakobovits' were soon to find out.

In his book, *If Only My People*, Jakobovits refers to American Jews as 'the only Jewish community in history to have settled as equals – as immigrants like all other Americans. American Jews feel they have arrived at their final destination. They seek equality not just as individual citizens but as a group.' Thus he found the Americans' relationship with Israel to be more measured, more distant. American Jewry – while always at the political hustings to campaign for Israel or make big business out of Zionist fund-raising – was nevertheless at peace with its identity. For Amélie particularly, whose bitter memories of European anti-Semitism were calmed, if not healed, by their life in Dublin, this image of brash, influential and voluble Jews, who did not need to tread softly or lower their voices, proved a mixed blessing.

It forced her to recognise, perhaps for the first time, that there could be for Jews a demarcation point between the old and the new worlds that had little to do with Israel; that was beyond and external to Israel in every sense. Yet the newly established and hard-won Jewish state spelled home for the diaspora. It was present in Jewish prayer, poetry and thought – a refuge from persecution, a metaphysical place hovering beyond space and time, which had materialised in the creation of the state in 1948. Ireland had taken this perhaps too literally. American Jewry appeared to have rejected it altogether.* How would Amélie and Immanuel balance two such opposing attitudes?

Privately, the couple had reached a tacit understanding with Dublin – a 'gentleman's agreement', as Amélie puts it – that ten years was the maximum they intended staying in the Irish Republic. While the job was nominally for life, Rabbi Jakobovits knew that after a decade he would have given his best and needed to move on to recharge his batteries. In this they were both profoundly influenced by Immanuel's sister, Lotti, who took the strong view that her brother would neither develop his personality nor grow in knowledge or stature if he stayed too long in Ireland. Immanuel rather more modestly suggests that after ten years the community also needed to rejuvenate itself with a new minister.

However, a very high priority in the proposed move to America was also their children's education. 'The Irish educational system, with its compulsory use of the Irish language, took much time away from general education,' Amélie points out, 'whereas the Jewish day school system in America was far in advance of anything our children could have received in Dublin. We were looking for a school which would give them the best combination of Jewish and secular education.'

The opening move in the family's exodus to the United States came in 1958, when Jakobovits was invited to give a three-week lecture tour on his favourite subject of Jewish medical ethics. He was urged not to return to Dublin without calling on a man Amélie describes as 'one of the great sons of Irish-Jewry', Hymie Ross. The son of a previous minister in Belfast who had been loved and well-remembered on both sides of the border, Ross was a Wall Street stockbroker. He was also one of the leaders of a Conservative Synagogue on New York's West Side.

Jakobovits was too busy to pay Ross a call, but on the point of flying home to Dublin he found the airport suddenly closed due

---

* Particularly as far as the US Reform movement had been concerned. It totally rejected Zionism in its Pittsburgh Platform of 1885, preferring to present itself as a religious community. This attitude changed over the years as the Central Conference of American Rabbis (CCAR) softened its own stance on the Jewish nation-state. The CCAR embraced Zionism only in mid-1997 under the influence of events and the impact of Zionist ideology. The movement, notably in the 1940s, produced significant leaders in political campaigns in support of Jewish statehood.

to a snowstorm. Left with unexpected time on his hands, he telephoned Ross, who promptly invited him to join him at his home. During the course of that evening, Ross delivered his bomb-shell: 'I have a group of very close friends on the East Side who are building the first synagogue dedicated 100 per cent to Orthodoxy just two blocks away from Temple Emanu-El. I have a hunch that you are the perfect rabbi for them.' Ross stressed that there had never been an Orthodox synagogue on that side of New York before, and asked Jakobovits to delay his flight home by another day so that he could meet the moving spirits behind the embryonic community.

As Jakobovits had already perceived, New York Jewry of the late 1950s was in the fast lane of city life – buoyant, talented and so well absorbed as to be virtually assimilated. Neither Zionist nor religious in Orthodox terms, the Jews tended towards secularism. Judaism survived within the Progressive movement – Conserva-tive and Reform – while Orthodox instincts were somewhat suppressed in super-trendy Manhattan.

Temple Emanu-El, the colonaded basilica which straddles the southern part of Central Park, virtually symbolised this concession to the power of liberalism. A cathedral atmosphere pervaded the part of Fifth Avenue which it dominated, while Orthodoxy itself was out of sight. The gang of five to whom Ross wanted to introduce Jakobovits had become disaffected with their own synagogue on East 62nd Street, when its hierarchy, clearly influenced by Progressive thinking, moved towards mixed seating. The leader of the proposed breakaway synagogue, the heating industrialist, Henry Hirsch, could not stomach such a capitulation. As Amélie reflects, 'The idea of separating men and women during prayer is less a sexual concern than to emphasise that when we go into a house of worship, nothing, no other person, should matter to you except your relationship to the Almighty. That is the whole idea – no more or less than the total immersion of your thoughts in the Almighty.'

Hirsch had 'this clear dream of a small jewel of a synagogue, beautifully built and with a relatively small membership, where everybody would be like a family closer to the idea of the *heim*, the *shtetl*, the *Beth Hamedrash*,' adds Amélie. His dream was pure nostalgia, envisaging less a formal synagogue than a place of prayer, which combined the social values of the traditional East European meeting place, where Jews could relax and discuss the issues of the day.

Intrigued by this proposal, with which he felt some empathy, Jakobovits agreed to stay another day in New York to meet the men. Apart from Hirsch, they included the author, Herman Wouk, Herman Merkin, Sam Elsowsky and Judge Saul Rozenberg. They were all powerful and influential men who wanted to make their mark on Orthodoxy.

In Amélie's words, when they met her husband, 'they fell in love with each other straight away'. The founders' next move was to rent an apartment on East 65th Street, where they began a prayer group in which they were soon joined by two or three dozen friends on Friday nights and Saturday mornings. Before long there were sufficient numbers to form an Orthodox synagogue on East 62nd Street. The dream became carnate and the community of the Fifth Avenue Synagogue – FAS as it became known – was born.

Unlike most embryonic congregations which have to struggle to afford a synagogue of their own, the history of the FAS was the very reverse. Its prime movers were wealthy enough to buy a plot on Fifth Avenue, arguably the most expensive area in the world, next door to the Plaza Hotel and within sniffing distance of that enshrined edifice to Progressive Judaism, Temple Emanu-El. Their next step was to find an architect. Jakobovits, who kept in close touch with his sister and confidante, Lotti, who lived in New York, returned to Dublin to discuss the proposals with Amélie, who was expecting their fifth child. Their daughter, Aviva, was born on 21 April 1957. Half an hour later Rabbi Jakobovits came to Amélie with a registered letter offering him the position of first rabbi of the Fifth Avenue Synagogue, a unanimous decision on the part of the founder members, it said. And a move of tremendous vision on the part of Hymie Ross, Amélie thought to herself wryly.

For Amélie and her young family, the priority now was to find the right home in New York. She was adamant that the family could not move until that home was ready and waiting for them. Thus the capable Lotti, who lived centrally in Kew Garden Hills, was charged with the task of approving an apartment or town house before the deal was sealed. In this quest she was aided by Henry Hirsch's wife, Myrtle. Jakobovits gave his own community six months' notice of his intention to leave.

He fulfilled his pledge to the new synagogue that he would officiate at its New Year service with eleven men as its congregation, but then returned to Dublin to work out his notice. The family settled down to wait for news of their house. Nothing happened. Jakobovits had promised the Hirschs that he would definitely be *in situ* to officiate at their daughter Karen's wedding on 20 December of that year. About four weeks before the wedding, Lotti telephoned with news of a 'wonderful, wonderful house that Mrs Hirsch and the other members had found on the corner of East 62nd Street and Fifth Avenue'.

Lotti was drooling. You could not possibly dream of a more fairy-tale home, she assured Amélie. It was a house on four levels with two self-service elevators, and her vivid description of it has remained with Amélie as one of those rare moments of hyperbole: 'It has these three wonderful bathrooms, all marble, and the taps are made of pure gold, Amélie. You have no idea what a wonderful house it is!' Amélie's romantic imagination swiftly caught the fairy-tale mood from her sister-in-law and, since the practical side of the deal seemed well in hand, she said to her husband, 'Let's go. We will be well in time for the wedding in December if we leave now.'

The Irish community was loath to let them go, however, and the family was fêted all over Dublin. Amélie recalls one party after another and the gifts they received reflected an excessive generosity. Daughter of a rabbi she may have been, under subtle pressure to remain ascetic as far as material goods were concerned, yet there was something very French in Amélie, something gleefully feminine and *jeune fille* that could not resist the ornamentation, the gilding and the sheer frippery. 'What I particularly admired was a tremendous candelabra standing at least two feet tall with four branches; in the middle was a huge glass bowl meant to be filled with fruit or flowers. It was a magnificent piece.'

The affection and largesse made it very hard for her to leave Dublin. But it also evoked the pain of leaving Paris ten years earlier, the awkwardness of the young girl embarking on a new life far from home, married to a man she barely knew. Now Amélie

131

recognised her deep attachment to what she describes as the 'sweet kindness' and the 'homely atmosphere both created by our Jewish community and our non-Jewish friends', just as she had missed what she considers the *joie de vivre* of her Paris home.

With more than a touch of sentimentality she mourned the first few years of her marriage while her mother-in-law was still with them. It saddened her to reflect that never again would she sit in the evenings in the study listening to classical music, doing Irish embroidery with Mrs Jakobovits. Amélie often reflects that her married life started back to front: sitting around doing embroidery would normally be the province of the retired.

Perhaps Amélie sensed that what she would miss in the transatlantic adventure ahead was the Irish richness of character and shared instinct for her own values – family life and morality. She dreaded leaving her familiar world and entering an unknown sphere. 'I have always said that it is much harder for a wife and mother to reshape her life. She moves on for the well-being of her husband's career. When he moves, he already knows what he is moving for and what he intends to do, but when you as a wife follow, you have to rebuild your own world not knowing what is expected of you.'

Amélie rightly anticipated the change of tempo in the American life that awaited. Despite her apprehensions, she felt her own temperament would harmonise with it, would move with the same beat. She curbed the sadness within her and, knowing that at the very least she would have her beloved Lotti for support, she tuned in to the life ahead.

18   The New World

AMÉLIE DID not yet realise how overpowering the membership of the Fifth Avenue Synagogue could be, occupied as she was with the move and the children's prospective education. The sisterhood – as the FAS termed its synagogue ladies' guild – were assembled at the airport to meet them, and presented Amélie with a huge bouquet of red roses. The family spent the first night with Lotti and her husband, Rabbi Fabian Schonfeld, at their home in Kew Garden Hills, near the airport. They planned to meet the Hirsches and Mirkins the following day after what Amélie somewhat hopefully anticipated as 'a good night's rest'.

However, this was not to be. That first night they had to call the doctor because baby Aviva had developed chickenpox before leaving Dublin, and on the plane her temperature had risen. The doctor was fairly cursory in his examination, upon which Amélie protested to him: 'You didn't examine every part of my baby, Doctor, you didn't examine her chest!' The doctor turned to Amélie, slowly glancing her over and said, 'Ma'am, would I tell *you* how to make gefilte fish?' Amélie's response was to burst into tears. 'I want to go back to Dublin,' she wept, 'nobody in Dublin would speak to me like that. *Nobody.* None of the doctors in Ireland would have the cheek. I'm not staying here!'

But worse was to come. Two days later Shoshana, then aged two and a half, managed to unscrew a child-proof bottle of baby aspirins and swallowed the lot. She was rushed to hospital, where her stomach was pumped out, and had to remain there overnight for observation. The child seemed to have come to no harm, but two days later she repeated the enterprise. 'So much for the supposedly brilliant invention of unscrewable bottles and the temptation of orange candy-coated baby aspirins,' sniffs Amélie.

Between rushing one child to hospital and caring for another at home, Amélie's petulant mood subsided and she accompanied Lotti and the children to the new house. She made a point of bringing the children because she refused to be overwhelmed by Lotti's enthusiasm and wanted to assess the practicalities of the place for the needs of her growing family. It was a large town house, which had an enormous hall graced with an impressive marble staircase and two self-service elevators. Downstairs were an old-fashioned but elegant kitchen and a scullery. The lounge and dining-room were on the first floor, and there were two bedrooms on the second floor with one of the lavish bathrooms Lotti had described. On the third floor were a further three bedrooms with magnificent bathrooms *en suite*. It was an undeniably splendid property.

Amélie went downstairs and told Myrtle Hirsch: 'I can't move into this house unless you give me the personnel, the staff to run it and make sure our little boys and the other children won't get stuck in the self-service elevators.' Mrs Hirsch implied that the question of domestic help was the family's responsibility. Jakobovits made no comment. 'My husband never interfered with my domestic needs,' says Amélie.

Subsequently, she discovered that the house had been offered to the community at a very low price because it could not be sold on the open market. Its recent history was tinged with the dark symbolism of crime fiction: someone had been shot dead in the house and the body had never been found. How much of this did the founding fathers (and mothers) of the FAS know? Amélie insists that they knew nothing beyond the fact that they had been offered the house at a knock-down price. She believes that it was her beloved grandfather, Natan Goldberger, who guided her away from accepting the house. 'Can you imagine – settling down in it and then being told there was a dead body somewhere!' (The house was eventually bought by the then US President Richard Nixon and Nelson Rockefeller, who pulled it down and built a condominium on the site. When Rockefeller moved into the house with his first wife, he was found together with his second wife-to-be, Rebecca, so clearly for some it was not the luckiest house in New York.)

There was a functional apartment above the new synagogue, but Amélie and Rabbi Jakobovits did not care to live 'above the shop'. The architect-designed building consisted of a vast hall suitable for receptions and kiddushim, with a small daily chapel or *Beth Hamedrash* next to the secretary's study and the rabbi's study, with the ladies' gallery on the third floor. Above was a huge gym and above that the potential rabbi's quarters. In Amélie's words, the synagogue was 'sweet and lovely and had a warm intimacy'.

On arrival, Jakobovits discovered that the only Orthodox rabbi on the west side of Manhattan, Rabbi Leo Jung, originally from Germany, had given his permission for the elevator in the new synagogue to be used on the Sabbath, provided it was operated by a non-Jew. Jakobovits was not satisfied with that arrangement and called in the engineers. Together they created a system in which the elevator would become self-operational for several pre-set hours, stopping on every floor and enabling people to enter and exit automatically. The lift was programmed to operate from Friday afternoon to the very end of Shabbat, and it worked successfully for twenty-five years and still does. Amélie rues the fact that neither she nor her husband had sufficient business acumen to patent the invention because it would have yielded a tremendous financial return. The lift was subsequently patented and introduced in many strictly observant hotels and private apartments in America and Israel.

Until a suitable home could be found, the Jakobovits family had to divide themselves between various relatives. Amélie, Immanuel, Aviva and Shoshana stayed with the Schonfelds in Kew Garden Hills, while Yoel, Shmuel and Esther went to live with their mother's family in Borough Park, Brooklyn. After a three-month search, they found two apartments on the first floor of Cumberland House, on the corner of Medicine Avenue and 62nd Street, one block away from the synagogue. These they knocked into one large apartment, which remains the rabbi's residence to this day.

It had three bedrooms, one of which doubled as a family room and playroom during the day, and the girls' bedroom at night. Amélie turned the other large room into a combined lounge-dining-room. There were two kitchens, one of which became a

Pesach kitchen, a conversion Amélie would not recommend since she soon realised the impracticalities of giving up a kitchen for a whole year that could have simply been a dairy kitchen. Theirs was the only apartment with a balcony, which made it ideal for a *succah*.* There were also three separate bathrooms.

On the day the Jakobovits family actually moved into their new apartment, Lotti instructed her sister-in-law on the dress code required for 'the most elegant area in the world'. The children, she insisted, must never go out with a button missing or a tear in their clothes, 'or G-d forbid, a stain. They should always look just so.' Amélie had to ensure that everyone would 'look up, not only to us but also to our children'.

It was with some trepidation that Amélie absorbed Lotti's advice on the journey. When they finally stopped in front of Cumberland House and the obligatory gold-fringed and studded doorman leaped towards them, it seemed that not just this highly paid functionary but all the power and glory of jet-setting New York had descended on them. How would the young family be regarded? Would they be considered arrivistes in a calculating, high-flying world they barely understood?

Anxiously smoothing her own clothes and gazing critically at her children, Amélie watched Lotti open the boot of the car. She will never forget the ensuing scene as her sister-in-law put her head into the boot to retrieve something, only to find her *sheitel* stuck on top of the car. So much for her etiquette lessons! Amélie and Lotti forgot everything and burst out laughing.

The community paid for the apartment, its renovation and contents, leaving the choice of decor and furniture to Amélie. Despite its manifestations of serious wealth and power, Amélie did not consider the community generous, and with hindsight regrets her own lack of expertise in failing to achieve sufficient financial security for the family. 'My mistake was not to realise how much we really needed for the numbers of people in our family, and also for the kind of work we wanted to do, particularly in regard to

---

*A four-sided, open roofed hut hung with fruit and vegetables in which Jews eat and sometimes sleep to celebrate the harvest festival of Succot, or Tabernacles, beginning on the full moon of autumn five days after Yom Kippur and lasting eight days (seven in Israel).

entertaining, which I love, not for the sake of it, but for being able to talk to people, for the stimulus. But while sitting down to discuss salary with the lay leadership, I never had anyone to advise me.'

Here Amélie is inclined to paint a picture of herself as an *ingénue* abroad, but then the scope of her vision tended as much towards the romantic as the practical: 'As my husband says, you are able to discharge your work – your dreams of what you want to achieve for your community – much better around your dining table than with a thousand sermons. Therefore our door was always open.' But to keep that door open was expensive. Amélie found herself footing their daily entertainment bill out of her own budget.

The idea of developing relationships in terms of a 'religious leadership couple' involved sharing the congregation's problems, headaches and heartaches. And behind that lay a more subtle purpose: 'taking the community deeper into the love of authentic Judaism'. Yet they had barely arrived in New York when they received a visit from Amélie's uncle, Rabbi Eli Munk from London, whose judicious view was not long in coming. 'If you had been my daughter, I would have advised you not to take your children into such an opulent congregation,' he declared. Uncle Eli feared that exposure to such rarified life-styles would adversely affect the children.

It was true, Amélie reflected. Only the wealthiest could afford to live in this community, and they naturally tended to be middle-aged or elderly rather than couples with young children. Even for those who could afford it, the location offered few good Jewish schools or recreational opportunities. Amélie felt spoiled by this ageing community, who seemed to regard her as a daughter or granddaughter. If she also felt short-changed over entertainment money, there were other compensations.

For instance, Amélie was often overwhelmed by the generosity the community extended to them when invited to the rabbi's home. Where most people might bring flowers or books, their guests would bring china. As a result, much of the Jakobovits household was built up from these gifts from individual members. For one Friday night dinner invitation Amélie would receive an entire tea-set, or a set of salad bowls, or crystal, or the most elegant coffee set. The gifts were generally of a practical nature. The community was so generous in this respect that Amélie would one day manage to replenish both their homes in Israel and London by the time her husband reached retirement age. Yet Amélie's incipient attraction for the expensive and the beautiful exposed her to a charge of materialism from her critics. In his authorised biography, *Lord Jakobovits*, Chaim Bermant alludes to her 'expensive taste in clothing and jewellery', which she would occasionally indulge, taking her place among 'the elegant matrons of the Upper East Side', although, he admits, with a touch of French chic entirely her own.

Amélie refutes Bermant's claim, but acknowledges the importance for an Orthodox woman to look good in a practical way: 'I don't think you could go through my wardrobe and actually find an expensive dress or suit or outfit. I have a lot of changes of clothes. I feel that it is important for me to present not only the office but also that Orthodox commitment – and make it attractive.' Here Amélie – perhaps unconsciously retaining the almost Svengali influence of her elegant Uncle Kohn – will invoke tenets of Judaism which urge everyone to make the best of themselves and to present the rituals in an attractive way. 'This doesn't mean that someone who has only plain earthenware dishes and just a little white tablecloth, or even a sheet, cannot make her Friday night table look as attractive as someone who owns a lot of silver and crystal.'

A contemporary has noted the expensive gifts given to the Jakobovits', while acknowledging that they 'came with the lifestyle. As far back as I can remember there has always been a feeling in clergy circles that the wealthier members of the community do not see the need for rabbis and their families to live in the style to which they themselves are accustomed. I think that view is wrong. Amélie always had the courage to go for what she thought was her due.'

If, by the nature of life within the elegant New York set, Amélie managed to arouse envy, she was disarmingly anxious to be liked, and her ability to succeed won general approval. As time went on, observers began to recognise one of Amélie's main gifts: the power to demonstrate to the community with 100 per cent success the value of family life. As she grew more comfortable in the community, involving herself with fund-raising and welfare work,

Amélie's efforts to advance her husband's prestige in the outside world through personal public relations began to be noted. However, she found it hard to come to terms with criticism, or to concede that it was an inevitable part of public life.

Thus she would become defensive to any charge of materialism. As the daughter of a great rabbi whose profound thinking had so influenced her, Amélie could hardly have been more wounded by such allegations. She was the last person, surely, to be attached to the world of transitory things. But being house-proud was another matter: 'I love pretty things, but very rarely expensive things which I would buy for ourselves.' For a Frenchwoman, the question is more one of style than opulence. It was in the States that the Jakobovits' developed a taste for caravan holidays, which were certainly basic, but Amélie would always pick a flower or a little weed in the fields, or leaves from a tree, with which to decorate their mobile holiday home. 'Each time I have found that nature offers something much more beautiful than anything you can buy or make yourself.'

Regarded by the New York sophisticates in her community, however, less as a social climber than a dedicated young Jewish mother, it took Amélie time to develop her own style as an Orthodox *femme du monde*, if that is not a contradiction in terms. Some contemporaries have observed her emergence from the unfashionable chrysalis stage. One Shabbat lunch chez Jakobovits is recalled vividly by a New Yorker in the advertising world: Amélie 'was this little, round, jolly lady with a *sheitel* that sat on top of her head in the environment of very chic socialites with luxurious apartments on Fifth Avenue, used to entertaining the Rockefellers and people of great affluence. She was very unsure of herself, coming from Ireland. It was a dramatic contrast. I must say, she was her mother compared with who she is now.' However, the slow change within her may have been too subliminal for Amélie herself to notice.

What impressed her New York guests about Friday night or Shabbat lunch was the way the young family behaved at the table. The father always addressed the children in conversation and included them in questions usually on religious topics. Observers noticed that at this time Amélie did not demonstrate any other outside interests apart from her family. Yet she was quietly absorbing everything around her.

In America Amélie was struck by the celebration of the new, the original, in sharp contrast to European tradition where things simmered over centuries. Here was the society of the instantaneous – whether a detergent or a rabbi – prepared for the soundbite to come. Soon, she remarked, everybody wanted to come along and see what it was like to be led by an Irish rabbi, as rare a being in their mythology as a fourth leaf on a shamrock.

For the founding members of the FAS, the originality of their experiment was to prove to the world that a strict Orthodoxy, in harmony with the secular hierarchies of art, science and business, was the ideal solution. It would require a spiritual courage, a great leap of faith that Rabbi Jakobovits found inviting, even though his own experience may have warned him that it was an unlikely marriage. Were they really about to witness the dawn of a new Enlightenment merging the secular philosophies with European traditional Jewish thought? The leaders of the community – all strongly entrenched in the business or intellectual worlds – clearly thought so. The service was augmented with traditional cantors, such as Barnie Bloomstein, originally a choirboy in London's Great Synagogue, followed by Joseph Malovani, reputedly one of the great cantors of the twentieth century.

As for the team themselves, Henry Hirsch, whose dream the new synagogue was, is described by Amélie as a very sweet, simple but very successful businessman, a pioneer of the air-conditioning business. Closely associated with him was Herman Merkin, a merchant-shipping magnate, who took on the presidency because Hirsch was considered the dreamer. Hirsch's wife, Myrtle, had a practical head and helped bring the dream to fruition. Amélie describes her as an elegant woman who had a great impact on the development of the congregation, although she preferred to take a background role. Henry Hirsch became chairman, which, in America, has a lesser function than that of president. Hirsch was a modest person who consistently refused to sit in the front, but always took a seat at the back of the synagogue.

Best known of the founding fathers, who perhaps embodied all the creative and religious worlds they wished to bridge, was the

American-Jewish novelist, Herman Wouk. He was celebrated for his classic novel, *The Caine Mutiny*, but the popular *Marjorie Morningstar*, later filmed with Natalie Wood, about a Jewish wannabe actress who adapts her name from Morgenstern in order to succeed in Hollywood, was frowned on by the Fifth Avenue community, who felt such exposure of the Jewish condition was really letting the community down. The US, of course, was not alone in publishing these neurosis-rippers. Such a mood of intellectual honesty similarly pervaded Britain during the late 1950s and 1960s, when writers like Brian Glanville, Gerda Charles, Lionel Davidson and Arnold Wesker all published revelatory plays and novels about the inner workings of the Jewish psyche.

For an Orthodox Jew in New York, however, this behaviour was not acceptable. 'The congregation was unhappy about [Wouk's] book,' says Amélie, 'and I well remember the day he came into my husband's office at the Fifth Avenue Synagogue, with a sweet, shy, rather self-effacing smile and the very first copy of his book, his personal manifesto of Judaism, *This is My God*, and he said to Immanuel, "This is my way of making amends for *Marjorie Morningstar*."' While Wouk drew back from justifying the writing of *Marjorie Morningstar*, the community preferred to see the book just as a moneymaker and could not quite equate it with his personality.

Wouk's mother headed the women's division of New York's Yeshiva University for many decades, for which she ran successful evenings at the New York opera house, the Metropolitan. She had devout beliefs herself, and Herman's own faith deepened over time, particularly after he suffered a great tragedy in his personal life when one of his young sons died after falling head-first into a swimming-pool.

Amélie's recollection of Wouk is of a tall, distinguished, calmly dignified yet approachable person, a man with a presence. She remembers him as a very serious, relatively quiet person known to study a page of the Talmud each day, for which he was noted at Marble Arch Synagogue in London as well as at Palm Springs in California. Amélie acknowledges him as one of the world's most deeply religious celebrities. She recollects a day in Palm Springs when her husband came home after morning prayers and told her that it had become increasingly fashionable for Orthodox men to place their prayer shawls over their head, in order not to be diverted from their prayers. When he took off his *talit*, he noticed that the Bobover Rebbe from New York was standing on his left-hand side, and on his right stood Herman Wouk, both of whom had their prayer shawls on and only discovered each other after removing them later. Wouk's membership of the FAS undoubtedly contributed to its cachet, and he also introduced several other members to the synagogue.

1. 'Oma', Matthilda Goldberger (Amélie's maternal grandmother) with her children, Nuremberg, 1916. The children, from left to right: Fanny (Amélie's mother), Heimi, Tossi, Baby Ruth, Malie and Etta.

2. 'Opa', Natan Goldberger (Amélie's maternal grandfather) with three of his daughters, c. 1918. The children, from left to right: Malie, Etta and Fanny (Amélie's mother).

3. Fanny Goldberger and Rabbi Elie Munk (Amélie's parents) on their engagement, early 1926.

4. Immanuel as a boy, 1926.

5. Fanny Goldberger just before her wedding, Nuremberg, 1927.

6. Natan Goldberger's warehouse in Nuremberg, 1928.

7. Exterior of the synagogue in Ansbach.

8. 'Opa', Shmuel Munk (Amélie's paternal grandfather), Ansbach, 1932. The children, from left to right: Jacki, Ruth (Amélie's brother and sister) and Amélie.

9. Amélie (right) and her cousin Eva, Nuremberg, 1934.

10. Mr Adolf Kohn, his wife, Ruth (Amélie's maternal aunt) and their three children, Gateshead, early 1940s. The children, from left to right: Tani, Livia and Miriam.

11. A discount card from c. 1945. After the war, de Gaulle instigated a discount scheme for families with more than 5 children to encourage the repopulation of France. It offered a 30% discount on travel and basic food stuffs such as bread, sugar and grain.

12. Amélie, Nice, summer 1948.

13. Dublin, 1956. From left to right: Yoel, Mrs Jakobovits senior (Immanuel's mother), Esther, Immanuel, Shoshanna, Amélie and Shmuel.

14. Rabbi Dr Elie Munk (Amélie's father), re-dedicating the Ansbach
Synagogue, 1964. (Photograph from Diana Fitz, *Ansbach unterm Hakenkreuz*,
Ansbach: Stadt Ansbach, 1994).

15. Lotti Schönfeld (Immanuel's sister), 1959. This is the last picture taken before she died.

16. Amélie and her husband, New York, 1966.

17. Farewell dinner of the Fifth Avenue Synagogue, 1967. From left to right: Amélie, Herman Merkin, Immanuel, Senator Jovits, Max Kettner, Henry Hirsch, Abe Jaffe, Sam Elowsky, Judge Saul Rosenberg.

18. From left to right: The Chief Rabbi and Amélie, Rabbi Rosen (Chief Rabbi of Romania) and a Clergyman of the Greek Orthodox Church, Bucharest, 1980.

19. Sir Immanuel Jakobovits after receiving his Knighthood, Buckingham Palace, June 1981. Back row, from left to right: Shoshanna, Aviva, Norman Turner (Shoshanna's husband), Elisheva, Amélie, Immanuel, Esther, Rabbi Chaim Pearlman (Esther's husband). Front row, from left to right: Israel Turner, Eliezer Pearlman, Zipporah Pearlman, Yehuda Pearlman. (Photograph courtesy of Sidney Harris)

20. Amélie with Felicia B. Axelrod, MD, 1984. Dr Axelrod is one of only two world specialists on Dysautonomia (an Ashkenazi genetic disease of the nervous system). Some 450 children worldwide have been diagnosed as suffering from the condition which requires 24-hour attention. The support group was started 20 years ago and new medical research has saved many lives.

21. Yehuda Pearlman, eldest grandson of Immanuel and Amélie at his Barmitzvah, 1985.

22. The Chief Rabbi and Amélie being presented to H.M. the Queen by Judge
Israel Finestein at the Guildhall reception to mark the 119th anniversary of
Norwood Child Care (now Ravenswood Norwood), December 1985.
(Photograph courtesy of Sidney Harris)

23. Elisheva being blessed by her father at her wedding, 1986.

24. The Jakobovits' children on the occasion of their father's induction into the House of Lords, 1987. From left to right: Elisheva, Aviva, Shoshanna, Esther, Shmuel, Yoel.

25. Ruth Winston Fox and Amélie, China, 1987.

26. Amélie with Jonathan Sacks, Chief Rabbi, September 1993.
(Photograph courtesy of John R. Rifkin)

27. Immanuel and Amélie at the wedding of their granddaughter, Zipporah Pearlman, to Eli Segal. Radleigh Close Synagogue, London, summer 1994.

28. Amélie with Tony Blair at a Jewish Care function, November 1994.
(Photograph courtesy of John R. Rifkin)

29. Margaret Thatcher at the opening of 'Schoenfeld Square,' Summer 1995. The square is a complex which houses an old age home and also offers sheltered accomodation for large families living in poverty.

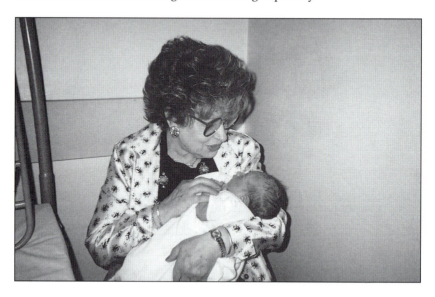

30. The second great-grandchild for Immanuel and Amélie. A little girl, Gila Nechama, for Yehuda and Chaya Pearlman, 1996.

31. The Emeritus Chief Rabbi, Amélie and the President of South Africa, Nelson Mandela, at a dinner in honour of the 10th anniversary of the Chief Rabbi of South Africa, Cyril Harris, November 1997. (Photograph courtesy of Shawn Benjamin Photography)

32. Amélie meeting H.M. the Queen Mother at the 75th Anniversary of the Stepney Settlement. (Photograph courtesy of Sidney Harris.)

19   *To Boldly Grow*

IN THE absence of her mother's good humour and homely philosophy to guide her, Amélie found a natural mentor and ally in her sister-in-law. Lotti had the kind of verve and tenacity that was highly attractive to Amélie. On moving to New York following the death of her mother-in-law in an air crash, Lotti began a community in her own right, launched in the basement of her close friends, Mary and Nat Saperstein. She also ensured that her husband entered the rabbinate at a time when he would have been quite content to remain a teacher in London at the Hasmonean Boys' School. Lotti planned that, on being ordained as a rabbi, Schonfeld would have his own community. It has since developed into one of the main Young Israel communities in America and Schonfeld has remained its rabbi, now assisted by his son Joey, thus ensuring that Lotti's desire for some of the family to become rabbis was realised.

For Amélie, too, it was time to consider the future of her family. The issue of the children's education was a priority. Despite the abundance of choice in America, they could not find the right school for their sons in the immediate vicinity. The right school easily presented itself for the girls, the Manhattan Jewish Day School on the West Side of New York, but in the case of the boys, the blend of education they sought was more difficult to obtain. After much research and deliberation, the boys were sent to the school begun by the lay leadership of Lotti's community, which offered a combination of religious and secular teaching near Lotti's home in Kew Garden Hills. Later, the boys commuted to a yeshiva high school in Queens. The cost of education, compared to Dublin where state aid to Jewish schools ensured that they were virtually free, was very expensive.

To Jakobovits' dismay and disbelief, Jewish organisations blocked a measure in the High Court to secure Federal funding for parochial schools. Committed as he was to the concept of religious education in schools, be it Jewish or Christian, Jakobovits welcomed the growth of Jewish schools since the war and recognised their need of state support. Now he feared that by their action American Jews were putting their very faith on the line. It has been argued that he failed to grasp the psychological differences between Americans and Europeans. American Jews descended from refugees who had fled religious persecution and now preferred to keep secular and religious education apart.

However, writing in the *New York Times*, Jakobovits predicted a 'generation of heathen hedonists, worshipping the idols of happiness and material success'. He further vented his views in *Journal of a Rabbi*, deriding schools which failed to provide religious training as 'career factories, turning out morally indifferent robots'. These fears were to fuel the lecture tours to come in which he would berate American Jewry for lapsing from Jewish life, for failing to replicate themselves, reflected by the low Jewish birth rate, and for their involvement in pornography. Perhaps more surprisingly for an Orthodox rabbi, he also deplored the Jewish tendency to become 'the most urbanised people on earth', insensitive to the 'thrills and quiet inspiration' of nature.

This love of the countryside, the ability to hear what he described as 'the mystic eloquence of a rushing stream' or the 'sweet, soothing music of a humming-bird', invited the latent poetry in the man, and this was something in which Amélie shared when they embarked on their caravan holidays in the country. It is tempting to speculate that this unusual attraction in an orthodox couple for the spiritual in nature may have been a reaction to New York life, representing as it does urbanisation at its most intense, materialism at its peak, the neurosis of high-rise living at its most threatening.

Meanwhile, Amélie joined two other Fifth Avenue women in the running of a kindergarten in the synagogue. Despite the dearth of young families in this, the wealthiest square mile in the world, there were still enough to justify the scheme, which was also intended to attract other young couples into the congregation.

The initial intake was ten children. It had never occurred to Amélie herself to send a child as young as two or three away from its mother for up to three hours a day, but one day one of the mothers asked her why she did not send her youngest daughter, Aviva, to the kindergarten. Disingenuously Amélie replied that it was her job to take care of her daughter for as long as possible. The mother replied that this attitude would persuade the other mothers that the rabbi's wife did not consider the kindergarten good enough for her own child. Amélie saw the point of this and she recalls how Aviva, the quietest of all her siblings, turned into a lively, communicative child as soon as she joined the other children in the kindergarten. It was a decision which made her re-think her earlier attitude towards mothers with very young children. When she saw how children thrived in each others' company and reflected upon the tremendous improvement in her own daughter, she became very much more involved with the activities of the kindergarten.

But barely seven months after the Jakobovits' arrived in New York, just as they were settling into the community, tragedy struck. The family joined Lotti and her husband in Candlewood Lake in the Kendal Woods, where they rented a small summer house to escape the unbearable heat of New York in July. Fabi suggested going swimming, but Lotti suddenly admitted to a pain in her left side which she had kept secret for the last few months, and claimed that she did not feel strong enough to swim from the side of the lake to the raft. As Lotti swam like a fish, her husband, known as something of a hypochondriac, became very concerned. He invited his wife to an open-air movie in town, which happened to be *The Ten Commandments*, but before going to the movie, he stopped at the hospital, where Lotti was examined, given blood tests and requested to return the next day for the results. The family had noticed that she was eating badly, but because she was such a staunch and feisty personality, the Number One of the family, nobody had ever questioned her. However, Amélie had noticed that for a long time she had been very tired and needed a lot of sleep. The following day Lotti was diagnosed as having an acute form of leukaemia. The family went into shock.

'I had a suspicion that Lotti knew what she had,' Amélie says, 'and to this day I still argue with my brother-in-law about it. For him, it is a sort of comfort that she didn't know. We had just left Dublin at a time when a little boy had died of leukaemia, and she knew all the signs because we had often talked about it; but she was completely unselfish and endured eight months of pain without telling anybody.'

Fabi took Lotti to hospital despite Amélie's pleadings to leave her with them over Shabbat, because the hospital insisted on an immediate blood transfusion. When Amélie wanted to visit her there, Lotti begged her on the phone not to leave the children alone out in the country. She feared the dangers of the lake close to their bungalows. 'If you want to do something for me,' she urged, 'just stay with the kids.'

Amélie never saw her sister-in-law again. Lotti died in hospital in that summer of 1959. She was thirty-six. She left four children, aged two to fourteen years. It is clear that even when Amélie speaks of Lotti now, years later, the deep bond remains, as does the pain of her death. 'I was so close to her and depended so much on her and could not visualise how my life in the USA would carry on without Lotti. She was so full of life, so beautiful.'

One of the secrets of the special relationship between the sisters-in-law was the fact that Amélie perceived something of her own mother in Lotti. 'She was exactly as if she had been born to my mother,' she says. Amélie had often been told by the Jakobovits family that they thought he was attracted to her because she so resembled his sister, something which gave Amélie great comfort and which she considers the greatest compliment anybody could pay her. Indeed, Amélie has a particular enchantment in her voice when she speaks of this soul sister destined to die so young. Lotti was perhaps the older sibling for whom Amélie may have sub-consciously yearned, forged, as she says, from Fanny Munk's spirit and with some of the same iron in Amélie's soul.

Immanuel was devastated by his sister's death; they had been virtually as close as Siamese twins. He gave voice to the inner darkness that consumed him on her death and in seeking comfort from the prophet, Isaiah, seemed to grow closer to the spirit of his sister as he reached towards the light she had always reflected to him. Certainly the attractive and dynamic Lotti would have been a welcome ally in the years that lay ahead for Amélie, particularly in her dealings with the élite corps of the Fifth Avenue sisterhood. But this road Amélie had to travel alone.

As members of an Orthodox community, the Fifth Avenue women made their presence felt very powerfully through their menfolk. Short of actually running the religious services, the women ensured that all the 250 members of the synagogue knew each other and were as actively involved in the development of the community and its projects as their husbands. One Orthodox contemporary who occasionally worshipped at the FAS, noticed certain tensions between Amélie and some of the more prominent members. She also points out that her husband was seen by some as 'maybe too religious'. Time and again on his lecture tours he demonstrated his unbending adherence to strict Orthodox values no matter the climate of opinion around him. As a counterweight to this, however, he was also far-sighted enough to observe that 'the fragmentation of Jewish religious life in the New World is approaching the stage when we have to think in terms of different Jewish denominations of the Christian pattern'.

If these or other more personal issues led to inter-communal tension, Amélie preferred to rationalise them. She accepted that the very closeness of the community in itself invited differences and occasional disagreements. Coming from a large family herself, she was well aware that people did not always agree with each other, but on the whole she found the synagogue had an atmosphere of friendship, patience and tolerance. The philosophical outlook nurtured by her mother helped her to temper any irritation she might feel with humour. This has taught her to 'completely forget' very unpleasant situations, while remembering difficult ones from which she could learn something.

Stress and exhaustion following Lotti's death and the need to take care of so many children – Lotti's, on a temporary basis, as well as her own – played havoc with Amélie's figure during this period. She put on nearly two stone through an eating pattern which many young mothers will empathise with – by 'finishing off the children's plates instead of sitting down and eating a proper meal myself!' Amélie's wry affirmation that 'I had become a very heavy girl' did not escape the critical eye of the svelte and sophisticated *beau monde* among whom she lived. On the second day of

Rosh Hashanah, Mrs Merkin suddenly whispered to her, 'Mrs Jakobovits, how can you let yourself go that way when you are married to such a handsome man?' This remark gave her a jolt, launched her on a successful diet and prepared her for the life-long battle 'between my body and myself!'

The wives of the founder members were very aware of their influence over the direction the community would take and the way their opinions infiltrated into the progress of the synagogue, certainly during the first five years of the time Rabbi Jakobovits was in office. This gave them the sense of equality with their husbands.

Apart from her involvement with the kindergarten, Amélie preferred at first to take a back seat, adhering to the principles she had formulated in Ireland, that it was fairer not to take executive positions with any committees, nor even attend meetings rather than invite invidious charges of favouritism. However, the strategies that worked in Ireland were clearly inappropriate in New York. After three months Myrtle Hirsch demanded to know why Amélie never attended meetings. In vain did Amélie protest that, of course, she was always there for anyone to share ideas with her. Myrtle told her in no uncertain terms that things in New York were different: 'As the rabbi's wife you are expected to turn up at meetings and show your involvement and concern in a physical way.' Amélie was particularly fond of Mrs Hirsch, describing her as 'my American fairy godmother – a very beautiful lady, not only attractive to look at but beautiful from within. She shared everything with me, pain or joy, and gave ready advice if I needed it.' So Amélie changed her tactics and started to attend meetings, just as Myrtle had advised, although she remained true to the principle of not taking executive office.

Years later Amélie was to recall Myrtle's special qualities when, in 1967, that lady became Chair of Israel Bonds and one of the first Jewish women to ask others around the world to surrender their jewellery to raise funds for Israel. She herself sold a diamond knuckle-duster of a ring and earmarked the proceeds for the treatment of soldiers. She then bought a fake copy, which she wore for the rest of her life without her husband ever noticing the difference.

Life in New York did have some difficult moments for Amélie, particularly where she found herself cast in the unwitting role of the *ingénue* among somewhat daunting women. She speaks of them with a certain ambivalence, regarding them as very powerful – 'only because they were financially more endowed than I was' – but, on the other hand, describing them as kind and patient and with a manner which did not make her feel inferior. She does however admit to – 'possibly some small incidents'.

One occurred during a dinner party, when, according to social rules, she did not tell her guests who else was invited. The first guest to arrive brought her wheelchair-bound mother, and Amélie casually revealed over drinks who the other members of the party would be. To her horror, her friend turned white and said, 'If they walk through that door, my mother will die.' Amélie barely had time to catch her breath before the doorbell rang. She went to the entrance door and asked the new arrivals, 'What am I going to do? She says her mother will die if you walk in!' The couple, active founder members of the synagogue, appeared very understanding and explained that Amélie had obviously not known that they were not on speaking terms. Courteously they offered to leave immediately and make up for it another day. A disconsolate Amélie made her excuses to her other guests and walked a couple of blocks with them towards their home, desperately apologising and trying to assuage in advance any hurt feelings that might develop later.

Yet Shabbat was barely over when she received a phone call from Myrtle Hirsch lambasting her for having seriously upset a founder member. 'What have you done, Rebbetzin?' she exploded. 'How could you see them out of the door when you'd invited them for dinner! We could lose these people, we could make a terrible name for the community. It's unforgivable what you did!'

Amélie went to pieces. She implored her husband to go with her to apologise to the wronged couple. 'But my husband is not a person who apologises. The whole Jakobovits family don't like to apologise. It's very rare that they can accept that they have actually made a mistake which requires an apology. But I was crying so hard that he acknowledged that it was not my fault and could not have known they weren't on speaking terms.' Gently, however, Rabbi Jakobovits chided his wife that the whole incident could have been avoided had she informed everyone of the guest list instead of sticking to her 'crazy unwritten law that you don't tell people who else is coming to dinner'. Eventually, Immanuel softened and accompanied his wife to make due amends to the party concerned. Amélie would not stop crying until they accepted the apology, but she had an uncomfortable feeling that the president of the community would be less forgiving.

Amélie went into a deep depression. She did not leave her bed for three days and had no luck persuading her friend who had caused the problem in the first place to intercede on her behalf with the chairman's wife. It seemed almost as though she were throwing herself willingly into the lion's den and insisting on being devoured, instead of walking away with dignity, having expressed her regrets over the incident. Myrtle Hirsch finally put Amélie out of her misery by relenting, but not without a gentle warning. 'Okay,' she reproved her. 'It was a mistake, that's fine; but I am sure you'll never make one like that again.' Amélie accepted the admonition, which was perhaps the one she had sought, and revised for ever her entire practice of whom-to-invite-to-dinner. It was, if you like, Amélie's induction into the world of diplomacy.

At this time the Jakobovits' had been asked to take in a paying guest, Rivka Landesman, who needed to live with a family near her Jewish high school. Amélie grew close to this girl, who became 'like our daughter', but one day Rivka told her that she knew there were some community members of whom Amélie did not think very highly, and could not understand how she could greet them on a Saturday morning with a warm and friendly smile. 'Isn't that very hypocritical?' the young girl asked. She reflected that she herself could never be a rabbi's wife 'because it follows that she has to be a hypocrite'.

Amélie had certainly never thought of herself that way. After thinking deeply about it, she admitted that although she may not like certain people, she had discovered that if only she had the patience to cultivate a friendship in someone she did not particularly admire, she would invariably find something good in that person and would benefit by deepening her own quality of mind and heart. Amélie learned equally from the question. Had the young girl not challenged her, she feels that she would not have made so many friends in the community. Meanwhile, Amélie's great talent for communication and her genuine concern for the sick were qualities that were beginning to make themselves felt among her contemporaries. Describing her as a 'great rebbetzin in New York', Ulla Merkin recalls Amélie's interest in the lives and problems of the congregation and admires her tolerance, particularly in the light of the various degrees of Orthodox observance it reflected. Amélie, she noticed, 'had time for everybody and everything'. She undertook every aspect of pastoral care, from hospital and home visits to staying with relatives of a patient during surgery, baking *challot* for Shabbat, and inviting congregants to her home and excluding nobody. Amélie was helped by a healthy lack of inhibition, Mrs Merkin noticed, and was always the diplomat, avoiding the inevitable frictions and clashes which defined a new community. The telephone was her great communicator. Sometimes she made up to a dozen calls a day, omitting private ones. 'I always envied her the gift of speaking on the phone and cooking or making cakes at the same time.' Most of all, Mrs Merkin praises her sunny, outgoing temperament, which, she claims, 'helped her and the Rabbi through thick and thin'.

Very soon the Fifth Avenue Synagogue became a vital part of the American Jewish scene and the community responded positively towards what Amélie viewed as an improvement in the Jewish community's way of life. The format of synagogue activities remains the same today as when Jakobovits first conceived it. There is a Monday night *shiur* (religious teach-in) for men on the Talmud, and one for women on Wednesday morning. He also innovated a ten-minute Friday night sermon before the service, which takes the form of a resume on the following morning's reading of the law. Many enjoyed this more than the Shabbat morning sermon.

The 1950s were years of war recovery offering tentative moves towards religious revivalism, of which the FAS was perhaps the most prominent example. But they gave way to a more dynamic era – the 1960s – in which the dawn of political awareness spread from Europe to the rest of the free world. Some of it was not at all to Amélie's liking. She somewhat cryptically refers to the 1960s as a decade riven with certain evils – in other words, student activism – and it revived memories of her own life in the Yeshurun movement in Paris, which was also marked by rebellious spirits who were very agitated about the adults around them. Amélie herself remembers as a teenager dismissing the adult society as the bourgeoisie, but came to believe during motherhood that the most intolerant people were the student bodies themselves.

As universities all over Europe staged sit-ins, some synagogues followed suit, often in some right-wing religious protest, notably the famous Rue de la Victoire Synagogue in Paris. Their successful sit-in was aimed at removing the mixed choir and organ in accordance with their interpretation of Jewish law, which forbids the use of a musical instrument on the Sabbath. The rumbles of religious discontent spread to America, too.

20   *The Sisterhood*

AS IT inspired other forms of political protest, student unrest also awoke the dormant spirit of feminism, which Amélie was inclined to dismiss somewhat disingenuously as 'nothing really new – remember the suffragettes?' There had always been a women's movement for one right or another, she declared. To religious proto-feminists, such an argument points to rude complacency on the part of the well-heeled women members of the FAS in the face of their sisters' struggle elsewhere for women's religious rights. Yet here Amélie points out that quite simply there was no battle: the Fifth Avenue women's involvement in the decision-making process of programmes planned with the lay leadership and the rabbi was total. Its remit included praying and socialising together on an equal footing, according to Jewish law, while the issues of Halacha (the code of Jewish law), as far as women were concerned, remained relatively minor because of the relationship between the rabbi and his community. Jakobovits had the time to handle any individual situation which might have arisen on these issues.

Unlike Britain, there is no central religious authority in America,* which gives each rabbi greater control over the decision-making of his community, leading to more freedom of action and leadership. Because each community in America has total autonomy over its destiny, any interpretation of the text and commandments concerning women's issues, for example, remains individual to each community.

The women of the FAS decided to form themselves, not into a

*Other differences between America and Britain include that of proving Halachic descent in the US, because of the lack of records. In Anglo-Jewry, however, all the archives are kept in the office of the Chief Rabbinate, where in Britain a person's roots can be traced back up to five generations.

ladies' guild, but that very American concept, a sisterhood. The sisterhood was an eclectic group, conscientiously rejecting a written constitution, becoming more democratic and less prey to 'women's lib agitation', in Amélie's words. Amélie was concerned that as such an affluent community – 'we were *à l'aise*, materially very blessed' – they should care for someone, adopt a project of true social consciousness. Amélie's proposal to take on one Israeli and one American charity project was well received by the sisterhood, and they began work on three parallel programmes: the development of the synagogue itself; the Maimonides Institute of America, then in its infancy; and a post-natal rest home in Bayit Vagan, Israel, where each mother was charged a token fee following the birth of her baby, in order not to feel she was receiving charity.

Amélie began to express her ideals of working on behalf of womanhood, the tacit idea of equality without making an issue out of it. 'I believe in preventive measures and if I act as a woman convinced of my equality with men, I can transmit that to any group of women who care to listen to my approach.' Amélie's attitude to the feminist movement was simply that men had one set of duties and women had another. Once she asked her husband whether his late father would have approved of her had he lived. Immanuel replied, 'Without any doubt my father would have loved you, Amélie, because you don't walk behind me, nor in front of me, but beside me.'

Raised by a father who taught her, from the age of four or five, that she was the exact equal of her brothers only different, Amélie could point to the powerful influence on Jewish life of the great matriarchs, Sarah, Rachel, Rebecca and Leah. If other women elsewhere were seeking more active participation in religious services, Judaism for the FAS remained a sealed and sanctified place whose members were content with the status quo. As another contemporary, who describes herself as a fringe member of the synagogue, observes, 'I wouldn't have thought these people would have had very much interest in seeking social, religious change. It was considered quite taboo for women to have their own services unless you were Conservative or Reform. They felt things should go on as before.'

To Amélie, secure in her Orthodoxy, such questions were largely irrelevant. But while describing herself as a feminist in her own right, she was always fundamentally opposed to the goals the feminist movement set out to achieve. They ignored, in her mind, an inherent wisdom: male aggression derives from a single source – men are biologically weaker than women and live with the constant fear of being proved so. Since they consequently have a sense of unconscious insecurity with women, they may become aggressive in certain situations, as a defence mechanism, in order to assert their superiority. Women, therefore, should be kinder, more sensitive, in dealing with them, she urges, instead of reacting to the false belief that men look down on them. To prove her point, she indicates the higher infant mortality among males, adding that biological factors prove that the physical make-up of the masculine gender contains inherent weaknesses in comparison to the female, facts which, she claims, apply throughout life for men. 'There is another factor: that men attain maturity later than women; hence in the Jewish religion the Batmitzvah of a girl is celebrated on her twelfth birthday, a year earlier than a boy's, because the Torah recognises that a girl matures earlier than a boy.'

Amélie has never seen any impediment to women's progress in the fields of education, social welfare or Zionism, so long as they avoid making a philosophical issue of their activities. Repeatedly she asserts her sense of equality with men. But where she parts company with 'certain religious feminists' is in her insistence that one of the great virtues of Jewish womanhood is modesty. It is enshrined, she says, in Jewish teaching. Therefore she urges women not to distort the facts of nature or to puncture male self-esteem. Her incipient belief in woman power would come to fruition later in life when challenged by an alternative viewpoint. Meanwhile, Amélie ignored the feminist revolution in the work-place, preferring to look to the man to secure the woman's future. For her, sexual politics are transitory events, while biological as well as religious factors represent eternal truths.

Amélie finds nothing in Judaism to stop women becoming great leaders – the religion has had its women judges and prophetesses – but this must be preceded by the building up of knowledge. She admits to never having studied any text of Talmud in depth herself, but then found that the women in her community were not as religiously committed as she was, lacking her particular background and the opportunity to study. She considers it arrogant for women who are Talmudically illiterate to insist on sitting with and pressing their demands on a group of judges in religious courts. However, if a woman has truly studied the texts and is sure of her facts, then she deserves to have the opportunity to demand her rights from the dayanim.*

However, here the very concept of the word 'right' becomes a complex issue. Jewish philosophy teaches that no human being is born for rights, only for duty. Extending the debate, Amélie believes that everyone is born to fulfil a task, to contribute to the betterment of the world. Therefore an obsession with rights can lead to hectoring demonstrations supporting a narrow and one-sided philosophy, often crushing other equally valid voices. This she defines as a 'very un-Jewish concept'. 'There are human rights according to the law of the Torah, but we are not supposed to demonstrate for rights for single parenthood, for instance, or on behalf of anything which is not moral according to Jewish law. It is by your actions in life, not your preaching, which will create a *Kiddush Hashem*, which is an honour in the name of G-d wherever you move.'

In the years ahead Amélie would see the flowering of many education groups for Jewish women all over the world, enlightenment and awareness study groups on the subjects of the Talmud and the Kabbalah, many achieving great depth. While there may still be the small voice within her which holds fast to the traditional, supportive role she has always envisioned for herself, she has no problems with the Kabbalah if it is taught properly. Many women teachers and lecturers in the Talmud, the Bible and other Jewish subjects would make their presence felt; among them Aviva Zonnenberg and Naomi Heller in Jerusalem and Fia Kimche in London. Such women were to win Amélie's admiration for developing depths of Jewish learning, which they would share as teachers with large groups of women without neglecting to create

---

*Highly placed rabbinic authorities who act as judges of the Beth Din, the Jewish religious court.

the nurturing homes and family life which were always her priority.

Yet, though Amélie's preoccupations were mainly Jewish ones as far as women's rights were concerned, it was impossible for her, as a maturing woman in New York, to ignore the impetus of the feminist movement. Dazzled but not fazed by its power, she became inevitably attracted to its oblique reference to the feminine power itself. While acknowledging its virtues, Amélie was tempted to blame the movement for a variety of ills in society. As she contemplated the changing family patterns that were emergent at this time, she noted that women as a group had surrendered their 'prime duty as builders of a home or a family', and she feared that such surrender would ultimately prove damaging.

It was in New York itself that some of these ideas began to take shape – New York with its twin edifices: the rising feminist movement and the potent but orthodox Fifth Avenue sisterhood, whose mores she had to study and skilfully negotiate. Against those towering rival monuments Amélie began to evaluate what was important in the life of a woman. She recognised that her thoughts would not be deemed politically correct and might invite criticism. She had always shrunk from criticism, whether directed at herself or her husband, but could not disguise her view that mass surrender of the traditional female role has led to so many more family problems, separations and divorces.

'If I have one resentment of the Women's Lib movement', she says, 'it is that those of us who commit ourselves to building our homes have been robbed of the pride which is the most precious of all gifts – the pride in the fact that G-d trusts us, as women, to be His partners in building up the security, the warmth, the love in the homes which we are called upon to build and which is in itself a tremendous art. If we had as secure homes in which to defend the future of our people as we have a secure army in Israel today, thank G-d, to defend the lives of our people, then we would in many ways feel very much better in every other way of life. And I deeply resent that this has been taken away from womankind.'

Amélie was always happy for women to develop careers as well as families provided the family remained the priority – not simply in physical but in moral and ethical terms, too. 'It means giving a lot of love day in, day out.' She found the courage to speak out against trends in New York which she perceived as debasing these values, but her preference was always for consensus not confrontation. 'I don't like to speak out against something. It's the dialogue, not the attack, that you need in any kind of process in human relations, whether it is with your spouse, your children, your friends or a political party. The attack will undermine everything which we are trying to achieve.'

She did not shrink from speaking her mind when addressing various feminist bodies, whether Jewish, non-Jewish or mixed. It was a point which she drove home with relentless persistence: that the tendency to undermine 'the other half of human society' will eventually cause them to damage themselves. 'Why not work on ourselves individually and collectively and accept that we are equal but different?' she asks. When Amélie offered this message to active feminists, she encountered many cliché-ridden arguments, but was gratified to find that her point eventually struck home.

She refers to the experience of leading American 1960s' feminist, Gloria Steinem, who ultimately went public with her admission that she had made many mistakes and deep down regretted having lost out on building a family. 'If she, the greatest exponent of the Women's Liberation movement, can have the courage to be a little old-fashioned, why can't I?'

But Amélie's basic belief in marriage stems from her mother's homily to her at the station on the threshold of her married life. From it grew her conviction that any woman has to work on her marriage to make it a success. 'I believe with all my heart that we women have the ability and the power in the palm of our hands to make a marriage successful – and the one who makes it work is more likely to be the woman than the man.'

In later years when she herself would counsel couples, she would invariably begin with her mother's words, which had been given in a light tone full of love and affection and had seared her mind: 'You had better make your marriage work, because I am not taking you back!'

21 Amélie's Ten Commandments

ONE DAY it would fall to Amélie and her husband, as Orthodox parents, to find partners for their sons and daughters. So while under the influence of major gender issues in America, Amélie began to develop her own Ten Commandments for a successful marriage and parent–child relationship. Many people are surprised at this list because of the order of its priorities. It reveals much about Amélie's self-awareness, her spontaneity, which can be read as impulsiveness, her alacrity in seeking solutions, which can be understood as impatience, her desire for cosiness in relationships, her inclination to pamper her man, but most of all a certain sanguine acuity in her recognition of all the facets of her own character. The Commandments take the following order: 1. Respect; 2. Patience; 3. Tolerance; 4. Caring; 5. Spouse priority; 6. Sharing; 7. Love; 8. Giving; 9. Praising; 10. Saying Sorry.

Respect is the first marital demand and the true basis of partnership. 'There will be times when you have arguments – and it would be very boring if there weren't any. You can still speak like children to each other, you can have a little shout, a cross word, but intellectually you know that the respect between you and your partner is always there.'

Her First Commandment, of course, involves self-respect. 'I have always felt within myself that only *I* can protect my self-respect. No one is going to take that away. For instance, if I applied to a school and was refused, my attitude would be that the school wasn't good enough for me, not that I was turned away because the school was anti-Semitic.'

In the early days of her marriage, one evening as she sat with her mother-in-law in their Dublin study listening to music and embroidering, Amélie, pregnant with their first child, had burst out to Mrs Jakobovits Senior, '"You know, if your son Immanuel had not wanted me, I would have taken the attitude that he wasn't good enough for me." She turned absolutely white, and said to me, as his mother, "That's what *you* think!" I've never forgotten it. But having said that, thank G-d he did think I was right for him.'

In ensuing years, Amélie and her husband nurtured self-respect in their children, and she believes it has paid off. But the quality must not be confused with self-importance, she points out.

As for Patience, her Second Commandment, Amélie is the first to admit that she herself is basically not a patient person, wanting everything done immediately. 'Immanuel is very much more patient than I am and he is a wonderful teacher. Over the years I hope I have developed or refined my patience, but it's a number two ingredient in a successful marriage. So just be patient if you can't understand each other; wait for another few minutes and then start talking about it again.'

From this follows Tolerance. 'You will see in my Ten Commandments that each one is linked to the other. It is likely that you will not have the same opinion about everything, for how can two human beings who have not known each other for the formative part of their lives get together within a matter of weeks or months and then be expected to get on immediately? Every person has certain idiosyncrasies in the eyes of the other person, so you have to develop this tolerance. There are no two partners who are totally alike and both love the same things, but it is important to have the same fundamentals and share the same goals, otherwise you can't make a go of any partnership, least of all in marriage.'

Tolerance extends to many things. 'You might discover that he only brushes his teeth at night –' what kind of behaviour is that when you've always brushed yours night and morning!' Or he may throw his pyjamas on the floor instead of putting them on the bed. 'I find that terribly irritating,' Amélie admits *sotto voce*. 'You have to develop patience because you will never really teach that person to change a habit which he or she has had all his/her life.'

Tolerance as it relates to mutual compatibility must be worked on a great deal, she considers, because this may only be discovered over time and within the intimacy of marriage. 'There are certain things you cannot discover if you are religious people until you actually get married and live together, because it is strictly against Jewish law.'

Looking back on her own marriage, she recalls the day, during the early months of her first pregnancy, when she was reproached by her mother-in-law for asking Immanuel to pick up the knife she had dropped on the floor. 'I am just speaking of details which can be very irritating,' says Amélie. 'They are all small things, because in the final analysis, what we human beings get upset about are small, insignificant things and that's why tolerance is so essential in a marriage.' Of course the issue Amélie describes here is less the issue of respect between her and Immanuel as between her and her mother-in-law. 'In my case', she sighs, 'I had both to deal with.'

Caring and Spouse Priority, fourth and fifth on the list, mean avoiding the assumption, after many years of marriage, that the couple no longer need to express their mutual feelings. 'Caring is saying that you care and acting accordingly. At the end of the week, come home with something special for the weekend. If you are not the kind of person attuned to care about another, at least make an effort once a week, a month, two months, certainly once every three months, to show you care. You have to show it. In my case, for instance, in order to express my care to my husband, I will never leave the house knowing that I'm not going to be home for lunch without leaving a tray for him. And he, in his turn, will never leave the house for morning prayers at 6.40 a.m. without bringing me a cup of coffee, even if I'm asleep. Now these are small things, but really they are great things because they cement your relationship.'

In the case of a working woman who has to leave the house at 8 a.m., Amélie advises her to 'try not to leave without saying a nice goodbye to each other, even if you send a kiss on the hand, but make sure that you do not leave the house without greeting one another. Make sure, too, that you never enter the house without saying, "Hi, I'm here."'

The Sixth Commandment, Sharing, is 'an utmost priority in life, because if the children and even your guests see that you share everything, it will only enhance your love for each other. For instance, share the morning paper with your wife. Have a cup of coffee together, instead of saying, sorry, I haven't time. If you share everything of material or spiritual value, it will add to the development of the marriage.'

The Seventh Commandment is Love. Love is placed seventh down the list because Amélie came early to understand, under the influence of her own parents, that the true meaning of love is encapsulated in the qualities she presents higher up the scale. 'I think that family background is very important. It's not a must, but it's a tremendous insurance policy. By this I mean someone who comes from a loving home. The security and warmth of a home is the background of a child and also a family who is well respected, of course, and is known to be a healthy family.'

Chemistry, however, is something no one else can judge, and she feels that if it is there, 'nothing will ever fall out of place – but that a marriage will never work unless the chemistry is there'. She rationalises the alchemy of attraction by taking a religious view: 'If the Almighty wants what in secular terminology we'll call chemistry, which means you are attracted physically to each other, then the other things you might not so enjoy about that person, perhaps even if the looks are not exactly what you dreamed of, or the intellect is stronger than the *joie de vivre*, you will always be able to adjust. There is no such thing as a 100 per cent perfect match because at least 10 per cent is missing in any partnership; if everything else is equal, then the 10 per cent will eventually fall into the 90 per cent and you will forget that the negative 10 per cent was there in the first place. When I say love each other, I mean say it from time to time. Let the children see that Daddy and Mummy love each other.'

Here Amélie distances herself from the religious view, certainly prevalent in Europe when she was growing up, which holds that parents should not kiss in front of the children. Yet the memory of her own parents openly showing affection to each other has confirmed in her and her siblings a sense of security in what she describes as 'the cradle of our family life'. She knew that her parents loved each other: 'we didn't only know it, but we saw it. We didn't speak about these things, but we felt them.' It was only later on in life that Amélie realised that the inner security she had experienced as a child, despite all the external hardship and danger to which she had been exposed, came from that certain knowledge of the depth of the love of her parents.

The Eighth Commandment, Giving, refers to how, according to Jewish law, a man and woman become one on their marriage. As Amélie and Immanuel consider themselves one unit, the concept of giving indicates to them giving generous amounts of love and knowledge to their children. It affects material concerns, too, but actually means giving of oneself as a person.

The Ninth Commandment is Praising. 'One should not fall into the trap of taking things for granted from each other. People may take for granted that they have a caring husband, who offers unconditional love. The husband may take it for granted that his wife will cook for him, change the beds at the right time, lay out his clothes. Never take anything for granted. Say thank you to each other, and when your partner achieves something special, praise is very important.'

Her Tenth and final Commandment conflicts with the view popularised by the book and film, *Love Story*, which holds that love means never having to say you're sorry. Amélie, more pragmatically, says never go to sleep without saying 'sorry'. 'Even when you are convinced you are right and he/she won't admit it, say sorry before you go to sleep, even at the cost of swallowing your pride. Otherwise the minor argument will become a little snowball which will grow as days pass, and you will eventually no longer remember what stupid little thing grew into this tremendous snowball.'

In Amélie's view men find it harder than women to say sorry because 'there's a little boy inside every man'. Perhaps she reflects an endearing aspect of diffident charm in Immanuel when she reveals: 'The greater the man, the more he's a little boy inside and therefore we women are not only spouses, we are also mothers in many ways and saying sorry is tremendously important. There is a wonderful parable which my husband uses in another connection, and that is when we say the end of part of every daily prayer, we go back and then we come forward, as if to say in order to make peace with each other, in order to come back to a certain understanding with each other, you have to give; you go back a few steps and then you come forward again. In other words, let's give a little bit.'

If Amélie's Ten Commandments seem more heavily pitched to a woman's sensitivities rather than to a man's, she would make the following point: 'My advice to any feminist is just to be a woman again and to avoid giving men an inferiority complex. The struggle is an artificial protest, as all the protests were, because in the last two decades the world has functioned on emotion, not intellect.'

22   Sous La Belle Étoile

IMMANUEL HAD often expressed his attachment to nature and his sorrow at not being able to achieve the greening of US Jewry. Amélie, too, yearned for the country life she remembered in the parks and forests of Ansbach, particularly when once she smelt the nostalgic scent of forest pine, redolent of how, as a Jewish child growing up under the Nazis, those places had become off limits to her.

Family holidays when the children were younger consisted of a short trip into the Catskills, where they would rent a bungalow. There the children played in a tree house whose secrets became their private and impenetrable possession, relished well into their own adulthood. But then as the children grew up, the family became restless, longing for the total freedom of an adventure holiday. They wanted to drive around America, staying at American motels overnight. Then one day Immanuel had to take a train trip to Baltimore and noticed a journal advertising a rare type of trailer, twice the length of a bus. It was not the sort of thing which would appeal to many people, says Amélie, 'and certainly not Jews, who preferred on the whole to go to hotels and be served'.

The trailer had windows all around, and behind the driver's and passengers' seats was a long area with a well-equipped kitchen, a hot and cold shower, convertible beds and plenty of storage space. Amélie and Immanuel were captivated by the idea of caravanning in such a vehicle which offered so much space. They picked up the new mobile in Denver, and Immanuel was given half an hour's driving lesson on it before they took it over. As Immanuel drove, Amélie was able to cook and to bake her Shabbat *challot* because all the newly acquired pots and the oven itself were magnetically secured.

They left Denver and travelled to the famous Hearst Castle in California, Las Vegas and Yellowstone Park, a remarkable nature reserve with its famous geyser, which stands many feet high and is known as Old Faithful because it comes up from the depths of the earth to produce very hot water faithfully every hour. They parked the trailer near a waterfall or well and rose daily at 6.30 a.m. to make sure that there was enough water to wash in and boil, moving on at night. The family passed through the Grand Canyon and San Francisco, admiring beauty spots such as the redwood forests containing the tallest and possibly oldest trees in the world, estimated at thousands of years.

On that trip Immanuel – who planned the route himself down to the smallest detail and discouraged any questions from Amélie about their destination because he wanted to surprise her – drove 4,500 miles from Denver on the coastal road right up to the Atlantic on the other side. He proved an excellent navigator, prompting speculation that had he not chosen the rabbinate (which itself required considerable skills of navigation), he might have become an explorer.

As Amélie fondly recalls, 'The memory remained with the children and with us as something very special. It brought us very close to each other because we often talk about it. Every day Immanuel would tell us, "Well, tomorrow we'll do something even more exciting than today."'

Right from the beginning of their marriage, Amélie and Immanuel had this desire for flight, for a primitive quest in their vacations. In their first Irish holidays they had stayed in a little bungalow which had neither water nor cooking facilities. Immanuel used to bring water from an outside well and they made a coal fire outside to boil it. 'The bungalow itself had been beautifully designed and furnished, but it was very down to mother-earth and it was called *My Lady*. The name didn't refer to me, but to a different lady, and you know what that means in Ireland!'

At Yellowstone Park something of this was regenerated for them. They would wash in a little cold river, which they sought out each night as a good area in which to park the caravan. Next morning *en famille* they would rise to say early morning prayers. Amélie describes these moments with a touch of the sublime, recalling the joy of peace and tranquillity they experienced as they stood together in prayer: 'Just to smell the sweetness of the grass and the trees, and to see the early morning dew slowly and gracefully disappear under the rays of the early sun, and to look at the sky, which is majestic whether it has clouds or is completely crystal blue. You can actually hear the silence of creation when you stand out there in the very early morning with those who are closest and dearest to you.'

Of course it was not purely the beauties of nature they shared. There were trips to Disneyland and Marineland as well as long forest walks. *Kashrut* proved no problem since they had a small freezer in the caravan and had made arrangements with their New York butcher, who had agreed to deliver deep-frozen meat to various railways stations or post offices for the next five weeks.

Each child was given a task to do in the caravan, and after tidying their beds the children studied Talmud with their father, who always insisted that they must take their homework with them and divided his time between them, helping them both with their religious and secular subjects. After this they would go on their trip, which always included the promised surprise. Armed with their picnic rucksacks they would walk or go swimming or hill climbing. 'My husband enjoys nothing more than to be on the top of a mountain or to see the rough sea,' says Amélie. 'I am a very outgoing and excitable person and I love a calm sea. I can sit on a beach and look at a calm sea for hours and he, on the other hand, is a very calm personality and he loves rough sea, the thrills of the noise, the musical noise which the waves make against the rocks. It is fascinating to consider how differently human beings connect with nature.'

At about 4 p.m. Amélie would start nagging her husband to make sure that they would find a spot to leave their caravan at night, preferably near a farm or a house, 'just in case something happened'. They rejected caravan sites because the idea was to get away from people and simply be on their own. They invariably knocked at someone's door if they found a spot which appealed to them. Sometimes it was near a waterfall, so there would be a cottage keeper somewhere, or a beach or a forest, where they could find a forester who would let them camp there overnight. Once

Amélie remembers the children being annoyed because she and Immanuel wanted to snatch half an hour on their own. This meant leaving them alone for a while, 'although then it was still safe to leave your children alone for half an hour'.

Of course their holidays were not without incident. Many of these were both pleasurable and memorable. Amélie describes her eldest son, Yoel, building a rowing boat for the lake – 'a raft, as some of our forefathers would do'. But she will never forget the evening in Yellowstone when their second son, Shmuel, then aged twelve, stood saying his evening prayers beside a garbage can that was built into the ground and covered to protect it from wild animals. Suddenly they heard a loud mmmmm mmmmm and returned to see what was happening. There was their son refusing to move because he was in the middle of his devotions, while a grizzly bear came steadily towards him. The child realised he needed help, but could not cry out. They reached him just in time for Immanuel to grab him by the shirt and lift him into the caravan.

Another terrifying moment came one Friday afternoon when they stopped at a beautiful lake in Texas and noticed a horse-riding range. The children begged to be allowed a ride. While Amélie prepared Shabbat lunch, Immanuel took the five children to the riding range, but looked up to see the ranger return alone after half an hour. Jakobovits went over to the ranger and asked: 'Are any of your guys in the forest looking after our children?' He replied, no, because Yoel seemed 'so sensible and so mature, so grown up and sure of himself, that we felt we could easily leave him in charge of his brother and sisters while I came back looking for more customers'.

Half an hour later Yoel, Shmuel, Esther, Shoshana and Aviva dutifully returned from their forest ride and were on the point of turning right to go back to the stable when Aviva's horse suddenly caught fright and bolted. A petrified Amélie averted her eyes and intoned the prayer for those who believe there is no hope whatsoever except for the Almighty to hear their cry. She was sure that this was the greatest danger she had ever seen any of her children in.

The horse was so agitated by now that none of the rangers or passing drivers who tried to help could get anywhere near it. How

Aviva, at eight years of age, who had never ridden a horse before, had the presence of mind and physical strength to hold on to the reins of the horse, her mother will never know. But after an eternity, which was in fact ten minutes, the horse actually settled down and found its own way back to the stables. The nightmare was over for Aviva, who sustained no ill effects either mental or physical. But for her mother it was less simple. Amélie continued to torment herself with guilt about whether she should have allowed the child to ride and how the rangers could have allocated her a horse so potentially dangerous, or permitted the children to be by themselves. 'Had it happened a few years later, we would probably have taken them to court, but in those days you didn't do those things, and in any case, our child was well.'

On some of their nature trails the family accepted the help of a guide. Amélie has fond memories of the day when little Aviva took charge, pretending to be a guide, allowing her imagination full reign. 'She would stop at the roots of a tree and say, "Now this pine tree, ladies and gentlemen, was planted some 4,000 years ago. It took root here in this particular spot through some pollen which has found rest here, and this is the magnificent result of G-d's magnificence in being able to create a tree out of a tiny scattering of pollen." Then she would stop at a big rock and continue to explain the age of the rock, and the material out of which it was made, the sulphur or whatever chemical, and it was absolutely fascinating to listen to this little eight year old, who had carefully absorbed the spirit of what the guides had told her, and even though it was not, of course, correct, her imagination made it work for her so effectively that you could easily have fallen for everything she was saying.'

In Rabbi Jakobovits' writings about his travels to the Indian desert in the US and elsewhere, he compares the Native American culture with Judaism and suggests that the former failed to survive because it was purely an oral tradition, whereas any culture depends on a literary tradition: the received wisdom, he asserts, must be written, which is the secret of Judaism's survival. When one suggests that much spiritual wisdom, art and creative imagination of indigenous culture has indeed survived, if not quite through a vast body of literature, then at least through a powerful, recondite tradition, Amélie is inclined to take this as a criticism of her husband. It is not so. It is merely a question of looking at something another way. She feels impelled, however, to rush to his defence: 'What the Indians have not left behind is the teaching which leads to your commitment to the law of morality. Immanuel's challenge from that is to make sure we will survive because of what we can hand on from generation to generation. These are the initial moral teachings which have come through major members of civilisation right down to our day.'

Behind this assertion lies a genuine fear on both their parts that Jews are not sufficiently aware today of this need and must concentrate on recognising, augmenting and preserving the beauty of synagogues, museums and even private homes. 'We fear', says Amélie, 'that we are no longer adding any originality to the great bequests from past generations on interpretation of our laws. Judaism was the first to receive the gift of divine law which has been accepted both by Christianity and Islam. Although I wish everyone had a chance to visit the Indian desert in the USA, because, yes, it is breathtaking and yes, they have left us this art, it was a culture and spirituality they were not able to hand on to the next generation, which can only be done through writings. My husband interpreted everything he saw on our trips in the USA to his commitment to Judaism.'

However, there were other things waiting to be discovered in nature and the nature of the Jewish spirit that were still less conventional. On one trip the family were invited by a member of the Fifth Avenue Synagogue to stay overnight at a hotel he owned in Las Vegas. Immanuel and Amélie resisted the temptation at first because of the hotel's inevitable gambling connotations, a fact of hotel life in Vegas, but as the temperatures that summer had soared into the 100's, they decided that sleeping in the caravan in such intense heat was not a good idea. They drove into Las Vegas at about 2 p.m., which just gave Amélie time to prepare for Shabbat, which came in at around 6 p.m., and they managed to disguise Immanuel, thus sparing him the embarrassment of being recognised in a gambling hotel! Amélie told him to remain in the caravan while she entered the hotel to register. Amélie introduced herself at the reception desk and explained that the hotel's boss,

Mr Entrata, was a member of the FAS. He had fortunately left a note with reception to this effect. 'Like most of the American hotels, the place was so big that the receptionist did not necessarily know who the boss was, nor that he was actually the owner of the hotel. My sons were wearing their skullcaps, and as I filled in the registration forms, some gentleman came over and tapped our eldest son forcefully on the shoulder and said, "Hi, young man, which yeshiva do you come from?"'

They were given an excellent air-conditioned apartment, where they hid Rabbi Jakobovits for the whole of Shabbat. On the Sunday before they left, Amélie went to Mr Entrata's office to thank him personally: he had arrived in Las Vegas some time after Shabbat. Under the glass top of his desk she noticed photographs of VIPs who had stayed with him over the years, which included half a dozen of a certain well-known rabbi from Jerusalem. Mr Entrata calmly revealed that the famous rabbi came to Las Vegas every year, where he gave him a considerable amount of charity for his institutions in Israel. Mr Entrata explained: 'This is a very good thing for my soul, because out of all this gambling, which I know is not 100 per cent according to Jewish religious law, I can give with all my heart to good causes.'

Intensified by the caravan holidays which helped bond the family to an appreciation of America's natural beauty, Amélie considers that the eight and a half years they spent in the USA offered them 'absolutely everything'. What helped, of course, was the presence there of all her family apart from her parents. Several years before the FAS offered Immanuel his consummate appointment, Amélie's siblings went to the USA, because in the early 1950s work prospects as well as Jewish education were considered so much better. Amélie's sister, Ruth, found a job as a French translator at the United Nations and married a professor of physics at Queens College. Her sister, Françoise, followed, as did Judith, both taking on the same position as Ruth and getting married there. When Amélie's parents returned to France after visiting them in America, all the Munk girls wept. Mme Munk turned to her daughters, a typically caustic smile on her lips, and reinforced her feminine credo, which was that the woman is first a wife: 'Now look here, I am very happy with my husband and I am going with him wherever he goes. You are each very happy with your respective husbands, so just stop crying and be happy where you are.'

'Okay, Maman, we'll stop. We'll never cry again when we see you off,' the girls sobbed.

Amélie looked at her mother and remembered how lucky she was, too, having discovered so much about rural America through her travels with her husband.

23 *Rabbi on the Hoof*

DURING THEIR eight American years, the Fifth Avenue Synagogue was visited by various personalities from Israel, France and Britain, including Isaac Wolfson, president of the United Synagogue of Great Britain and the Commonwealth, the large and historic grouping of synagogues in London, and founder of Great Universal Stores, who had family and business interests in New York. Sir Isaac stayed at the Pierre Hotel, or the Plaza or Westbury, and invariably worshipped at the FAS, where he became acquainted with Jakobovits, a relationship that would be more fruitful than the rabbi could have envisaged.

In the early 1960s some people expressed their commitment to Jewish scholarship in rather unusual ways. Two brothers visited several Jewish communities to raise funds to build a yeshiva on the upper West Side of New York. When they came to the FAS, they took a very high-handed attitude, having assessed everyone's business interests and how much money each member could afford. Jakobovits was intensely irritated and refused to allow his flock to give money under duress. 'You do not collect money to teach Torah by blackmailing people,' he said. The brothers lost patience and staged a sit-in in the synagogue lasting several days and nights. Jakobovits had to resort to what Amélie calls 'outside physical help' to forcibly remove the men. But the following Sabbath the men held a service in the street outside the synagogue. This went on for two or three weeks until some visitors, seeing them outside, came to the conclusion that the synagogue was so crowded that they couldn't get in and so they joined them outside in the street. Within half an hour there were fifty people outside, fervently praying, the women sitting behind them. The brothers, however, did not succeed in their aim and eventually walked away empty-handed.

Meanwhile, Jakobovits was putting many hours into the community, yet still finding time to develop his interest in Jewish medical ethics, which was to prove an enduring mission. He started work on the first compendium of Jewish law relating to medicine with its code of practice in hospitals. He had joined a small group publishing a pamphlet for the guidance of doctors in hospitals regarding Jewish patients, which is still in use today thirty-five years later.

Jakobovits had a dream to extend the FAS, which now had a worldwide reputation, by adding a centre of Jewish ethical teachings, which would include medical, business, marriage and consumer ethics, but the membership was less than enthusiastic. They told him that he had created for them exactly what they wanted. They demanded no more; they had no interest in opening another dimension of Jewish life, for which there was also no offer of financial support. While Amélie privately criticised the membership for their short-sightedness, she realised later what she could not see then – that their objections opened her husband's mind to other offers, including the chance to look very seriously at the invitation from Sir Isaac Wolfson in 1963 to become Chief Rabbi of the United Hebrew Congregations of Great Britain and the Commonwealth in succession to retiring Chief Rabbi Israel Brodie.

At the time Amélie and the children were not in the mood for change. The answer then was a categorical no. Amélie was in love with the New York cultural scene as well as its religious life. The world-renowned museums, theatres and operas attracted her like a butterfly, and the couple still basked in the approval of the community for their efforts in improving the Jewish way of life. Jakobovits remained then very much in the midst of building the FAS, his programme of lectures in medical ethics was well underway and the children were still very young. 'We had everything. There was no reason to consider going anywhere else.'

Yet the ethos of America was changing. The years 1961–2 saw the start of American involvement in the Vietnam War, and Amélie made no bones about voicing her displeasure and her disagreement with President Kennedy about entering the war. She felt it was his way of showing the world that he could combat Communism, but feared that, as time went on, the price would prove too high. It devastated her to think of so many young conscripts sent far away to fight a war that could not be won, in a place far from their homeland.

In 1963 President Kennedy was assassinated. The war he had launched escalated, and one of the more perceptible results of this tragedy and the consequent guilt that began to consume America was that many young Americans turned to drugs.

At about this time there came an offer to succeed Chief Rabbi Bernard Casper in South Africa, which was rejected out of hand. Neither Amélie nor her husband felt inclined to take their children to South Africa at that time. They considered it dangerous. The FAS was a very responsive community and offered an excellent Jewish educational system for their children. Why go to South Africa, which was inflamed with political problems, when they still felt needed in the heart of New York City?

In 1970, when they would make their first visit to South Africa to be 'wined and dined like royalty', Amélie thought back to that invitation and was grateful that they had decided not to accept the call. She disliked the underlying immorality within the attitude of the whites towards their black servants. Although she noticed that civilised people treated their servants well, paying for their children's education, clothes and for their homes in the townships, she was very much opposed to the apartheid system which treated them as secondary citizens. Sadly, even Jews, she noticed, were not immune from this tendency, which had insidiously worked its way into the national culture as a whole. Surprisingly for an altruistic couple, there was an even deeper fear of being imperceptibly sucked into that system themselves. 'I have no doubt that it would have happened to us as well,' she says. 'We would have slid into the same way of life.'

Of course the Rabbi could have looked upon this offer in another way; as a call to help South African Jews facing a moral dilemma find a moral solution. How would they have identified this offer as a religious calling? Perhaps it is Amélie's pragmatism that convinces her it was not. They still had work to do in New York, unable yet to see that their efforts to take the FAS one stage further would end in frustration. 'We were nowhere near ready for another challenge,' Amélie insists.

In fact, they both reacted as Jewish parents first and as a religious leadership couple second, as evidenced by Amélie's reflection that had the call come later, they would still have turned it down. 'We both felt very deeply and instinctively that the future of our children would not be assured, and we would have to separate from them much earlier and I wasn't willing to do that.'

Perhaps a clue to their problem with South Africa came much later, in 1977, when Jakobovits caused controversy with an article published in the *Jewish Chronicle*, in which he sympathised with the difficulties of South African Jews in speaking out against apartheid. 'If they have not proclaimed the Jewish abhorrence of racial discrimination as loudly as we and they would like, it is precisely because the only alternative to tacitly accepting the system without protest is to leave the country,' he wrote.

Chief Rabbi Casper was succeeded by Rabbi Cyril Harris in the late 1980s, when the apartheid system had begun to crumble. 'Cyril and Ann [Harris] were very courageous and are very successful and deeply appreciated in their work and their relationship with the black community,' says Amélie. Meanwhile in London, Sir Isaac Wolfson, a man not used to being turned down, had his eye firmly trained on Immanuel Jakobovits. He waited in the wings.

24   *The Reconstruction of Anglo-Jewry*

LONDON, 1966. While in New York Rabbi Jakobovits and Amélie were busy weaving the complex strands of Jewish thought into a cohesive Orthodoxy, London was suffering fallout from a spiritual bombshell destined to split Anglo-Jewry.

Rabbi Dr Louis Jacobs, brightest star in the Jews' College firmament and tipped to succeed the retiring Principal of the college, Dr Isidore Epstein (which was the nominal path to chiefdom of the United Synagogue), had, before his appointment, written a radical book, *We Have Reason to Believe*, which was the fusion of intellectual enlightenment with spiritual quest. Revelation, suggested Jacobs, did not end with the Five Books of Moses on Mount Sinai, rather it began there. He dismisses the literal concept of Moses being given *The Pentateuch* by divine dictation, in favour of a more dialectic approach. The Five Books were divinely inspired, he said. Man's spiritual journey is boosted by G-d provided man does the work himself, over time. Thus, he argued, *The Pentateuch* is a composite of various historical periods, conveyed to the Jewish people through their own historical experience.

The Manchester-born rabbi with a penchant for open, discursive debate rather than recondite philosophy was the product of Gateshead Yeshiva and the distillation of all that is disciplined and joyful in Judaism. If not quite the parallel of the martyred German Christian, Dietrich Bonnhoefer's theology that G-d requires man as much as man requires G-d, Jacobs' view is that G-d offers man a dynamic, spiritual journey rather than a defined chronological one. His beliefs were honed at London University, which exposed him to a world of challenging religious opinion.

Ironically enough, some time earlier he had worked as assistant to Amélie's cousin, Rabbi Eli Munk, at his Golders Green Beth Hamedrash.

While Jacobs' opinion was not inconsistent with Conservative Jewish thinking in America, it shook mainstream Anglo-Jewry and its religious powerhouse, Jews' College – where Dr Jacobs was lecturer and moral tutor – to the core. Jacobs' 'heresy' was to apply critical analysis based on modern scholarship to an area of faith. Orthodox opinion held that if you rejected the theory of divine authorship of the Torah, there was no reason to accept any of the Commandments. On the contrary, Jacobs would argue, Judaism is not a religion graven in stone. Indeed, in his preface to the fourth edition of his book, Jacobs explains: 'I *reasonably believed* at the time that the book was fully compatible with the somewhat tepid Orthodoxy then prevailing in Anglo-Jewry. When I presented the book to Chief Rabbi Israel Brodie, he accepted it without the slightest objection to any of its contents, though I still do not know whether he bothered then to read it.'

If Anglo-Jewry had not been at that moment on the brink of a vacuum, perhaps no one would have batted an eyelid. For centuries Jewish thinkers had applied various interpretations to the question of the divine influence in man's affairs. Yet with the imminent retirement of Jews' College principal, Dr Epstein, and the need to groom a successor to the Chief Rabbi, the question of the tutor's unkosher thoughts became a matter of serious concern. The outstanding candidate was seen as a Trojan horse.

Epstein was a very precise and erudite man whereas Brodie was regarded as more pastor than theologian. Jacobs' book had been in Brodie's possession for three years and, as Jacobs says, he had never remarked on its controversial passages. Contemporary observers believed it was the more scholarly Epstein who took issue with Brodie over the Jacobs Affair, complaining that a man of Jacobs' opinion could never head Jews' College. The passages in his book, he said, disgusted him.

However, according to Rabbi Jacobs himself, the prime mover in the case was neither of these two but Dayan Grunfeld of the Beth Din, who was anxious to placate the right wing of the United

Synagogue and drew Brodie's attention to the offending passages in *We Have Reason to Believe*.

Either way, the Orthodox establishment was set for a show-down. In 1962 Chief Rabbi Brodie vetoed Jacobs' appointment as principal of Jews' College. Jacobs resigned as tutor and lecturer and, despite the loyalty of his own congregation at the New West End Synagogue in Bayswater where he officiated, his job there went too. He was now *persona non grata* in the United Synagogue.

The *Jewish Chronicle* (*JC*), under the editorship of William Frankel, took up Jacobs' case and turned it into a long-running *cause célèbre*. The Jacobs Affair, as it became known, was the accident waiting to happen in a society which had become so complacent that vast numbers of serious-minded young Jews were now estranged from Judaism. Frankel, who edited the paper from 1958 to 1977, was concerned about this drift and his sanguine, practised eye told him that Jacobs, with his mild ways yet ferocious intellect, represented the radical seeker they could identify with.

Whether fired by concerns for halachic purity or mere envy of Jacobs' achievements, the controversy was destined to rumble on and cause a seismic split within Anglo-Jewry which would slowly tear it apart over the next thirty years. The initial volcanic thrust created the bedrock of the Masorti or British Conservative Movement. Jacobs' supporters at the New West End Synagogue immediately reformed themselves into the embryonic New London Synagogue, a blueprint for an independent progressive movement way to the right of the Reform, based on Jacobs' liberal theology – traditional Judaism with an open-mind on revelation. The movement grew to capture much of what *JC* journalist Simon Rocker describes as 'the religious middle ground'.

It found many sympathisers. Jacobs' ideas inspired support from people like the late philo-Semitic Christian scholar, Dr James Parkes, who in 1966 condemned Orthodoxy for branding those with differing views as heretics. Judaism, he felt, in an echo of the *JC*'s views, should become more relevant to the community. One year later, in 1967, Rabbi Abraham Heschel, Professor of Jewish Ethics and Mysticism at the Jewish Theological Seminary of America, feared that there was too little emphasis on Jewish thought in theology and a belief that thought itself could threaten the existence of Judaism. Patrick O'Donovan, writing in the London *Evening Standard*, spoke of the heartbreak of communal disunity caused by the Jacobs Affair. The tragedy was that nobody seemed courageous enough to enter the debate in a cool-headed, rational manner. Suddenly the cult of personality, so prevalent in the West at the time, was alive and kicking within Anglo-Jewry, too.

Again, Jacobs argues in the latest preface:

> The modern Jewish theologian has to try to understand how, now that Judaism is seen to have a history (which means there is a human element in revelation), the traditional view of *Torah Min Hashomayim* can be reinterpreted while still retaining its ancient vigour and power. The solution is to see the whole process in dynamic rather than static terms, that G-d gave the Torah not only *to* the Jewish people but *through* the Jewish people.

And he continues: 'The attempt by some traditionalists to preserve the old picture by rejecting all science and all modern thought is futile. There can be no going back.' In an almost conciliatory note aimed at his critics, he adds: 'The Torah is still G-d given if the "giving" is seen to take place through the historical experiences of the Jewish people in its long quest for G-d.'

However, there was to be no consensus on the issue. A breach existed in Anglo-Jewry which its power-broker, Isaac Wolfson, was anxious to heal. The man he had persistently head-hunted for the job was Rabbi Immanuel Jakobovits. But if there were signals of incipient frustration in his own career with the Fifth Avenue Synagogue, Jakobovits was blinkered to them. He remained happy and fulfilled in New York, giving lecture tours around the country on the issues of law and medical ethics and fêted as a leading personality on legal-ecclesiastic affairs. It was an irresistible mix of spiritual and intellectual challenge with celebrity status, milked the way only the Americans knew how. Clearly Jakobovits was not ready to move.

In 1966 the highly respected Rabbi Yaacov Herzog stepped into the breach upon Brodie's retirement, with his wife, Penina, at

Wolfson's request, but after only six weeks he developed an incurable blood condition that forced his resignation within months.

Meanwhile, in the wake of Vietnam, America was turning increasingly into a drug culture. The Eldorado of spiritual optimism was becoming for Amélie a Carthage of burning despair. And besides that, the FAS had gone cold on Jakobovits' vision to augment its now international reputation with a college of Jewish ethics. His brilliant dawn of enlightenment was beginning to fade into a deepening twilight of realistic awareness. There was no doubting the fact that he had pushed the FAS as far as it would go. Amélie remembers her husband having sleepless nights for lack of sufficient challenge. Yet, as Jakobovits laments in *If Only My People*,

> nothing was further from my mind and ambition than to exchange my freedom and comparative comforts of the material as well as vocational rewards in America, for the headaches and constraints of an awesome office in which my manifold duties would be rigidly defined by constitution and tradition, which would allow me little time to pursue my favourite academic and literary interests.

Indeed, an Anglo-Jewry riven with controversy and despair was the very antithesis of their dreams. The integral spiritual challenge it represented was far tougher than South Africa's had been, and since the amiable Louis Jacobs had by now achieved virtual martyr status, their arrival in London was not likely to guarantee much popularity. From New York Rabbi Jakobovits continued to resist the offer now from the altruistic belief that he could still restore Louis Jacobs to the fold. 'Jacobs had the strictest Orthodox background, and I thought I should try, before taking office, to persuade him to rethink his views. To be truthful I wasn't sure if I could achieve it,' he said. Yet the letter he wrote Jacobs was regarded by the latter as 'nasty'.

'It accused me of arrogance,' said Rabbi Jacobs, 'because I said I put forward views that would be accepted by all scholars today. But I wasn't being arrogant. I mean I've got my share of arrogance, but I wasn't saying they agreed with *me* but that I agreed with *them*.'

Jakobovits' letter has been seen by some as a political intervention to launch his own candidacy for the top job in Anglo-Jewry.

'Wolfson was pushing him like mad to become Chief Rabbi and to heal the breach again,' says Jacobs. 'And when he came he tried to do that, but what *could* he do?'

Despite what sounds like despair on Rabbi Jacobs' part, he does admit that Wolfson had urged Jakobovits to 'make *shalom* with me otherwise it won't work'. Jakobovits himself 'wanted to make friends', he adds. Jacobs also acknowledges Jakobovits' efforts to pour oil on troubled waters by avoiding further eruptions in the delicate area of sanctioning Masorti conversions and marriages.*

For his own part, Jakobovits' objective attitude towards Jacobs avoided the hysteria shown by other critics. In London on a peace-seeking initiative, Jakobovits and Jacobs took long, ruminative walks together in the country. Setting aside his own future for the moment, Jakobovits had committed himself to giving Louis Jacobs the opportunity to rejoin the ranks of the United Synagogue. There must have been moments of intense debate and soul searching between them, driven by a certain nostalgia. It was a moment of history for Amélie, waiting in the wings. There was something deeply moving in the way these two profound thinkers, who held each other in such long-standing mutual esteem, tried hard to bridge a fundamental difference. Amélie describes Jacobs as having been a 'wonderful student' at Gateshead, but steers clear of the philosophical issues that were to drive that inevitable wedge between him and the United Synagogue. 'Rabbi Jakobovits wanted to take him back in the fold,' she says, with that cosy sentimentality of hope, that doomed longing for an ideal Jewish world without rifts or breaches. Perhaps deep down she knew that the Jacobs Affair would prove a place of no return to that world, for both of them.

It was a moment of truth for Jakobovits, too. This may have been

---

*One of the main controversies arising out of the Jacobs Affair related to the Beth Din's refusal to recognise Masorti conversions and marriages. It was Chief Rabbi Jakobovits who achieved a delicate consensus with Jacobs over these issues, although the subject flared up again in 1988 when Jacobs blamed the London Beth Din for blocking unity over Jewish status in Anglo-Jewry. In 1995 Chief Rabbi Jonathan Sacks denounced Masorti as 'dishonest and dangerous, consisting of 'intellectual thieves', who posed a danger to the future of British Jewry, condemning their marriages as not halachically valid and refusing to recognise these as well as Masorti divorces and conversions, out of fear that moderation may lead to annihilation.

the subliminal issue which had caused him to resist the challenge for so long, rationalising the issues raised by the Jacobs Affair: 'Jacobs' views were heterodox rather than orthodox,' Jakobovits reflects. 'His principle that there were human elements in the handing down of the Five Books of Moses was not a communally accepted view. Brodie needed a supporter; he was under siege, so I felt I owed it to him to do what I could.' But there was another motive behind his decision to move to London. It was at least partly inspired by his gratitude to Britain for having saved his life and those of his family. He felt a moral obligation to give something back to Britain and the Anglo-Jewish community. In this view Jakobovits was deeply influenced by Amélie's father, Rabbi Elie Munk, then the head of Independent Orthodoxy in Paris, who told him that he 'had no moral right to turn down such a call'.

So Jakobovits finally accepted the invitation to become Chief Rabbi of the United Hebrew Congregations of Great Britain and the Commonwealth. And from his first days in London he could already predict the future of Anglo-Jewry – according to Louis Jacobs. He told him that it lay with the right wing; with Stamford Hill. 'Why?' asked Jacobs. 'Because they have large families. And they are sincere,' Jakobovits replied. 'So you see he was starting off at the beginning by being careful not to offend them,' Jacobs says.

However, on arrival the Jakobovits' found things at a very low ebb. The Chief Rabbi Elect had stepped into the breach, but at a cost. The community was split and the Jacobs Affair continued to resonate with those Jakobovits sought most to influence. He also had to contend with the brouhaha unleashed by the *Jewish Chronicle*, which was not going to die down. 'When I came, the residue was still so powerful that the *JC* virtually boycotted me,' recalls Rabbi Jakobovits. 'They ignored my first official visit to Australia and wanted to denigrate the office of Chief Rabbi. It carries on to this day. I was faced with these terrible problems – the chance of the break-up of the community; the dissident movement. Jacobs rode into a storm. The rumbles could still be heard – the grim aftermath of the Jacobs Affair.'

Still licking his wounds, Jacobs, ever the challenger, declares tartly in his Preface: 'I sometimes wonder what exactly these Chief Rabbis have meant by *Torah Min HaShomayim* since none of them has ever tried to spell it out. It is not for a Chief Rabbi to define Jewish dogmas in Papal fashion!'

Jakobovits, on the other hand, knew that there could be no peace until he moved to calm the storm. On his first pastoral visit, to Glasgow, he achieved a slender but key victory. He visited a synagogue on the brink of breaking away from the United Synagogue to join Masorti. 'There was a minister there sympathetic to Louis Jacobs. I exposed myself to a public grilling by the leaders of the congregation. But the after-effects were that they supported me. It could easily have joined the dissident movement, but it did not and there was an end to the rebellion.'

For Amélie, whose feathers were always ruffled whenever her husband was attacked, it was another matter. 'Amélie always gets very upset when I am criticised,' Jakobovits admits, 'taking it as a personal attack on me. I myself do not take it that way. I am not an emotional person, although it is possible to suffer pain even if you are not emotional.' Taking the flak for something over which he had no control would have sent a lesser man into turmoil. For his wife, however, whose respect for her husband had been reflected in the community they had just left, the London experience was initially difficult.

But if Jakobovits' challenge to the post-war generation was its failure to add new dimensions of originality and thinking, and Amélie's, that its materialism outweighed quality, neither of them could accuse the Anglo-Jewish community they entered in the late 1960s of lacking in intellectual debate. If Amélie felt any regret over leaving the USA, she could be consoled by the many letters she received telling her how lucky they were to leave America before the drug culture became widely practised.

25   Amélie's View

NEW YORK, June 1966. Looking back, it had been like a dream. Amélie had lain among flowers in the plush Sinai Hospital on the East Side of Manhattan, nursing their new-born sixth child and fourth daughter, Elisheva. The luxury of the hospital was a far cry from the birth of her fifth child in Ireland eight years earlier, when she had been literally strapped to the bed and not allowed to get up, even to bathe. Here she had her own shower in a room so garlanded that off-duty medics would pop in to join her with tea and coffee in what swiftly grew into a botanical garden, and Immanuel would drift in at night like a ghost in a pristine white coat and mask. Beside her bed was a pink telephone to denote the sex of her child in order to spare doctors the trouble of asking.

Illness after Aviva's birth had prompted doctors to advise against more children. Yet eight years later, here she was nursing her new, much longed-for baby. Her husband would call Elisheva his American souvenir.

'Coming up from the pit of creation,' in John Updike's graphic phrase, it was Amélie who received the telephone call from Sir Isaac Wolfson offering her husband, who was absent on a lecture tour, the top ecclesiastical job in Anglo-Jewry. Sir Isaac, whose powerful voice had boomed down the phone, had also exclaimed, 'What! A girl. That will be expensive!' Amélie said to Aviva, 'It's happened to us twice; once after you were born, when we were asked to leave Ireland for the US, and now after Elisheva's birth. That's it. I'm not going anywhere any more!'

Certainly there could hardly have been a worse moment to contemplate a move, but negotiations for England began almost immediately. Reluctantly Amélie left baby Elisheva with a tiny but efficient maternity nurse, a refugee from the Nazis named Mrs

185

Gluckstadt, while she and Immanuel flew to London to discuss the offer. Amélie was, however, seriously worried about how the new position might affect the family. She had researched the history of the Chief Rabbinate throughout the decades and discovered that, in the majority of cases, the children of past Chief Rabbis had been negatively affected. Amélie became desperately worried. As a mother and a wife, she believed that the first question she would be asked on Judgement Day would be: what did you do for the spiritual and physical well-being of your husband and children? And then the second question would be: what did you do for your society? 'I was always aware, as a woman, of my partnership with the Almighty in giving life and I was very concerned that I would not be able to carry off what I think is my major challenge in life.'

Meanwhile in London, unaware of their inner turmoil, Sir Isaac offered them the luxury of the Savoy Hotel. While Jakobovits went into a series of intense meetings with the leaders of the United Synagogue, Amélie made contact with a cousin of Mrs Ulla Merkin, wife of the president of the Fifth Avenue Synagogue. Erica Lawson was to prove a great ally to Amélie in the months which lay ahead, particularly in her instinctive assessments and her ability to guide her new protégée every step of the way. Amélie admits that for their first few years in London, she could not have done without Erica. If Myrtle Hirsch had been her fairy godmother in America, certainly Erica assumed that role in Britain. 'My London mentor' is how Amélie describes her. Erica always knew when she was needed and would instinctively ring the bell of their official north London home at Hamilton Terrace whenever there was a crisis in Amélie's life. She still thinks of her with gratitude.

One of the first pitfalls Amélie discovered in these early days was that the Jewish day schools in Britain did not offer anything approaching the standards of their US counterparts. She was advised by religious families to send the children to a good secular school and employ home tutors for Jewish subjects. When she first heard this, Amélie had second thoughts about coming to Britain. The decision also meant leaving their sons, Yoel and Shmuel, behind because they were just finishing their high school education, which in the States is the equivalent of Britain's first university year. She need not have worried. Eventually, Yoel went to Baltimore Yeshiva, majored in bio-chemistry at John Hopkins University and joined his parents in Britain, where he qualified in medicine at University College Hospital. Shmuel elected to go to Kerem Beyavneh Yeshiva in Israel, later making *aliyah*. Esther had great difficulties settling in because she was nearly fifteen and at high school. After A-levels, she left for the embryonic Michlala College in Jerusalem under its founder-principal, Rabbi Yehuda Coppleman, who was originally from Ireland. Shoshanah and Aviva, being younger, settled more comfortably into the primary school system – Menorah Primary School in London's Golders Green and later Hasmonean Grammar School for Girls.

However, neither Amélie nor her husband could predict that all this would fall into place when they first arrived in Britain. Uneasily they went to visit Chief Rabbi Brodie at his official residence, Hamilton Terrace, a twenty-room house which included his offices. The Jakobovits' looked around them and saw, in conflict with their own credo, that the Brodies, who had married late and had no children, definitely lived 'above the shop'. In fact, when she first saw Hamilton Terrace Amélie shuddered: 'It was a dungeon, painted all in dark brown.' Lady Wolfson, Sir Isaac's wife, seemed to intuit her feelings and promised: 'If you accept, it will be decorated the way you want it.'

Lady Wolfson in fact moved fast. She had a door removed which stood in front of the staircase and reached the ceiling and had the original carved rosewood staircase restored. She also thoughtfully added a child gate to match the staircase in case baby Elisheva learned how to crawl down. During the three days in January 1967 that Amélie spent in London to decide on decorations, she stayed at the Wolfsons' London home at Portland Place and went off in the Rolls-Royce with Lady Wolfson to the Houndsditch Warehouse, a then well-known furniture wholesaler belonging to Sir Isaac. On their decision to accept the offer, Amélie's sense of French chic was brought in to play. She was given *carte blanche* to do what she wanted. The most important change was to introduce light into the house. She rejected the idea of an interior designer because, she says, 'I am impressionable and if anybody talks me into something which I hadn't thought of, two years later I will realise that I didn't like it in the first place and yet allowed myself to be influenced.'

The upstairs offices were transformed into the children's bed-rooms. Brodie's office became a guest suite with an *en suite* bath-room decorated in orange, while the rest of the house was painted in light colours, mainly magnolia. The guest room was destined to be the place where the Jakobovits' daughters stayed to recuperate after the birth of their babies, and it was the room in which Amélie's mother-in-law was to pass away in 1973. Although this orange room saw illness, it remained for the family a happy place reflecting light and also change.

The house had a small reception-room downstairs flanked by a dining-room on the right and a larger reception-room on the left, which overlooked a garden full of fruit trees and cactus plants surrounding a lawn, with a rockery and pond at the top encircled by steps. Amélie designated the room between the dining-room and the sitting-room as her study, and had the white painted doors to the sitting-room replaced with glass. This room became the small reception area where most of the meetings were held, but in its less prestigious role it was their breakfast-room with a round table. During the few weeks of her husband's incumbency Penina Herzog had already planned the division of the kitchen into milk and meat, but her choice of a beige carpet throughout the house led Amélie to tears of frustration as it bore the constant stains of extensive use. Not being able to afford a carpet cleaning firm as often as was necessary, and not having the heart to ask her staff to do it, Amélie spent hours on her knees after each reception trying to get the stains out until the carpet finally grew threadbare and she was able to cover it with rugs. Her physical struggle with the carpet proved an ironic metaphor for the more spiritual struggle she had endured in Dublin trying to emulate her mentor, Penina Herzog's mother-in-law, Sarah, in whose name the Sarah Herzog Hospital in Jerusalem was later established. Amélie was to become actively involved in this hospital for elderly psychiatric patients as its patron. Perhaps now, more than ever, in the key role of wife of Britain's Chief Rabbi, she remembered her influence – 'she was a tremendous inspiration to me – a model of what a rabbi's wife should be' – despite the irritating way people used to exalt her as an icon, creating an impossible act to follow.

But for the moment Amélie was totally occupied with creating a home for herself and her family, a place where she and the Chief Rabbi could entertain world leaders, clerics, politicians and congregants alike. Amélie placed her husband's study on the first floor near the main bedroom and *en suite* bathroom. The bedroom itself was decorated in pastels with off-white drapes set off by the silver silk-patterned bedcover given to them by Lady Wolfson.

The Chief Rabbi's study, which Amélie lined with bookshelves, contained an antique desk in the centre, two reclining chairs and a chess set, as he is a consummate chess player. The study, which in a previous incarnation had been occupied by the Labour MP Greville Janner's wife, Myra, a niece of Sir Israel Brodie, led on to a balcony, while at the front of the house were three further bedrooms with two more bathrooms. The garage was built underneath, but on top of that they designed another room as a bedsitter for the boys when they came home on visits.

The Jakobovits' arrived at Southampton in March 1967. Amélie and her four girls were left to find their way, by train, to London while Rabbi Jakobovits was whisked away by car. Only one United Synagogue officer, George Gee (who later became President of the United Synagogue), accompanied Amélie and the children from Southampton to their new home. By the time they reached Hamilton Terrace it was evening. Amélie will never forget her first glimpse of the house, glowing with lights from every room. The reception-room had been prepared for breakfast in the morning, and on entering the kitchen Amélie found the fridge and cupboards filled with food. This was the work of Lady Wolfson. The house was already a home. Amélie's predecessor, Lady Brodie, a teacher by profession, was not the most domesticated of women, 'and hardly knew how to make a cup of tea,' according to Amélie. 'She had had a housekeeper who didn't care that the kitchen looked like the continuation of the cellar, although by the time we arrived Penina Herzog had already made some alterations.'

Amélie was surprised and delighted to find when she went to bed that first night that not only was the heating on, but in every bed, including the baby's cot, was a hot-water bottle. 'For us Americans [*sic*], we had never come across a hot-water bottle before.

Amélie had brought three armchairs from America, one beautiful antique table, a gift from a member of the congregation, and the rocking-chair her husband had bought on her pregnancy which was destined to undergo many colour changes and serves him in his study to this day. The furniture in the house was a mélange of antiques, including the dining-room suite with Chippendale chairs. The Jakobovits' had also invested in Chippendale chairs in Ireland and found they exactly matched those Lady Brodie had chosen. However, keen to introduce the practical modernism of the 1960s, Amélie had asked Lady Wolfson to provide built-in cupboards in rosewood which offered plenty of room. 'I wanted as little furniture as possible. I love homes with the minimum of furniture. For my taste every piece has to be useful.'

The large reception-room was painted in light beige with blue drapes. The small lounge had a similar colour scheme. The dining-room provided a stronger contrast, with the walls draped with the same material used for the curtains – a deep bordeaux wine – 'which flowed into each other and lasted the full twenty-five years in which we stayed'.

Amélie used the morning-room as her working room. It was a cosy place with a round table flanked with armchairs and many family photos, and lamps and flowers to replace the art she would have loved but could not afford. But Amélie soon noticed that frequently, after a stand-up reception, some of her little *objets d'art* vanished. 'It seems that this is what people do when they go to Buckingham Palace,' she says. 'They take things as a souvenir, without meaning any harm. I soon learned not to leave out anything of too emotional value.'

One thing Amélie sought to change was in the area of neighbourly relations. Having moved from an eclectic, open society such as New York into the chillier emotional climate of London, Amélie felt that it would be good to open up Hamilton Terrace, a stately Victorian street, into a friendly neighbourhood. This was Amélie's brainchild alongside a devout Catholic couple, Michael and Sally Petal, who both felt that it was rare in London for neighbours to become friends. Their project was to have luncheons and tea parties at which the other neighbours of Hamilton Terrace were the invited guests.

Her circle had begun with two journalists from *The Times*, David and Susan Spanier, who originally lived next door before moving away, and included Chief Rabbi Hertz's daughter, Josephine Hertz, who remained at 103, Hamilton Terrace, until her death, since that house also belonged to the United Synagogue. The family's friendship with David Spanier proved of particular benefit. In the early 1970s they would come to discuss the plight of Soviet Jews together. Spanier took on board what had been said to him and a few weeks later one of *The Times* editors wrote the first supportive piece on Soviet Jewry which changed the climate of media opinion on the issue. Amélie considers that the best articles to emerge from that decade by Bernard Levin in *The Times* were on the plight of Soviet Jews, possibly influenced by the fact that the Jakobovits' were neighbours of the Spaniers.

So now Immanuel Jakobovits had reached the pinnacle of his career. He had become Chief Rabbi of the United Hebrew Congregations of Britain and the Commonwealth. For Amélie, too, there was more than a sense of reflected glory. Here was the opportunity they had both subliminally worked towards. Jakobovits, in terms of broadening his scholarship and his will to expand communal educational awareness, now had the chance of greater scope for his talents. Amélie found that her loyal support of her husband and perception of his powers were fully vindicated.

Yet, despite her gratitude to those who had made her welcome and smoothed the domestic path for her family's arrival – notably Lady Wolfson and her niece, Miriam Martyn, with her husband, Herman – Amélie's first five years in London were not entirely happy. She missed both the buzz of New York, where they had started a congregation from a community of eleven and watched it grow, and the small-town familiarity of Dublin with its 5,000-strong Jewish community. In Britain she knew almost no one and was to discover that the British mentality was quite different and more introverted. A friend recalls Amélie's open admission that her first years in Hamilton Terrace were 'terrible'. She often cried on the stairs. Her difficulties were probably intensified by her strong and effervescent personality and her sense of being suppressed in an English society which expected her to stay at home with her children, apart from attending official functions. This contributed to her initial loneliness.

So for Amélie there was a part-grudging sense of homesickness. 'American Jews are much more outgoing, have a wonderful sense of *joie de vivre* and remain grown-up children all their lives,' she recalled. Anglo-Jewry, by contrast, reflects the 'more sedate maturity' of the British people. It was hard for Amélie, whose passionate nature craved warmth and response, to reflect on the contrast between the excitement of their welcome to New York – 'Whoever had heard of an Irish rabbi? Whoever knew there were even Jews in Ireland?' – with the cooler, more measured British attitude of wait-and-see. Apart from this, Amélie felt very bitter about the sustained campaign against the Chief Rabbinate by the *Jewish Chronicle* over the Jacobs Affair. 'The *JC* never gave us the chance to say in our first years – wait, this guy from the USA didn't have to come here; he only came to help us out – but that was never said.'

She still feels let down by two things promised by Sir Isaac Wolfson. One was the offer to start another newspaper in competition to the *JC*, 'with more balanced reporting', and the other was to launch a centre for the Chief Rabbinate away from Woburn House, providing a more independent centre for the religious courts. She claims that her husband regrets to this day that there is no other serious national Jewish newspaper to rival the *JC*, especially as far smaller Jewish communities, such as Australia and South Africa, have at least two major communal newspapers. 'But at the time of any controversy he simply said a person must put his head on the pillow at night with a clear conscience and be prepared to take the criticism.'

26 Kitchen Cabinet

IN ORDER to glean a better understanding of the community he was now to lead, the Chief Rabbi cultivated special links with many leading personalities whom he would consult from time to time, even if they held no formal office in the community. Thus he would occasionally turn for advice to such diverse figures as Victor Mishcon, lawyer and politician; Joe Gilbert, chairman of the Bnai Brith Hillel Foundation; Arthur Snowman, chairman of the Association of Jewish Youth Religious Advisory Committee and the Boys Welfare Committee of the then Board of Guardians (who was to lead the 1963 negotiations for the creation of the Norwood Joint Committee); Dr Bernard Homa, academic and writer and leading proponent of orthodoxy; Vera Braynis, doyenne of Jewish women's organisations, who later won the present Chief Rabbi's Prize for Work in the Community; and Greville Janner, the politician and Jewish rights campaigner. Over the years other voices added their influence, and eventually this practice became formalised into a virtual Chief Rabbi's cabinet.

As the only woman on this ex-officio privy council, Vera Braynis' role was to represent women. While the committee concerned itself with purely communal issues, the combined sagacity of its members was occasionally used to prevent the newly incumbent and still naive Chief Rabbi from doing something that they felt might damage his reputation. He was grateful not to put a foot wrong so early in his British career.

This group helped Chief Rabbi Jakobovits study the shape of the English community and learn how to deal with everyday matters. It was at their Monday night briefings when Vera Braynis went into the kitchen to help Amélie make the tea that they became good friends, consolidating their relationship through their involvement with the League of Jewish Women and other women's and general charities. Mrs Braynis found her to be one of the easiest of people to know. 'If I wanted one word to describe her it would be 'compassionate'. If it hadn't been for her, Jakobovits' task could have been very much more difficult.'

Vera Braynis' views would one day be reinforced by others, including Alan Greenbatt, a future director of the Chief Rabbi's Office, who observed how the Jakobovits' 'refined each other', and the Most Rev. and Rt Hon. Dr Donald Coggan, Archbishop of Canterbury, who was to praise Amélie's 'supportive' role, while Clive Lawton, a future chief executive of the yet unborn Jewish Continuity, winsomely remarked that Amélie 'warmed Immanuel up … and gave colour to black and white issues'.

Vera Braynis certainly discovered that Amélie enjoyed being with people and helped many who were in trouble. She remembers the day she arranged for her to see an Israeli woman living on her own, who had used all her savings to come to Britain for a lung-and-heart transplant. At the last moment, however, Amélie had to see someone else who was very ill. Vera Braynis was furious. Amélie, unconcerned, simply promised to visit the Israeli woman later that night. It transpired that Amélie looked after her, in every way, through visits, arranging Friday night dinners and seeking medical information. Although, sadly, the woman died three weeks later, Vera Braynis cannot forget how, during the time she was in London, Amélie made her life liveable.

People like Vera Braynis – one of a group of four powerful, vocal and intelligent women at the time whom Amélie knew were critical of her – were quick to perceive her qualities of empathy and sincerity, her complete lack of 'airs and graces', even if they also sighed over the unpunctuality that inevitably resulted from such an excess of compassion. Amélie would breeze in and out of meetings out of her fervent desire to be everywhere and fit twenty-six hours into twenty-four. This was a characteristic that she maintained all her working life. It was difficult for her critics at first to understand the pace at which she worked. Perhaps, a friend reflects, it might have been better had she cut out some of the other good works she was doing, but 'she was enjoying life so much that it would have been like smacking a child if you'd criticised the way she behaved'.

Undaunted by criticism, Amélie tried to study the behaviour of these powerful and cultured community women and learn something from them. But she was haunted by insecurity about her own educational achievements. When she heard Lady Brodie speak at a function one day, she was so impressed with her scholarly wisdom that she burst out to Lady Wolfson: 'I can never do anything like that. How can I speak in public?' Lady Wolfson soothed her by urging her never to emulate anyone else: 'Just be yourself'.'

Amélie took this advice on board and developed her own credo: to speak from the heart. Some people have been irritated by a touch of cloying sweetness in her tone or a sense of female sublimation, yet one can usually hear a pin drop when she speaks because the innocence and simplicity of her delivery is often more effective than that of the greatest intellectual heavyweight.

In tandem with a more confident and mature style, Amélie started to develop her own educational interests on Jewish themes, which would take her into the next twenty years. Over this period she would give a series of teach-ins in preparation for the High Holy Days and other festivals. In the future, could she but see it, were lectures on the events of the Holocaust, on marital and family relationships, and on specific issues within Jewish education covering a wide area of human development, as well as purely religious ones, such as on prayer or the week's portion, for organisations like the Spiro Institute.* Interfaith would one day be another area for her to explore, as would her series of lectures on the Ethics of the Fathers – 'where we can find all-encompassing lessons on the deepest wisdom and teachings of our sages'. She could hardly have imagined then that she would develop the panache and the style to teach successfully.

In fact, it would take five years before Amélie felt that she really knew the community. It was the marriage of their seventeen-year-

---

*The Spiro Institute for Study of Jewish History and Culture was established in 1978 under the founding directorship of Robin Spiro and his wife, Nitza, who was educational director of its cultural and language programmes. The purpose of the Institute was to intensify Jewish identity and awareness, to which end it launched a widespread educational network of Jewish history and culture, which included Hebrew and Yiddish, aimed at schools, universities and adult groups. The Institute today also concentrates on providing educational tours, public cultural events, concerts, film festivals, exhibitions and teacher training courses.

old eldest daughter, Esther, to Cambridge economics graduate and Talmudical scholar, Rabbi Chaim Pearlman, that 'broke the ice in our link with the Anglo-Jewish community, and from then on I made a super effort which I had neglected to do before to find my niche'.

In the meantime, Amélie had her family to look after. Esther and Shoshana were growing up in a large house into which state dignitaries and people of high political office became part of an ever-changing landscape. It may have been alien to the experience of most of their schoolfriends, but they came to accept the normality of this life, partly because their parents took the whole thing in their stride. Despite Amélie's spirit of adventure and irrepressible pride at the presence of eminent people in her home, her Jewish values helped her strike a difficult balance between religious observance and what must have been a natural curiosity on the part of their daughters about a lifestyle so different from that of any of their contemporaries.

Both Esther and Shoshana seemed untouched by the sense of British politics impinging so closely on their lives, while at the same time being well aware of the key role their father played in the drama on the British political or ecumenical stage. Shoshana remembers her status as Chief Rabbi's daughter only in the way other children at school tried to touch her. Esther has an image of looking up at a big spiral staircase at school and seeing people staring down at her. Sometimes there would be a meeting in the house when they came home from school. The Prime Minister might be inside. But Amélie loved it when the girls came in because it restored the natural order of the home. Both girls found that they were never made to feel different from other children. Quite the reverse. Their parents became irritated when they heard people urge the children to behave because they were the Chief Rabbi's children.

Their mother's past experiences would frequently arise around the Seder table as she recounted her personal exodus from the Nazis. They grew up with it despite the exhortation of their grandfather, Rabbi Munk, to Amélie not to dwell on the subject. The children became particularly aware of their parents' honesty and the palpable affection which their mother aroused. As a mother, Amélie demonstrated this same equality, tendering her affections to each of her children, 'making each one of us feel we were her favourite'. Shoshana believes that because she had gastroenteritis as a baby, her mother felt 'more sensitive towards me than the others'.

Esther had few friends when she first came to England and was considered remote. As the eldest daughter, her memories are the keenest of coming to London into a totally different environment and a home which had never been used to children.

When Jakobovits was invited by the United Synagogue to visit as many British communities as possible, Amélie insisted that she would only come if she could bring their four children. The honorary officers bowed to Amélie's demand that the family must stay together.

One Shabbat they were in Stamford Hill staying with the president of the community. The hospitality was lavish, but on Friday night, when they went to bed and the lights had gone out, Esther knocked on her parents' bedroom door, crying. 'I'm not going to bed,' she protested. 'I can't find my bed in the dark.' So together they crept along the corridors, touching the walls in a bizarre reminder of what Amélie had done in Paris as a child, afraid of the dark, until they fell on to a bed which Esther could just make out was all black with black nylon sheets. Esther said, 'No way am I going to sleep in black nylon,' and she sat up all night in Amélie's bed. 'Then I was ready to go back to the USA,' recalls Amélie. Yet years later, when Esther got engaged, her party was held in the apartment of this particular host and hostess in Jerusalem, and they became close friends.

The Wolfsons, whom the Jakobovits' always called Aunt and Uncle, as they did the Brodies, were a strong influence on Amélie and she describes them both as legends in their own lifetime. The birth of Amélie's sixth child, Elisheva, had reminded Lady Wolfson of her own thwarted desire to have more than one child. It would have been so much better for their son, Leonard, if he had had siblings, she confided, since she felt that she had spent so much time with her husband at the expense of her son.

While Sir Isaac had made his name as a millionaire benefactor, Amélie recalls a story of his early days in Glasgow shortly after the

First World War, when he was not yet wealthy. The first appeal for Jewish charity was made in the synagogue in Glasgow on behalf of the local Jewish Board of Guardians. Wolfson, who was sitting beside a millionaire, rose to his feet and said that his neighbour pledged £50 and he himself would pledge £25. He then went to the bank manager and demanded a loan of £25 (a considerable sum in those days), which he promised to repay within six weeks. The manager gave him the money, which he duly repaid.

When Amélie thinks of Sir Isaac, it is often an amusing anecdote about his family which comes to her mind, something which brings out the child in her. One of his sisters was a member of the Fifth Avenue Synagogue and Amélie used to sit next to her. 'One Saturday morning when I saw her come in, I greeted her before I went into my prayers and noticed immediately that she was wearing one of her false eyelashes upside down. That was the end of my devotions that particular Saturday morning. It took all my willpower not to go into stitches!'

27   A Call to Arms

6 JUNE 1967. Amélie and Immanuel had travelled to Gateshead, where he was delivering a lecture, when word came through that war had broken out in the Middle East. At the request of the late Lavy Bakstansky, then secretary of the Zionist Federation, and the Rev. Reuben Turner,* then director of the Zionist Federation's Synagogue Council, they took the first train back to London. They were met at the station by community leaders, who informed them that a huge communal gathering was due to meet at the Albert Hall that night which the Chief Rabbi was to address.

Jakobovits had only taken office three months before and when he stood on the platform staring at 10,000 people, all highly charged and waiting for a response from him, he understood that this moment was his first real emotional exchange with his community. Amélie will never forget it. 'G-d gave him inspiration that night and he carried the whole community with him. He, as leader, lit the hope of his community that peace would come soon.'

As they left the hall, a young Israeli woman approached them and said, 'Rabbi Jakobovits. I cannot pray. Will you please pray on my behalf?' Her words seemed almost a metaphor for the polarisation between the Jewish religion and the Jewish state, evoking the most spiritual longings expressed in the writings of Amélie's father, Rabbi Elie Munk, and the reality of war. The Chief Rabbi looked at the young woman, deeply moved. He recalled the incident frequently and was fated to meet her again, in 1973, at the

---

*Rev. Turner later worked with the Youth and Education Department of the Jewish National Fund and subsequently came into close contact with the Jakobovits'. The relationship bore fruit when his son Norman and the Jakobovits' daughter, Shoshana, eventually married.

outbreak of the Yom Kippur War, when she repeated her request to him for a prayer.

Amélie paid her first visit to Israel just after the liberation of Jerusalem in 1967. She could barely contain her utter excitement and disbelief as the plane began its descent, waxing lyrical about her emotions: 'Can I ever forget the beating of my heart at such a speed that I thought anyone could see it!'

Her most vivid memory is of walking with her husband through the streets of Jerusalem on the saddest day in the Jewish calendar, Tisha B'Av, which commemorates the destruction of the Temples. It is a day of total desolation, when religious Jews sit on the floor rather than on chairs, wearing plimsolls and fasting. Yet on that night they were among 100,000 other Jews who came streaming from every street in Jerusalem, all of them dressed in white, floating like surreal Chagal figures towards the Western Wall, which was illuminated for the first time in over 2,000 years. To Amélie it was a divinely inspired experience. 'What was supposed to be the saddest day of the year turned into the most glorious and exciting *Yom Tov* that you could imagine – an answer to the prayers of our people throughout the world.'

Later memories would be less euphoric and would resonate with the symbolism of the Israeli woman who did not know how to pray. One of Amélie's most poignant experiences was during a visit to Britain of a group of soldiers wounded in the Yom Kippur War. 'It so often happened that one of our wounded soldiers would approach the Sefer Torah and ask, "What do I do? I have never been so close before to a Sefer Torah."'

It would be a few years, too, before Immanuel Jakobovits would reach a conclusion on his long, hard and brave reflections on the nature of the Arabs' quarrel with Israel. He had the political foresight long before most other rabbis to envision that doing nothing to help the Palestinians in their refugee camps would breed a dangerous hatred. Also, more altruistically, he condemned the moral failure of the Jewish people not to draw world attention to this situation, thus tacitly endorsing it. This would lead him into future conflict with his old friend, South African Chief Rabbi Casper. In 1980 Jakobovits' public support for an accommodation with the Arabs in order to achieve peace in Israel sent alarm bells ringing in South Africa, drawing fire from Casper who condemned him roundly from his Johannesburg pulpit for 'stabbing Israel in the back'.

The Six Day War had a dramatic effect on the Jewish community. Fund-raising for Israel reached unprecedented heights and numerous volunteer groups suddenly sprang up as if from nowhere.

Even internally, and particularly in the structure of the Chief Rabbi's Office, the war left important and permanent marks. At an emergency meeting of rabbis and ministers, the Chief Rabbi announced that he would open an Israel office for the mobilisation and organisation of volunteers and other Israel-related activities. Rabbi Maurice Unterman of the Marble Arch synagogue offered to take charge of this Israel portfolio, and this was soon followed by other departments being opened within the Chief Rabbi's office. Leading ministers took on the portfolios of education, welfare, Jewish-Christian relations and gradually some others too, to enable the Chief Rabbi to be more actively involved in all facets of communal activity, both by being represented on the major organisations responsible for these activities, and by being more closely involved in their activities through top-line representation.

Soon, these heads of departments became the Chief Rabbi's Cabinet, responsible for advising him in all these areas, and at the same time increasing the religious influence on the conduct of all activities within the community. After his retirement, the system was carried on by Rabbi Jonathan Sacks.

When the Yom Kippur War broke out, Amélie was in Ilford with her husband in accordance with their custom of spending every Jewish festival with another community. As happens with the minutiae of major catastrophes, she recalls every moment of their journey to Ilford the preceding day – from the time they left Hamilton Terrace at 2.30 p.m. to the congested roads with all the traffic lights against them and major road works at each roundabout adding two and a half hours to their travelling time. They arrived in Ilford at 6.30 p.m. instead of 4 p.m. in a highly tense state. Although they had eaten at home before embarking on their journey, they were still expected to share a meal with their Ilford hosts. But it was too late for that; they just had time for a glass of tea before leaving for the synagogue.

The news of the Yom Kippur War reached them at about 5.30 p.m. the following day, just before the Chief Rabbi went up to lead the service personally for the penultimate and deeply moving prayer of the Day of Atonement, the Neila service. As he mounted the steps, one of the leading synagogue members whispered into his ear that they had just been told that Israel was at war with its enemies once again. The Chief Rabbi did not mention it to anyone; he just led his congregation into the prayer. 'It is traditional for the community rabbi, if he has anything of a singing voice, to lead his congregation in that very solemn prayer at the end of Yom Kippur when the gates to heaven are still open and the Almighty receives our very last appeal before they are closed and the judgement is sealed,' Amélie says. 'It was only after the service was concluded that he announced from the pulpit the dreadful news of the Yom Kippur War and called for special prayers.'

The following day they were preparing their *succah* for the forthcoming festival of Tabernacles when Gerald Ronson and Cyril Stein, two of the most dynamic lay leaders of Anglo-Jewry, came to obtain permission from the Chief Rabbi to set up a blood bank to enable blood to be sent to Israeli soldiers. It would have to function daily and throughout the following festival, namely Succot itself.

This placed the Chief Rabbi in a religious dilemma since Jewish law prohibits any work on a festival, with the exception of saving life. From the religious point of view, he could only grant permission if the blood donated by British volunteers would be flown to Israel for immediate use. As he pondered the question, he explained to the two leaders his difficulty in coming to a decision unless he could assure himself that this religious condition would be met.

'As lay leaders, they couldn't understand even the slightest hesitation, and the Chief Rabbi was aware of that too,' Amélie recalls, 'and I remember hearing a loud discussion through the door, and finally my husband came away from that meeting quite agitated. The only way I can detect his restlessness or agitation is by him becoming very, very quiet and hardly conversing, not even with me, and so I knew this challenge was weighing very heavily on his conscience.'

Over the next few days the Chief Rabbi tried in vain to get a reply from Israel's army chaplain, Rabbi General Shlomo Goren. By Tuesday night the dilemma intensified. He knew that if he couldn't allow the community to volunteer for the blood bank at St John's Wood Synagogue and Marble Arch Synagogue, he would antagonise many members as far as religious commandments were concerned. They would simply not understand. On the other hand, he could not sanction the blood bank unless he was assured that the blood would only be used for life-saving purposes to the army on the combat fields. At last Goren's call came through assuring the Chief Rabbi of Britain and his religious court that the blood would be used immediately, and hence the bank was launched. Amélie was deeply affected by the positive response from the entire community. An army of taxi drivers volunteered to go from the blood banks to the airports several times a day to transport the fresh blood. This rallying to the cause continued for some three weeks.

As far as the Jakobovits family were concerned, for medical reasons only Esther's husband, Chaim, and Amélie could give blood. Amélie was photographed with the wife of the then Israeli Ambassador, Mrs Michael Comay, as the first volunteers. Esther, then eight months pregnant, volunteered to help people from the bed where they gave blood to a chair in order to rest and receive a cup of coffee. Her first patient, a 'huge six footer', slipped through the hands of this slight, pregnant woman and fainted on the floor.

However, as events later proved, the massive blood-bank appeal was quite unnecessary. The blood was never used at all. Other nations, including the French, had also sent supplies in vain because, in fact, there was sufficient blood in Israel to help those who had been badly wounded. But for Amélie it was at least gratifying to see how it was possible to harness the emotional involvement of the community.

It was around this time that Immanuel's mother, who had followed them to Britain shortly after their arrival, became seriously ill with Parkinson's Disease followed by glandular cancer. Upon her illness she moved into her son's home at Hamilton Terrace and stayed in the orange guest room. Amélie developed a deep attachment to her dying mother-in-law. Some instinct or sixth sense told her before she was asked exactly when and what her mother-in-law wanted.

Amélie speaks movingly of this deepening bond of affection with the woman whom, at the beginning of her marriage, she had certainly found difficult. As Mrs Jakobovits Senior grew more frail, the Barmitzvah of her grandson, Jonathan, son of Immanuel's brother, Joseph, loomed. Amélie felt very close to Joseph and his wife, Maya, and could not bear to reflect on the unthinkable – that her mother-in-law might die during the celebrations – and realised that only a blood transfusion would keep her alive through this period. The problem was that it was illegal to do this at home. Finally, under great pressure from Amélie, the late Dr Ian Gordon, who specialised in cardiology, agreed to a transfusion, which enabled his patient to live through the celebrations. After the Barmitzvah, Amélie had to persuade her two brothers-in-law to delay their flight home because she did not believe their mother would live much longer. 'They were very annoyed with me,' she recalls. 'One of them said to me, "How can you have such little faith?" I replied, "I don't have such little faith; she is, thank G-d, comfortable, but the facts are that we nearly lost her last week, and I don't think it will be long. Stay for another few hours."'

Initially they refused and went to the airport, but when they phoned from there they were finally persuaded to return to be with the rest of the family to bid their mother farewell. Amélie describes the final gathering around her bedside in almost celestial terms. She asked Immanuel, who had not seen his mother for a couple of days having been out of town, to go up and sit with her. 'He then realised that the end was very close and there was a feeling in the room that she waited for him. He took a stool and sat next to her and held her hand and said prayers with her, including the final confession, which is the proclamation of the *Shema*. Everything was very calm and quiet and she asked her children to lower their heads; she wanted to bless them, and then she asked for me.'

Up to this time Amélie had held back, remaining discreetly in the background, unwilling to disturb a deeply emotional moment between mother and children. 'The room was half dimmed: we had closed the curtains. One really ought to do that if you feel the presence of the Angel of Death; one shouldn't see it too much, so the room was very subdued and peaceful. All the family took turns to stay with her and finally everything was beautiful in the Divine sense, and my brother-in-law, Solomon, recited Psalms as we do when we feel a person is on the verge of moving on to the next world, and at 2 a.m. he knocked at our door and said that was it, Mami had passed away, gone on *aliyah* into the next world.'

One of the problems of living a high-profile life that Amélie and her husband shared with religious leaders and top politicians alike was that of security. In December 1973, just before her first grandchild was born to her daughter Esther and her husband Chaim, Edward Sieff, a leading member of the Anglo-Jewish community, had been shot and wounded in a terrorist attack by the Black September at his home in St John's Wood. Returning home to Hamilton Terrace after first visiting him in hospital and then seeing Esther and her son, Yehuda, Amélie was confronted with 'four huge Scotland Yard security men. I went to phone my husband only to be told not to touch the phone, and for the few hours my teeth refused to stop chattering with fear and my French imagination started asking questions like, how do I know these men are actually Scotland Yard guys and not terrorists?'

One of the men offered to bring extra reinforcements needed to protect the twenty-room house. When the doorbell rang, Amélie was told not to answer it. Petrified, Amélie was grateful that Shoshana was with her. Then some security men went to Woburn House to pick up Immanuel in a car escorted by two armoured police cars in front and behind. Another security man entered the house to be informed by Amélie: 'You really look like an Arab', to which he replied, 'Well that's the idea, ma'am.' Finally Amélie found the courage to ask how she could be sure they were security men and not terrorists. They replied, 'You are quite right, Mrs Jakobovits, there is no way you can tell even though we have shown you our identity cards. But we promise you that we are Scotland Yard men.'

The first two weeks were very tense and unnerving. Amélie had the conflicting emotions of gratitude to Scotland Yard and awkwardness at having strangers in her home, which naturally made normal communication difficult. She describes the security officers as kind and caring. Seven-year-old Elisheva was taken to and from school, and Amélie had her work cut out feeding and looking after the men. 'It was good to hear a bit of gossip after they left that my wonderful cheese-cake was missed! One day, returning from shopping, I asked the driver to help me bring the bags in, but he said he could not do so because he needed both hands free – just in case.'

For the next ten days the men remained with the family until the alert was called off, and from then on the Israeli Ambassador, the Chief Rabbi and the head of the Joint Israel Appeal (the JIA) continued to receive non-stop surveillance. Amélie learned to her surprise that the two British personalities most guarded by Scotland Yard were the Israeli Ambassador and Margaret Thatcher, even more than the Prime Minister or the Royal Family.

The major international event for the Jewish community in the early 1970s beyond the continuing struggle to reach a peace agreement in the Middle East, was the movement to free Soviet Jews who were not permitted, under secular Soviet domination, to practise their religion and faced serious economic persecution, or even risked being sent to Siberia, once they applied for exit visas for Israel. The groundswell that delivered the pressure group, the 35's, led in Britain by women such as Doreen Gainsford and Barbara Oberman, created a flowering of protest on behalf of these criminalised citizens of a country most British Jews up till then had never visited. The 35's Group was a pivotal force formed by a group of women aged thirty-five who pledged to free thirty-five-year-old refusnik, Ida Nudel.

On a bitterly cold day in December 1970, Amélie led the first Anglo-Jewish march on behalf of Soviet Jewry, which took place along London's Bayswater Road to the Soviet Embassy and attracted some 3,000 women marchers. The initiative came from the women, Amélie recalls, and the men followed suit. In fact, many developments on behalf of the beleaguered Soviet Jews were launched from the lounge at Hamilton Terrace. It was a new, painful and yet exciting challenge for Anglo-Jewry. The Iron Curtain, as the Soviet power bloc was then called, seemed closer to the world of spy fiction than to the comfortable predictability of Western society.

Whether their protest was galvanised by memories of the Holocaust and the pathos of six million helpless deaths, or whether it aroused an even deeper sensitivity to all the past agonies of European exile, this time Western Jews were not going to sit back. The Chief Rabbi of Britain, too, was in touch with all the demonstrations, marches, candlelit vigils, telephone campaigns to the USSR and constant lobbying of MPs.

When he was invited to visit the Moscow community in 1975 – the first Western rabbi ever to be invited by Moscow – the Israeli authorities were against the visit since they felt the Soviet Government would gain all the political advantage of the trip to the detriment of Russian Jews. Yet the Chief Rabbi felt, as did Amélie, that if he had the opportunity to shake hands with only one Jew behind the Iron Curtain, how could he possibly say no?

In fact, when the Chief Rabbi accepted the invitation, he saw at first hand what the true meaning of freedom was. The synagogue elders could not decide to allow him to speak, since they were not sure whether his invitation had come from the president of the Jewish community or from the Kremlin itself. Eventually, he was invited to speak and addressed them in Yiddish since only older people attended synagogue that morning. The younger members, who belonged to the refusenik movement, stood on the pavement across the road from the synagogue but did not enter.

Later, Jakobovits was approached by an elderly man, who gave him three challenges in Yiddish. He said, 'We hear you making a lot of noise and demonstrations in the West for us to be allowed to leave the Soviet Union and make *aliyah* to Israel. But how many of *you* go on *aliyah*? You are in the free world, completely free to come and go as you like, and it appears to me there isn't such a big *aliyah* from the West either.' The man's second question was: 'Why is it that visitors from the West who come here on business and campaign for Soviet state approval for Jewish education can't say the blessings themselves when called up to the Torah? Why do they have to be helped to say the blessings and repeat them after us? How come, when they can get their education freely, they haven't got it? Why is it that you protest for us and do not, it seems to us, protest for them?' The third challenge the man offered him was, 'Who will say Kaddish* for me on my death?' Amélie understood that this was not a challenge on his own behalf but very much a *cri de coeur* on the part of Soviet Jewry. The Chief Rabbi was much troubled by these challenges about which he thought deeply, yet told his interlocutor he couldn't answer.**

On the same trip Jakobovits was asked to speak on medical ethics to a refusenik group to which Natan Sharansky belonged before being sent to Siberia. Unexpectedly they were given a car by the Soviet Government to take them to the meeting, and later Sharansky questioned him closely on the subjects he had raised. Amélie describes Sharansky as being as 'courageous and tenacious as he is small in physical stature. He is a strong personality with an enormous amount of willpower. Without this he would never have survived the atrocities and interrogations which he suffered in Siberia for seven years.' After the meeting Sharansky remarked, 'I never realised Judaism had anything to say about anything. When I grew up, I was always told by my parents that being Jewish is a kind of illness, a virus which you carry with you, and should never tell anyone about, and I was ashamed. I was fearful that any of my friends should find out that I was carrying a virus and would run away from me, so it is only now I am beginning to discover that Judaism is not a virus but is actually a religion, a belief, and I have decided to study its ethical, moral teachings.'

The questions from the man at the Moscow synagogue and Sharansky's revelations certainly fired the Chief Rabbi's mission to stimulate Jewish education in Britain. 'We wanted to rally more and more people together,' says Amélie, 'to boost Jewish education and try and find a message to advocate the same challenge as that given by General de Gaulle in 1947 when he offered families inducements to have more children.' It gave Amélie and her

*Ancient Aramaic prayer for the dead, said daily for one year by a parent, spouse or child of the deceased.
**The three challenges to which Jakobovits was subjected by this man gave rise to speculation as to whether the questioner was a KGB agent planted at the synagogue in an attempt to undermine Jewish unity.

husband great satisfaction to see that by the late 1980s there was a flowering of Jewish day schools in many parts of Russia, ironically pledged as it had been under Communism to the erosion of religious identity. These facts bear out Amélie's point that Judaism derives much of its strength from adversity. 'Many Jews who came out of Russia and studied Judaism and its moral and ethical idealism learned to know it and therefore love it, just as a painter loves his work with all his heart.' There were many others, however, who left Russia knowing nothing about Judaism, and she feels they are not contributing greatly to the communities in which they find themselves, particularly as many went to Israel purely as a means of securing an exit visa.

Those Western Jews seriously committed to helping them became involved on their behalf in projects launched by inter-community groups in Britain and Israel. Amélie was forced to acknowledge, however, that the majority of Soviet Jews remained secular, but she accepted that it would only be the minority who would become more spiritual, a fact borne out throughout Jewish history. There is not enough awareness of the importance of remaining a people of spirituality, morality and ethics, she believes. And she echoes her father's words when she proclaims that this was G-d's purpose in creating the Jewish people in the first place.

Amélie reflects that pressure groups fighting to free Soviet Jews adopted as their slogan the Biblical phrase, 'Let My People Go', and sent them aid, cultural and religious items, and books, but unfortunately the second part of the sentence – 'To Serve Me' – was left out, which meant a weakening within the more spiritual aspects of the campaign.

Chief Rabbi Jakobovits' first visit to Moscow had posed three challenging questions and introduced him to Sharansky, an indomitable fighter who was in some way almost a born-again Jew. On Jakobovits' second visit to the Soviet capital, he was handed a small bag of bones. They were the remains of a teacher given to Jakobovits by his devoted student, who had prayed since the 1940s to find someone to take them to be buried in Israel. The day after her husband's return, Amélie was due to fly to Israel. She agreed to take the bones, out of 'a deep sense of responsibility and a desire to do something for a soul which I felt was watching us'. The request sent her to Haifa, but she was advised not to keep the bones in her room because there might be some descendants of a priestly tribe* in the same house. So she left them on the balcony and handed them over to the Burial Society the next day. The funeral took place the following day amid a great sense of privilege and a feeling of a mission being accomplished. To Amélie it would be remembered as one of the holiest tasks she had ever been asked to perform.

Family life remained the central pivot of Amélie's experiences, much as it had been for her mother throughout the chaos of war. Now that she had been exposed to countries undergoing political upheaval in the Communist world, she began to reflect on the problems of raising a family in such places. During the mid-1970s, she and Immanuel met Romania's Chief Rabbi Rosen and his wife, Amelia, on a flight to a small Romanian Jewish community. Amélie was shocked to be told, in fairly matter of fact terms, that when the Rosens married in the early 1950s, they had had to make a choice as to whether to have a family or give themselves totally to the work of the community, which was still very dangerous for Jews under the Communist regime. They decided not to have a family. All this was so alien to Jewish thought, for Amélie. She could not recall a single precedent throughout Jewish history, but what particularly disturbed her was why the couple felt the need to speak about it. 'I have never heard of this idea of not having a family because you have to serve your people. On the contrary, your children contribute enormously to the dedication of your community. It is what leadership is all about.'

As for Chief Rabbi Rosen's personal qualities, Amélie assesses him as a great leader and saviour of his people, who contributed more than anyone to Israel's survival by ensuring that some 370,000 Romanian Jews left for Israel in the 1950s. She nonetheless perceived in him a totally Communist mentality. Amélie's opinions find resonance in George Weidenfeld's autobiography, *Remembering My Good Friends*, in which he admits to having been criticised for

---

*According to Jewish law, Cohenim, members of the priestly tribe of Israel, are not permitted to attend a funeral or have contact with a dead body.

publishing books by people like Rosen, widely condemned for colluding with the Communist regime. But Lord Weidenfeld takes a similar robust attitude: 'He saved some hundred thousand or more Jews by hobnobbing with the horrible Ceauşescu regime and procuring their exit visas to Israel.' He adds: 'Some fine men and woman have been unjustly accused of collaborating with the enemy when in fact they were appeasing him in pursuit of loftier, humanitarian aims.'

28   *Jewish Education on the Map*

THE MAN most credited with helping Chief Rabbi Jakobovits develop the educational direction of the community was the late Moshe Davis who had been army chaplain in the Middle East and to the British Army in the Rhine, and later worked as executive director of the Jewish National Fund's education department. In some ways Amélie's infallible intuition contributed to his appointment.

Amélie recalls the first impression Moshe Davis made on her when he asked a question following a lecture given by her husband on Jewish medical ethics. On the way back she told him, 'The young man tonight who asked you a question seems to be just the right type of man you need to succeed Rabbi Moshe Rose [who was leaving to go on *aliyah*] as your executive director.' It was not simply the question Davis posed, but the way he phrased it, the challenge within it and its intelligence, respect and profundity – a rare combination of qualities which Amélie pounced on.

He was duly appointed executive director of the Chief Rabbi's Office in March 1973. Amélie continued to pour praise on him. 'Moshe understands Mano's [Immanuel's] dreams.' This was as important to her as his demonstrable empathy with people from all walks of life. He also had the knack of getting them together to work in a group. It was generally accepted that Moshe Davis helped put the Chief Rabbinate at the centre of the Anglo-Jewish community. He was considered a master chess player, a quick thinker, able to assess difficult situations quickly, and with considerable energy and love for his work.

However, Davis was not only an administrator and educational adviser with a razor-sharp mind, a practical nature and a healthy cynicism. There was another side to the man that has been described as a sensitive inner consciousness, and it was this which inspired his poetry, since published in an anthology. Both qualities were required to foster the Chief Rabbi's ambitions in the late 1970s. Jakobovits set up the Jewish Educational Development Trust, which Davis ran from November 1972 until his retirement in May 1984 due to ill-health. But it was not in education alone that Davis was the standard bearer. He had the political acumen to guide the Chief Rabbi in the right direction, helping him particularly avoid the danger zones likely to ignite the growing schisms between the Progressive and the Orthodox wings of Anglo-Jewry, which were to erupt after Jakobovits had retired from office. He and Amélie also began working together in the field of Jewish counselling.

Geoffrey Paul, editor of the *Jewish Chronicle* from 1977 to 1990, looks back on the role of Moshe Davis as that of *chef de cabinet* – the supremo without whom Jakobovits made no move. 'Moshe would tell him what to do and how to do it. He was like a son to him.' 'With Moshe we entered the most perfect ten years of the Chief Rabbinate,' says Amélie. 'It was something in which I was able to take more more part in the later years.'

Yet as far as education was concerned, it took much longer than ten years – more like twenty-five – to realise Jakobovits' dream of creating new schools of higher educational quality. The Chief Rabbi had many occasions to be haunted by the words of the Soviet Jew outside the Moscow synagogue regarding the apathy of the free world towards its own spiritual enlightenment. Jakobovits only recently asked from a Hendon pulpit: 'Do we have enough education, do we have enough day schools and enough *quality* of Jewish education? Will we make sure that we have a high enough birth rate? There is a high birth rate only among the very right-wing Orthodox section of our people all over the world. There is not enough within the middle-of-the-road section anywhere. With intermarriage, opting out and general apathy, we just cannot survive.'

In support, Amélie looked vainly for the spiritual push from the State of Israel itself to 'increase our numbers worldwide'. While the Chief Rabbi admired the Jewish Day School Movement launched in Britain in the late 1930s by the late Rabbi Dr Solomon Schonfeld, it was the intensity of education that he sought. Both he and Amélie worried that Jewish secondary school education lagged far behind America's, as they had experienced in the case of their own children. They would have to wait a long time to see the launch of two new Jewish schools in Southgate and Redbridge, while Immanuel College in Bushey – Anglo-Jewry's answer to Eton, and named in his honour – would not materialise until 1990.

It was scant consolation for Amélie to learn of the high regard in which Jewish day schools were held by Gillian Shepherd, Minister of Education in the last Conservative Government. She was bitterly disappointed at the length of time it took for her husband's dreams to reach fruition. Education had been the primary factor that kept the couple in Britain, frustrating their desire to make *aliyah*. Amélie could not help feeling irritated at the close and lengthy scrutiny to which everything seemed to be subjected in Britain. Living in the Anglo-Jewish community, constrained, self-regarding – where the antique was valued over the new – was like existing in a perpetual goldfish bowl. For Amélie, not gifted with patience, it was particularly hard to wait for the measured British response.

It was the same pattern with the many meetings which took place in their Hamilton Terrace home, over weeks, over months. Amélie recalls hours of serving coffee – she once calculated with Moshe Davis that she served 700 cups of coffee a week. When a meeting was over, she would often go to the window in the hall and watch another meeting taking place outside often for yet another hour which cast doubt on everything that had been agreed in the original meeting.

29   Entertaining Amélie

AS ANGLO-JEWRY's first lady, Amélie was able to indulge one of her favourite passions – entertaining. Hamilton Terrace offered all the scope she needed to welcome *serious* guests, including the Prime Minister, Margaret Thatcher, and her entourage, world leaders, politicians, the editor of a national newspaper and the Archbishop of Canterbury. In order not to cause offence by singling out any specific Jewish caterer, she did most of the cooking herself, sometimes for up to sixty people – something which was hardly *de rigueur* in the rarified atmosphere she had now entered. Amélie always laid her own table, another love of hers. 'My mother used to say that if the table is laid, then if something is burned your guests will not taste it, because what you see is more powerful than what you taste.'

Yet the highly placed contacts with which she now mingled had required at first a softening of the slightly gamine awkardness of her younger New York self. Her image had vastly improved, as had her fashion sense, once she acknowledged the natural French flair with which she had been endowed. Nonetheless, at the beginning there had been situations – which, as her mother would say, she had to prevent from growing into problems – and not all of them could be avoided by the good sense of her friend and adviser, Erica Lawson.

After three months in Britain, at about the time of the Six Day War, Amélie was asked to open her home for a coffee morning sponsored by the women's division of the Joint Palestine Appeal,* at which the wealthiest women in the community could sell their

*A major Jewish charity which first changed its name to the Joint Israel Appeal (JIA) and later to the United Jewish Israel appeal, or the UJIA.

jewellery to raise funds for Israel. Two days later she received a phone call from a well-known member of the community, who thanked her for the coffee morning and requested a private meeting. After the obligatory niceties and cooing over baby Elisheva, she said: 'I have always been Mrs Brodie's fashion consultant and I would be happy to do the same thing for you.'

'Why?' Amélie asked in surprise.

'Because', the woman replied, 'what you wore the day before yesterday is not the kind of thing a Chief Rabbi's wife should wear.'

'Why?' Amélie repeated, disoriented, trying to remember. 'What did I wear?'

'A brown jumper and brown tweed skirt,' came the answer.

'Did you see a stain on it?' asked Amélie.

'No.'

'Did you see a hole?'

'Oh, no.'

'So what was wrong?'

'It's not the kind of thing a Chief Rabbi's wife should wear. She should wear much classier dresses.'

At that point Amélie asked her to leave. She was used to the potent wealth of voluble New York women, but nothing had prepared her for the subtler, elitist vanities of the Anglo-Jewish dress code. Amélie could not understand how, at a time of war in Israel when elegant women were asked to donate their jewellery in order to provide first aid for soldiers, anybody could worry about clothes. Amélie, of course, likes clothes as much as any other woman, but perhaps the difference is best illustrated by Geoffrey Paul's recollection of her visit to his wife, Rachel, shortly after the birth of their son. 'Rachel recalls only too clearly how the youngster soiled her very with-it silk dress and Amélie calmly wiped herself down and carried on the conversation as if there had been nothing untoward.' However, loath to fall out with any member of the community, Amélie eventually phoned the woman who had criticised her tweed skirt and they became 'very close friends'.

Another time she was asked by a guest to reveal her recipe for the 'delicious' coffee she had supplied at a meeting. Tantalisingly she refused, saying that she never divulged these secrets. But that caused a furore in the community, until Amélie telephoned the guest and apologised for having offended her. 'I understand you are upset, but how could I have told you on that morning that I only had four half-empty jars of coffee in the house and I mixed them all together in order to have enough!'

From the early gaffes and fiery initiations that marked Amélie's launch into Anglo-Jewish society, she grew into a hostess of some prestige, managing to straddle two almost irreconcilable worlds. Amélie was both a welcoming Jewish mother and a dignified society doyenne. Before long she would be a welcoming Jewish grandmother, and whether it was her children or her grand-children who were running around Hamilton Terrace, she had no intention of keeping them away.

As for the Chief Rabbi, Geoffrey Paul recalls the 'intense sense of partnership' between Amélie and the Chief, not just in public but also in private, to which he was party during breakfast meetings with him at Hamilton Terrace. 'Amélie would cook and serve, hovering for a moment to make sure we were well settled and then withdrawing so discreetly that you did not realise she had gone. Then she would come back and – it was uncanny – but she would have arrived at the same point of the conversation we had reached, although she could not have heard it. Incredible. She knew the way the conversation would go before it happened. She knew the drift. She could be at the end of a conversation before it began. She knew where she wanted conversations to go. And she got them there. She is a smartie. A very quick thinker.'

It is with wry humour that Paul remembers the Friday morning telephone inquests to which he was subjected by her after the paper appeared. After softening him up with some family news or harmless tittle-tattle, she would reach the point of criticism and put her husband on to take up the conversation where she had left it – and Paul, floundering. 'Immanuel would react as a victim. "You have made me suffer," he would cry, or "I am suffering because of …" I don't think he's an actor. He takes on the mantle.'

To Paul, a seasoned observer of the machinations of Anglo-Jewry, there is no doubt that the couple were a joint Chief Rabbinate. 'He's very gracious socially. We weren't intimates. I don't think he's a man you could really be intimate with. You stand a little back from him because he carries this aura of religious authority without becoming menacing or anything. Where he leaves this cool zone around him, she fills it in. She's busy running around, putting down the cakes and ale. There is Amélie and there is everybody else. As they say, you can't compare apples with oranges. Amélie is this unique fruit which is just there in its own glowing colours. It's Amélie.'

These were the days of the 'rubber chicken' official dinners which Jakobovits would avoid, sending Amélie instead as his eyes and ears. The meals she cooked at home, served by waitresses, kept many tired politicians for long hours at her table. Amélie basked in the knowledge that her highly placed guests had the sense of being welcomed into a Jewish home.

Shimon Cohen, the dynamic and successful publicity man who stepped into Moshe Davis' shoes on his twenty-third birthday when Davis retired in 1984, recalls a late dinner at Hamilton Terrace with Leon Brittan, then Conservative Home Secretary, when everyone was desperate for him to make a move to leave because they simply wanted to go to bed, but soon forgot their tiredness because Amélie helped make the evening so exciting and enjoyable.

Then there was the troop of Jakobovits grandchildren coming to meet Margaret and Denis Thatcher when they came to dinner. Like the famous staircase in Downing Street graced with the portraits of prime ministers, the staircase at Hamilton Terrace featured those of the Jakobovits grandchildren. The guests, no matter what they had come to discuss – from the forthcoming elections in South Africa to the proposed banning of sheep by the Swiss Government – were always taken on a tour of the grandchildren. 'A completely crazy thing to do when you are a major public figure entertaining other public figures,' smiles Cohen, 'but it meant she had these people eating out of her hands and that was her great skill.'

Amélie, in other words, was an ice-breaker *par excellence* if things became too formal or there were too many awkward silences. Cohen admits that there were many occasions when people would call him after a meeting and make it clear they thought she had been a liability at a certain event by reducing the serious to the frivolous. 'I am not a sycophant, and if I felt that she overstepped the mark, I would certainly tell her, but nine times out of ten she would be the one who would actually lay the tarmac for the road that was going to get us to the decision we wanted. She would never de-focus or take them off track. She was aware all the time of the sort of issues you were to discuss.'

During the time of delicate negotiations with the Government over *shechita*,* Cohen took part in an informal delegation to protest at a number of recommendations that were not acceptable. The Government at the time was caught between the imprecations of the Chief Rabbinate and the Farm Animal Welfare supporters, and after a compromise solution was reached with the former, the extreme right wing of the community objected. A meeting of all the religious factions at Hamilton Terrace resulted in impasse. 'One particular little old chap did not understand the political system – the give and take – and they were all refusing to budge, and it was getting horrible, really awful. And then all of a sudden we heard the rattling of tea cups and suddenly a woman had entered what was the equivalent of the holy of holies, came up to the man who was causing all the trouble, took the cup off the tray and held it out to him, so he had absolutely no choice but to take the cup. And from that minute the meeting started to improve. It was just one example of how she broke the ice by doing something that was a little bit mischievous, a bit naughty, but it worked.'

Shimon Cohen was indeed the ears and eyes of the Chief Rabbi, a grand vizier moving in all circles and playing a role in formulating policy through feedback from the key people. His brief was to bring the Chief Rabbi in touch with people at the highest echelons of society whom he needed to influence. Amélie, he felt, played an exceptional role in all this. Her views were valued, and she would often be called in for her expertise and ability to talk in a more human language. Often a meeting failed because she had not been present. Cohen's views are endorsed by Jonathan Kestenbaum, chairman of the United Jewish Israel Appeal: 'You had a sense that she broke through the protocol, and that's not because she's an intemperate woman but a naturally warm one.'

* The method of ritual slaughter used in abattoirs, which renders meat kosher.

Observers often chuckled at the way Amélie's bustling homeliness reduced the awesome dignity of her husband, as though in some way she desired this, was more comfortable with it. 'She would welcome people into her home and say, "I'll call my husband,"' says Cohen. 'And suddenly this great man, who had such stature and character, was no longer this great man but this rather bubbly, vivacious, excited lady's husband who would talk to you as though he were your grandpa.'

As far as the Office was concerned, it was troubled by one very delicate issue concerning a key member of staff. This particular staff member had worked closely with Amélie on counselling members of the community, but it was brought to the Chief Rabbi's attention that the man, who was married, was having an affair. He was asked to give up the liaison. Amélie drafted a proposed letter for him to send to his mistress ending their liaison, to which he agreed in principle but could not bring himself to write. To add to the moral dilemma, the man was also dying of cancer. Eventually, a formula was agreed for his resignation. He found other work in the community, but died not long afterwards.

The dilemma here is one which so exercised John Major's Conservative administration, as it did Margaret Thatcher's before him, and has more recently re-emerged with the Robin Cook affair. How much more did the issue plague the Chief Rabbi, who could not be seen to sanction adultery, and yet deeply valued the man, an exceptional human being, who had made a vast contribution to Jakobovits' work and was himself in a state of terminal illness and emotional turmoil?

As a leading figure in the community put it, 'I would say in that context, without any question, to me the behaviour of the Jakobovits' at the time was inexplicable. They could have found another way of dealing with the situation. Of course, the employee himself didn't help. But then try and get into the mind of a man who knew he had cancer and had found somebody who gave him warmth and affection, which possibly his wife did not find easy to give in the way he needed it anyway. He was seizing at the last moments, knowing he would be cold and lonely very soon. As for his wife, I believe, wonderful soul that she was, that with great generosity, she welcomed the woman into her home in his last weeks.'

Was Amélie wrong to press the man to give up his mistress? There are probably no clear answers. It is the eternal question of the straight and narrow path of unflinching Orthodoxy pitted against the open mind on an issue where compassion might have won the day. Amélie, the inheritor of both worlds, whose Orthodoxy and compassion are bred in the bone, made her choice.

30   *The Chief Rabbi and the Tory Party*

MANY PEOPLE have placed the Jakobovits' firmly in the Conservative Party camp largely because of the open admiration that the then Prime Minister, Margaret Thatcher, expressed for him during her prime ministership. She conferred a knighthood upon him in the Queen's Birthday Honours of June 1981. The Chief Rabbi's supporters and critics have spoken of him as Thatcher's guru, as though she favoured him above all others, including the Archbishop of Canterbury, when it came to gleaning ethical or spiritual advice. Such a glib reputation, even if it contains some truth, has sat uneasily on Jakobovits' shoulders, however, as his retiring nature shuns the glare of any kind of political mirror. Those who know him best like to think of him as his own man, as has been borne out by the unpopularity he has courted both over his statements on the Palestinian problem and the issue of homo-sexuality.

According to the then socialist MP, Greville Janner, the Chief Rabbi was a great defender of Margaret Thatcher. 'I could not get Amélie to understand that politically we were different, which had nothing to do with my feelings for the man himself.' But whatever associations people made about her husband's political colours, they never bothered Amélie, who always felt free to cultivate her own political opinions and remained determined to preserve a simple public attitude: she was the wife of her husband and the mother of his children, and her views became irrelevant when they needed to. She does, however, take enormous pleasure in the thought of the great and the good flocking to her husband.

A pivotal debate between the Archbishop of Canterbury and

the Chief Rabbi took place in 1985, when Dr Robert Runcie was researching a document later published under the title, *Faith in the City*. This was the response of the Church to the civil riots during that summer in Liverpool and parts of London, and reflected concern at the lack of godliness in peoples' lives contributing to disquiet and disharmony. It was very critical of government policy at the time.

The Chief Rabbi and the Archbishop were on first-name terms and good friends. Dr Runcie sent Jakobovits a private copy of this document before it was released, requesting his views. He wrote a response and his office sent it privately to the Archbishop. It was fundamentally opposed to Dr Runcie's conclusions, but the Archbishop wrote back, effectively urging him to publish and be damned so that they could both enjoy an intellectual debate in the newspaper columns.

Janner rounded on the Chief Rabbi, vehemently supporting Dr Runcie's arguments: 'I profoundly agreed with the Inner Cities Report and he did not. He made the statement that blacks should be like Jews in the sense that they should pull themselves up by their bootstraps, and there I disagreed with him in a parliamentary debate.' Janner did not think it appropriate for the Chief Rabbi to compare Jews of their time and circumstances with blacks and theirs, and could not persuade Amélie to understand that political differences did not erode his personal respect for her husband.

It so happened, however, that the Chief Rabbi's espousal of self-help and reliance on the family struck a Conservative chord, within Margaret Thatcher in particular. This happened not because she valued and trusted him more than she did the Archbishop, say observers, but that she considered the Archbishop to be a socialist and she thought Jakobovits was not. She also had more in common with him in intellectual and political terms than she did with Dr Runcie. Out of this embryonic relationship Jakobovits was soon able to lobby Mrs Thatcher on issues relating to Israel and Soviet Jewry. She was a passionate supporter of Soviet Jewry, so, as their friendship developed, he was invited to sit on various government commissions relating to family policy. He sat on the Commission for Embryology, he debated medical ethics issues as well as those relating to the health service. He participated in various seminars relating to disarmament, because he had very strong views, based on Jewish teachings, on the dangers of the arms trade and they would correspond. Margaret Thatcher did not, according to Shimon Cohen, ever look to him for spiritual guidance about how she should lead the country. For any such personal issues she would consult only her husband, Denis.

'For her,' says Cohen, 'Jakobovits was a man whose intellect was honest, and by that I mean he was not ever going to be elected to serve or continue in office, he was never going to have to be reappointed by his shareholders, he didn't have to look over his shoulder towards the election, so his views were intellectually honest views.' They were based not on the Jewish religion but on Jewish ethics, the work ethic. His views of society were not formulated by Margaret Thatcher but by Jewish teaching. The fact that Thatcher found something akin in Jewish teachings to the formulation of her policy brought her closer to the Chief Rabbi, rather than the other way round. 'She found him,' says Cohen, 'he did not find her.'

They first met officially when, as Secretary of State for Education under Edward Heath, she was invited to open a north-west London Jewish day school. She was later to recall a remark he made to her which really impressed her: '"You are really the Minister of Defence," he told me. And he meant, of course, that after what is learned in the family, it's what's taught at school that keeps the nation whole and strong.' In Margaret Thatcher Jakobovits found somebody with whom he could do business. As the MP for Finchley she certainly respected Jewish people and was surrounded by them. It was a relationship based on the converging of ideas, and where his philosophy, formulated on Jewish teachings, found kinship with her own in theory and practice.

'People have this idea that she came to him for absolution and compassion and things,' Cohen remarks, 'but that's absolutely not it at all.' Nevertheless, it was a romantic concept and one which must have been irresistibly flattering. The respect of the then British Prime Minister changed the perspective with which the community regarded the Jakobovits', and also broadened the Chief Rabbi's personal perspective. His philosophy derives from a phrase from the Prophets – 'Jews should be a light unto the nations' –

which was a guiding principle of Amélie's father, too. It was not difficult to perceive that this renewed esteem in which the Chief Rabbi was held in the country was an opportunity to be exactly that – a light to the nations. It was perhaps only half in jest that Paul Johnson wrote in the *Daily Mail* in the mid-1980s, that the Government should appoint Jakobovits Archbishop of Canterbury.

What Mrs Thatcher found stimulating about Jakobovits was his sense of the possible. He had a practical view of life; he was an optimist who believed that things could be done. Both of them were ideas people and, after talking to him, she could envisage a pragmatic application of her philosophies.

Amélie, who loved meeting people and took particular pleasure in seeing the esteem in which the Thatchers held her husband, recalls the night they all had dinner in the *succah*. She says, 'Both Margaret and her husband were always full of questions and wanted to know as much as they could from the Chief Rabbi about our rituals, the meaning of Jewish law, the meaning of Jewish ethics, and the explanations. They always offered a very intellectually inquisitive, genuine and very intelligent reaction to anything that one tried to explain to them and teach them – if I may say so.'

Amélie appreciated not only the mutual social intercourse, but also the intellectual intercourse they all enjoyed at the Jakobovits' table. She was personally impressed with Mrs Thatcher's thirst for knowledge and for discovery, particularly on the scientific front. She also discovered that contrary to popular opinion, Denis Thatcher, who always gave the impression he was not involved in any of his wife's decision-making, certainly had a major role to play. 'He told me more than once that Margaret discusses everything with him. Margaret is a person who needs very little sleep; she's a workaholic, and many, if not all of her decisions are discussed with him. So he is very much an adviser to her, a springboard and a tremendous rock of stability and security.'

Amélie found Denis Thatcher easy to communicate with and very intelligent. At official dinners or receptions, Margaret Thatcher's attentions went naturally to Immanuel, so Amélie usually found herself talking to Denis. 'I was very impressed. I admired their relationship as husband and wife, and I think he's been a great help to her in public life and in her work.' Perhaps in Denis Thatcher Amélie saw her opposite number, observing the same supportive restraint that she offered her husband – though at home she has been seen to be somewhat bossier, bringing him down to earth when he appeared vague because his thoughts were on a higher plane. She is the only one who could bully him, Shimon Cohen has observed. 'And at times he needed to be bullied!'

On state occasions or official dinners at her home, Amélie did not participate in her husband's conversations with the then Prime Minister as she was busy entertaining other people. She knew that they had discussed the attitude of the free world towards terrorist activities. Margaret Thatcher did not ask his advice in an obvious way, but made it her business to read his writings, then take guidance from much of them. 'There are a number of sentences which she has used in her premiership which I know for a fact she has taken from Immanuel's writings or TV and radio appearances,' Amélie says. She was intensely proud of this. She was once heard to remark guilelessly at a WIZO fund-raising lunch at the Guildhall, where the Prime Minister was the guest speaker, 'Look how Margaret Thatcher is looking at my husband. She really admires him!'

It was one thing for Amélie to entertain world leaders in her own home, it was quite another when they were invited to attend official dinners and receptions. The question of *kashrut* always had to be handled with diplomacy. The Brodies had made do with endless rounds of fruit, which led, they grudgingly acknowledged, to equally endless bouts of indigestion! Amélie did not care for that idea and devised a discreet plan in which a list of kosher caterers could be supplied to their official hosts before a function. Their names would be used in strict rotation in order to avoid offending anyone. It has now become second nature among the British establishment, first to issue the invitation, and second to volunteer the question, 'Which caterer would you like?' without any prompting. Normally the caterer would try to match the menu being served as far as possible.

During the mid-1970s Amélie found herself sitting next to Barbara Castle, then Labour's Minister of Education, at the 100th anniversary dinner of the TUC Congress at the Guildhall. When it came to the dessert, Barbara Castle looked at Amélie's strawberries and asked, 'How come your strawberries are so much bigger than mine?' Each strawberry was, indeed, at least four times the size as all those served to the 798 guests. Amélie looked at her coolly and said, 'Well, it's simply that mine are kosher and come from the State of Israel.' And Mrs Castle said, 'Really? Do strawberries have to be kosher as well?'

One day during John Major's premiership they were invited for brunch at the Prime Minister's country residence, Chequers. However, the phone call requesting the name of a preferred kosher caterer never came. Amélie recalls that they 'set off that morning for Chequers, and Immanuel asked whether I had made any arrangements for our food. I said no, they never phoned, but you see it will be okay, and if the worst comes to the worst, we'll eat a tomato, a cucumber salad, or some other salad which isn't cooked.'

Upon their arrival John Major welcomed them at the door with the warmth he extended to all forty of his guests, as though they were his best friends. After about an hour someone suddenly tapped Amélie on the shoulder from behind and took her hand. Amélie glanced up to see that it was the Prime Minister. He said to her, 'Amélie, let's lead our guests into the dining-room.' They walked into the dining-room followed by all the guests, where a buffet was set. Major took her to a round table in the centre of the room and said, 'Look, there are a dozen different types of vegetables here. We have cleaned them, we have cut them, but we didn't cook them because we wanted to make sure that everything would be okay with you.' Then he added, 'And here is a platter of smoked salmon and here a platter of smoked trout, and there is also a box of tea *matzos* and a bottle of wine with a corkscrew and – I hope that's okay – a bowl of fresh berries.' Then he looked at Amélie with a quizzical expression and asked her, 'Now, have we done everything correctly?' It sounded to Amélie as though he and his wife Norma had prepared everything themselves.

In the meantime, all the guests had assembled around the table and listened to the Prime Minister very carefully explaining to them the laws of *kashrut*. 'It was a wonderful experience we shall never forget. Everybody was very moved, and, of course, this was much more of an effort than simply calling in a caterer to do it all. There was so much thought and kindness and warmth in that act.' 'We enjoyed it, too. It is part of the challenge, isn't it?' was Norma Major's recollection of the incident.

Amélie has praised John Major's thorough sincerity, goodness and kindness. She considers both the Majors to be genuine people of patience and refinement. 'Those who have never heard him speak on social occasions cannot visualise that he also has an excellent sense of humour in his after-dinner speeches, but it is his thoughtfulness that most impresses me.' She equally admires Norma Major, the biographer of the soprano, Joan Sutherland, and author of a book on Chequers, as a sincere Christian who had a very strict, religious upbringing. 'I remember how she told me when they were in our home that they were not allowed boyfriends, and had to cover their hair when they went out of the house, as little girls.' But Norma Major was less convinced that her equally traditional attitudes towards family life stems from the same source: 'I don't know whether I am religious. At different times we tried a hotch-potch of different churches. My father was Jewish. I had a Jewish grandmother.'

Amélie does not believe that Norma Major had any idea how much she would share her husband's position when he first took office. From Downing Street, when Norma Major was still first lady in 1996, when the Conservative Government was beleaguered by the beef crisis and experienced, in her own words, 'a gruelling few weeks', Norma Major recalled Amélie's support in writing to them regularly, whether about the beef crisis or the Dunblane massacre. 'Hardly any of our difficulties pass her by. She would always write, "Keep at it; we are thinking of you and praying for you." I would like to think that she's a Tory. I couldn't make a briefing statement, but I have the impression that she is.'

Norma Major sensed an indisputable closeness between Amélie and Immanuel as a couple, as well as a sensitivity to what the Majors were going through during the final decline of the Tory Government. Amélie gave her the impression that she accepted that John Major believed he was doing the right thing and that most politicians were genuinely decent people, 'who are doing things in the way they believe is right'. She was amused and delighted upon hearing Amélie refer to John Major as a *mensch*.*

Although John Major had little exchange with Jakobovits as Chief Rabbi – 'they were going through the transition when we came here' – Norma Major noted that Amélie 'has done a tremendous amount of work in the educational field. I think the warmth does strike you, and the enthusiasm. She is full of life.'

Mrs Major – unexpectedly spotlit for her 'natural homeliness' to boost her husband's flagging chances during the doomed May 1997 general election – has referred to her own conflict of interests between supporting her husband and her writing career, about which she sounded frankly half-hearted. 'It's something you've achieved, but it's been a conflict of time. I don't know that Amélie needs something that is independent, as it were. Obviously it is linked to her husband's work and his office as well.' Mrs Major has some advice for the more emotional Amélie on the question of taking criticism of her husband personally: 'You get used to it. You accept that it's the role that gets criticised rather than the individual.'

Amélie was particularly affected by the way John Major went into the kitchen and shook hands with all the girls who had helped her to prepare and serve a dinner to which the Jakobovits' had invited them. As she accompanied him to the car, Amélie told him how rare it was to see someone in high office thinking of anybody else except his equals. It seemed as though Amélie was drawn to John Major for those very qualities which may have contributed to his downfall. 'On the one hand, this is John Major's greatness, but I think on the other hand it is probably what sadly, tragically, affects his ability to govern. He's just too kind and thoughtful, too sweet, and I think people take advantage of that. He's not a strong leader, but he's a very genuinely well-meaning leader who does not like to hurt anybody. Margaret Thatcher, who is also quite a thoughtful person, was certainly a very much more determined, severe, unbending, inflexible personality who also came from a relatively modest background.'

Amélie remembers being invited by the Queen to attend an intimate dinner party to bid farewell to Lech Walesa, then Prime

*Yiddish for a person of true heart and character.

Minister of Poland. Margaret and Denis Thatcher were present. Although black tie was specified on the invitation, Immanuel returned from a function in his evening lounge suit. Amélie wore a three-quarter-length evening dress. She admits that she did not look properly at her invitation, because she is normally very particular about the way her husband dresses. When she saw the assembled guests formally dressed in evening suits, Amélie was overcome with embarrassment, but Lady Thatcher, by then no longer Prime Minister, approached them and remarked, 'Oh, thank G-d your husband is wearing an ordinary tie! Denis is also wearing one.' Amélie presumes she, too, did not study her invitation properly. Immanuel was hardly a man to be over-concerned about the niceties of dress, issues which he left to his wife to sort out. With a touch of insouciance, Amélie is inclined to joke that he would hardly notice if he were wearing pyjamas.

31 _Diana and the Royals_

SUCH FORMALITIES are clearly not the things by which Amélie lives, but there is no doubt that she has a paradoxically romantic fascination with the glitz and protocol of British high society. There is no question that, long before Princess Diana transformed the royal landscape for all time, one of the highlights of Amélie's role as wife of the Chief Rabbi was their invitation to dinner at Windsor Castle in the spring of 1975 where they were to meet the Queen, Prince Philip, the Queen Mother and Prince Andrew. While the excitement of the experience was still with her, she wrote a letter to all her family and friends listing the event in every detail. The effusive letter written forty-eight hours later is full of the wide-eyed wonder of a little Jewish girl catapulted into royal society.

'Where – oh where should I begin?' she starts. Her letter is full of adjectives, such as 'anxiously looking forward', 'elated', 'absolutely overwhelmed', and then, as the hyperbole dies down, she describes their arrival at Windsor Castle just before 7 p.m., where they were received by members of the Royal Household, including a valet for her husband and a lady-in-waiting for her.

> We had a magnificent suite in King Edward II Tower. It consisted of a huge and beautiful lounge, two bedrooms and two bathrooms. Flowers, fruit, everywhere! We were allowed five minutes to change and were then escorted to one of the Castle's magnificent reception-rooms to meet the Royal Family for cocktails.

Invited with them were the then Home Secretary, Roy Jenkins, and his wife, the Duke and Duchess of Norfolk, the Earl and Countess of Antrim and Lord and Lady Nugent of Guildford.

A sudden stone-like silence overcame the room as the Queen

231

entered, surrounded by four of her corgis. We were introduced and then equally suddenly everyone relaxed again and started chatting. Immanuel was chatting with the Duchess of Norfolk, while I was entertained by Lady Rose, the Queen's Lady-in-Waiting. You can imagine my great shock and amazement when quite suddenly the Queen was standing right in front of me and starting a twenty-minute chat about how and where I had met my husband.

Here Amélie recounted the tale of their courtship and the beginning of their romance at the top of the Eiffel Tower, which so amused the Queen that she motioned to the Queen Mother to come over and listen while Amélie repeated it. Then she asked Amélie how her husband had become Chief Rabbi. Had he been trained since childhood? 'I explained and then she went over to my husband. I was terrified she would ask him the same question and he, no doubt, would give a different answer. Thank G-d that didn't happen. They chatted about the general world situation.'

The Chief Rabbi presented the Queen with a mounted frame of five copies of the Orders of Service held by the Anglo-Jewish communities for the coronations of four monarchs – a gift which Amélie saw moved the whole Royal Family. On returning to their rooms before dinner at the Queen's request, they found everything prepared, including their baths, and their cases unpacked. At 8.30 p.m. they were escorted back to the Queen, with whom they walked into the state dining-room, a sight which Amélie describes in effusive detail: its seven large candelabras, seven 'fabulous' flower arrangements, its array of crystal and china, the plates costing over £250 each, 'even though they used our own caterer's china. Four courses were served with speedy elegance.' Then she describes a scene where courtliness was blended with the common touch:

> At 9.30 p.m. or so the Queen stood up, left the room followed by her mother and all the ladies present; the men staying behind 'for port'. The Queen offered us to 'go and powder our noses'. Some of us did, then we all sat down together and *shmussed* about a hundred different things, the Queen telling us how she loved walking with her children in the Balmoral countryside and just getting lost.

Amélie heard them discuss the difficulties of being oneself, of being watched and reported, of feeling like a goldfish in a bowl. To her surprised ears it must have suggested a touch of the intrigues of the House of Borgia rather than the modern House of Windsor. The Queen told her that there was only one place in the entire world where she felt herself, and that was at Balmoral, where she had grown up and could have fun, and where, even today, the local people would not disturb her when she walked in the street. She was delighted when someone came up to her there and said, 'Good day, are you local around here and can you tell us where this or that place is?'

While it must have given Amélie an insight into the private character of the Queen, it was at this dinner party that Amélie felt so drawn to the Queen Mother. While chatting, she kept on playing with the lace frills of her dress. 'I really fell for her. She is so adorable and always smiling, speaking very softly and getting very involved in what she has to say.' Yet Amélie acknowledges that the Queen herself has the shyness of her father, 'this inability and possibly even dislike of being too close to anyone'.

A two-and-a-half-hour walk through the Castle corridors followed, with explanations by the Royal Family about the portraits on the walls. They ended up spending an hour in the private library, where the Chief Rabbi and the librarian had a fascinating discussion. Both the Queen and Prince Philip asked the Chief Rabbi a variety of questions on the Prophets and other issues relating to the Old Testament. During this time, Amélie was invited by the Queen Mother to read a few pages of the then Princess Elizabeth's diary written at the time of her father's Coronation.

When the Queen said goodnight at around 1.30 a.m. Amélie asked for permission to express her innermost feelings. She told the gathering: 'Considering that only a few years ago my husband and I and, by extension, most members of the Anglo-Jewish community and its Commonwealth were treated like animals just because we were born Jewish, for us both to be celebrated tonight as we have been by the Royal Family, is a blessing which neither of us, nor our friends within the Anglo-Jewish community and its Commonwealth will ever forget.' The Queen Mother, with tears rolling down her cheeks, replied: 'Amélie, when people come to spend an evening with us they will always thank us for a lovely evening, but my daughter, my family and I, are so grateful to have been able to hear you say that we have given you and our friends of the Jewish community so much pleasure.' This was, no doubt, one of the most moving moments in Amélie's life.

When they returned to their room, Amélie found everything prepared for bed, down to the glass filled with water and the toothpaste already on the toothbrushes. Her husband's suit for the morning was carefully prepared, his pockets emptied with every item well laid out in his room. Even the money was carefully piled and ordered with the Queen's face on top. His prayer shawl was also carefully laid on the bed, as though they thought it was part of his pyjamas.

At 7.35 the following morning, a tray with orange juice and coffee and all the newspapers was brought to them in bed. 'Luckily I got up about ten minutes before and put on my *sheitel*. I asked my husband if he had slept well and he said, "No. It's really too exciting." Can you imagine? Actually neither of us had slept well that night, as we talked for ages.'

Being entertained in that rarefied presence brought Amélie closer to an awareness of what constant media attention meant for those in its spotlight: a relentless, pervasive attention seeking out every silent, private place, making judgements from which there was no appeal.

Amélie's conviction that there should be restrictive legislation preventing its excesses, recommended by her friend William Rees-Mogg, then editor of *The Times* (and later Chairman of the Broadcasting Standards Council), was intensified in the years to come by one of the most turbulent incidents of the dying century – the tragic death of Diana, Princess of Wales, in a Paris car accident in August 1997. For both Amélie and Lord Jakobovits, the sadness of her short life and violent death was a tragedy of Biblical proportions. Amélie reacted emotionally alongside a vocal section of the public and the media, sensing that the crowds surging to Buckingham Palace and St James's Palace to place flowers and messages of love to their fallen Princess demanded more than what was judged to be a stiff, token acknowledgement of the Royal Family immediately after the crash. This was a rare moment in a nation's history calling for understanding and sensitivity, she felt, not the cold hand of regal protocol Amélie has frequently condemned. Although she has privately admitted that she is never comfortable with such mass demonstrations of emotion for one human being as they cannot help reminding her of Hitler's magnetism, Amélie was to perceive something else within the mourning crowd. This was the spiritual longing for which Diana's death had become an emblem, a sacrifice. Both Amélie and Immanuel had long been aware of the power of great personalities to change a mood, alter a state of mind to convey something beyond themselves. It could work either positively or negatively.

Long before the tragedy, Amélie had expressed fears that Diana's divorce from Prince Charles would, given her charisma and popularity, send out a negative message on marriage as an institution. While the Church of England remained mealy-mouthed on the subject of their divorce, Lord Jakobovits did not flinch from venting his feelings in the media about the need for those in high public office to set examples and moral standards. Under banner headlines in the *Daily Express* of 23 April 1996, he called for an eleventh hour reconciliation between the royal couple and lambasted both the Church of England and the Prime Minister of the time, John Major, for failing to prevent their break-up.

'My husband has always felt, as I do, that every time there is a tragedy in one marriage, it psychologically affects every other marriage – and can create a chain reaction,' says Amélie. In speaking about the Royal Family, Amélie was receptive to Diana's magic, her luminosity, compassion and also her fragility. She knows herself that such a large dose of personal charisma in one human being shines even brighter by exposure to the neediest in society. In some ways, perhaps, she saw in the tragic Princess a reflection of her own work in the community, for, while there are no paparazzi to mirror her work to the world, Amélie is nonetheless lauded for her charitable efforts and her personal charm whenever she visits those in need.

One man about to undergo by-pass surgery said that after Amélie's words of comfort to him in hospital, he passed through to the operating theatre in an almost euphoric state – 'on a cloud', he said – so powerful was her radiance and goodwill. Others have expressed similar sentiments. These are the words frequently spoken of the late Princess Diana, but the degree of support for the needy is harder to evaluate in a rabbi's wife than a glamorous royal able to reflect her angelic image through the world's media.

Amélie sometimes rushed in where angels feared to tread, among the suddenly bereaved who sometimes resented her intrusion on their private grief, as well as among those who clung to her and depended on her support. Amélie could never predict how she would be received. It took courage as well as a spontaneity sometimes bordering on foolhardiness. She faced open resentment once when she rushed in to offer home-baked *challot* to a bereaved woman, but she would not give in, and over time she managed to break down the woman's resistance until they became friends. When she speaks of this incident, Amélie admits that she has learned from her mistakes and would do things differently now.

Amélie shrank from the prospect of Diana's *Panorama* interview because of her dictum that respect for leadership will diminish with exposure of too many private thoughts and emotions. Yet admiration – 'in spite of myself at her incredible performance' – became Amélie's unwitting obituary to the star-crossed Princess. 'It was a really tremendous performance. She never hesitated in her answers, never tripped over a word; she was in total control. To me she was as cool as a cucumber, and some people watching with me were convinced she was reading from a telescript, but it couldn't have been, because she lifted her eyes, do you remember her enormous ability to use her eyes? She didn't even need to answer the questions, you could tell in her eyes what she was saying.'

Listening to Diana speak of her post-natal depression and bulimia, Amélie, never one to favour counsellors and therapists, took the view that professional help was needed here. 'But more important than everything else was the support of husband and family. Diana did not have that because nobody understood it; her husband didn't understand it, the Queen, presumably, didn't have the time to understand it, so there was nobody to give her support.' Amélie acknowledges Diana's covert attack on the Royal Family in her interview. 'I think it was remarkable that when she suffered bulimia, the rest of the world didn't notice it. Yes, she did fight back; she took an enormous gamble by fighting the family she felt she had been hurt by.' She added that she believed Diana's

Panorama interview, 'in which she exposed herself and her sufferings to the world, will go down in history for ever'.

Amélie rushed to the Princess' defence over Nicholas Soames' attack on Diana's 'large dose of paranoia' after the programme, dismissing his remarks as 'a typically masculine, unpleasant and nasty thing to say'. She added, in a phrase that has its own poignancy in the light of Diana's death, 'if she were paranoid, would it be any wonder, with the entire world, every camera on top of her? I think she is a miracle. How does she survive it altogether?'

Amélie believes the monarchy will change. She would like the Queen to give up some of her aloofness and become more communicative, to draw the royals into a new, more approachable era, such as that which has long dawned over Holland and Denmark. Clearly Amélie longs for the human face of royalty which she believes died with Diana. Amélie is not alone in demonstrating a certain confusion over what that should be. Like many, she wants the 'magic aura' of majesty to continue. Amélie has criticised both Charles and Diana for the openness which she suggests diminishes that majesty, and yet dislikes the remoteness with which it may yet best be preserved. She was disappointed with the Queen's failure to visit her mother for five days after her hip operation. Describing the Queen Mother as a 'very courageous nonagenarian who is an example to the world through her courage and sweet, warm dignity', Amélie believes that the Queen has stifled those human qualities that the Queen Mother demonstrates in abundance. 'I think all other members of the Royal Family have lost that characteristic. The Queen has always behaved as an institution rather than as a wife, a mother, a human being.'

Through Amélie's belief in a woman's power comes her censure that the Queen failed to give the world a message of what it is to be a daughter and, by implication, a mother-in-law. For this, Amélie blames the very heavy work schedule and weight of tradition to which she thinks the Queen has 'sacrificed part of her femininity'. She considers that the Queen was born with a streak of apparent coolness, unlikely to have ever indulged in a warm, friendly relationship with anyone, totally committed to her work, which results in a certain aloofness that Amélie noticed at Buckingham Palace garden parties.

Amélie considers that, in the absence of parents with the time to give counsel or provide role models, the more mature Charles made the mistake of marrying a very young girl he didn't love, despite his long-term friendship with Camilla Parker Bowles. 'He should have been kind enough not to marry this very vulnerable young woman who wasn't even twenty and who obviously at her age had the right to dream of a fairy-tale,' she protests. In Amélie's words there is perhaps a hint of the nineteen-year-old French girl who married a great man and who was to discover that happiness unfolded gradually. She, herself, was fortunately supported by a mature and well-rooted family.

But it is the mother in her who remembers with affection Diana's visit to Ravenswood Village in June 1985 when she sat on the ground with some of the disturbed Ravenswood children.* The way Diana connected with the children was 'inspirational, very moving, without fear of catching any illness. I would have loved to see her as a happy person within a good marriage, working as an ambassador on behalf of Britain.'

Sadly, of course, that was not to be. But as far as Prince Charles is concerned, Amélie believes that with the right guidance, 'which he desperately needs', he would be a good king. She recalls a dinner party given by the Prince on her husband's retirement, at Kensington Palace, where Jakobovits had been very impressed by the Prince. From interviews with others who had met him, she had the impression of a searching soul – a soul in quest and occasionally in turmoil.

'It would be a wonderful gift for the British people and the entire world,' she adds, 'if the Royal Family could demonstrate what family life ought to be.'

---

*Diana arrived by helicopter at Ravenswood Village on 25 June 1985 and remained half an hour longer than scheduled because she stopped to speak and shake hands with as many residents as possible. The climax of the visit was the opening of the Ravenswood Rose Garden when she was presented with a beautifully sculptured rose as a memento of the occasion. The following day a letter was received from Diana, saying how touched she was by the wonderful atmosphere of the village.

32   *Amélie's Universe*

FAMILY LIFE for Amélie has always been lived between the philosophies of two men: her husband and her father. Despite what some might regard as the rigidity of Orthodoxy, Amélie is defined by the flexibility of curiosity; a recognition of differences and an awareness that you cannot preach to your children what you do not believe yourself. Her children were brought up within strict parameters, but she is often heard repeating a personal doctrine: what is not suitable for children to watch on TV is not suitable for adults either. 'It breeds immorality, cruelty, crime.' Thus it may be a fond hope, but Amélie anticipates a time when campaigns against crime, for instance, can be run without showing all the negative details on TV. 'As my husband says, there is the truth and the entire truth, and there is a world of difference between them. The media never lies outright, but put the comma and the full stop in the wrong place, and you have changed the story.'

Although she cannot stop the invasion of the superficial world, Amélie's story is a universe of husband, children, numerous grandchildren and several great-grandchildren. The residue of other peoples' lives – her family, her friends, those who come calling, reflective, Orthodox men with beards, women in *sheitels* and headscarves, as well as people whose lives are barely touched by religion, those in need, her many charities – all these fill her home; a nucleus of intensive thought, an Anatevka of activity and many shadows, few of them silent. She travels everywhere: to Jerusalem, where they have another home, to Kiev, to Minsk, to the USA, where some of her children and extended family live, to Australia not long after they first arrived in London and faced such hostility in the community. Her favourite city, she says, is naturally Paris. She is, if not by birth, then certainly by natural endowment, a

Parisienne. But then she also admits to a great love for London, 'more than any other city – oh yes, except for Jerusalem and Israel generally'. She likes walking, especially in the country, preferably the mountains; the bleaker the better. They have visited Scotland, and she admires Norway and New Zealand. Mountains, fjords, forests, water, lakes – these are all dramatic aspects of her desire for flight, to drive a caravan with her husband away from civilisation and into the more ethereal planes of the unknown. And yet she is also firmly rooted in the soil. Some have said she is the grounding influence in her husband's life.

Amélie is honest about her own imperfections: not just her impatience, or her inability to take her time and wait for an answer. She questions and challenges her intense curiosity about people, life and death. It may take her to places within her soul she fears to recognise, but she will not resist it, even though those questions penetrate like missiles in the night, for she usually gets to the point quicker than anyone else.

Once she spent two or three days in the South African bush, in Mala Mala. There from the open jeep she watched a giraffe stand on its hind legs and could see the baby emerge from the birth canal down the leg of its mother until it was able to stand up against its mother's leg – an unforgettable memory. But here comes the darker side: on the same night as she watched the birth of the giraffe from the jeep, she saw the teller notice a sudden movement. He told the ranger to go out and look: it turned out to be a leopard chasing a young gazelle. The leopard seized its quarry by the neck and ran up the full height of a tree. 'Our jeep and all the other jeeps in the bush surrounded the tree. We all stood hypnotised, then we experienced the thrill of seeing the kill, and I held my husband by the hand in order not to move and frighten the animal, because one is an onlooker. And then I asked myself, why am I enjoying watching the kill? I realised that human beings are made so, that they have that streak of cruelty. The Almighty gave us the ability to discriminate, and I was very grateful that at that moment G-d gave me the sense to lower my eyes. So I had the experience of enjoying the kill of one of G-d's creatures. On the one hand, I was shattered and felt guilty and, on the other, grateful for this understanding of free will.'

240

It is an attitude redolent of the current British controversy over fox-hunting. Where Amélie differs from many proponents of this traditional country sport is in her acknowledgement of man's enjoyment of cruelty for its own sake. Many whose pleasures were threatened by recent government proposals to ban the blood sport reject any notion of its incipient cruelty and prefer to stress its value as a means of keeping the balance of country wild-life.

However, Amélie will not dwell on the aspects of her own nature which disturb her. She is more driven by action than thought. Having acknowledged them, she will move on. Then she will laugh and admit, 'I don't really want to know myself. I was a very lucky girl, born to outstanding parents, and the first grandchild of a very special grandfather, who, even now, I speak to every day either to thank him or ask his advice.'

She considers that her first years were very much blessed – on the one hand by *force majeur*, and on the other through parental instinct which delegated responsibility at an early age. Amélie was also influenced by what she calls 'the dynamics of the rabbinate'. In her counselling, she claims to make unceasing efforts to understand the person facing her, and she acknowledges two special gifts: her organisational skills and her energy. She does not require an awful lot of sleep.

In her role as Chief Rebbetzin, Amélie's day could begin with a couple of meetings about social cases: one welfare case here and one in Israel, families possibly with serious illnesses who required her to raise money for them and to counsel them on the right doctors worldwide. Or she might attend a meeting set up by the Jewish World Relief Organisation, which used to be called the Central British Fund. Her weekly lecture, or *shiur*, to the Spiro Institute on the meaning and the beauty of prayers to women from all different backgrounds, from right-wing Orthodoxy to Liberal or Progressive, might be on the day's agenda. And in the evening she might address a group of senior citizens or a gathering of divorced and separated people. At one such gathering, the pain was palpable. The women gathered around her in a circle and she clearly saw that she must deal obliquely with the problem she was there to address, revealing her own family bereavements rather than raising the subject of betrayal and separation. She saw that since she had no experience of this, it would be inappropriate for her to touch their anguish with direct words. At one point when a young girl broke down crying, Amélie simply left her chair and took the girl in her arms. Amélie's attitude at most of these gatherings might vary from compassionate restraint to sharp curiosity. Sometimes opinionated, she will nevertheless cock her head in that bird-like way and listen intently to an uncommonly held view. Some people may be surprised at her open-mindedness and tolerance, while never losing sight of the clarity of her own religious convictions.

Amélie remembers praying since she was a little girl for whatever was 'Divinely ordained' in her life to come about, and that sooner rather than later she would 'see the hand of G-d on what it's all about'. On her return to Paris after the war, she promised herself that she would stand for the whole day of Yom Kippur, which only a few men do, in gratitude. She tried to do this inconspicuously by standing by the wall and hoping that everyone would leave her alone, but in fact somebody told her father's friends about it, and the following Sabbath every man who was called up to the Torah offered a special prayer of well-being to the daughter of Rabbi Elie Munk. Standing there gave her so much, she felt, that she did it the following year, again hoping that no one would notice. However, her father advised her against it on the grounds that a person should never do anything three times consecutively that is not part of law. 'Otherwise', he told her, 'you have adopted it for life; you have created your own force of law.' He further advised against it because she was a woman and he did not consider it healthy once she married and had children. 'By the third year I was already married, and my father called me in Dublin that Yom Kippur in 1949 and said, "Please no standing this time, okay?"'

Her beloved father suffered a stroke in the early 1970s. He and Fanny left Paris two years later to live near the majority of their children, in Brooklyn. There, despite Rabbi Munk's dwindling health, they remained independent, and still, in Amélie's words, the 'crowning head of the family'. Apart from Amélie, it was easy for their children to visit them several times a day. The adaptable pair quickly acclimatised to their new surroundings, used as they were to their itinerant life during the chaos of the war years. They did not allow material or mental obstacles to interfere with their general demeanour.

Amélie visited them frequently from London. Watching her father's ebbing life propped up by the wires and technology of life support during the final days of his illness at Maimonides Hospital, Brooklyn, sent images of the man he had been flashing through her mind. When they had crouched together under the nose of the Nazis at the Swiss border, hardly daring to breathe. When she had sought him out in a Foreign Legion boot camp near Albi, in France, and seen the expression of amazement on his face. When he had publicly thanked his son, Max, on his Barmitzvah for saving the family's lives. And then it came to her that she could no longer pray for his recovery. She called her husband in London several times a day with the repetitive question, '"What do I do? What do I pray for?" And that's when I learned that there are times when you can start praying for *Rachamim*, which means mercy, so that the soul of the person will pass on into the next world peacefully, with the minimum of pain. Prayer helps, if only for ourselves, because there is nothing else we can do.'

It had been difficult for Rabbi Munk to speak about his devastating illness, which he endured for twelve years, but his eldest daughter had the consolation of knowing that he was sustained right to the end of his life by his absolute faith in the Divine. 'He was most certainly one of the few saints totally able to accept the decree of G-d.' When she speaks of his loss, she describes the strength of his presence felt by his children, which, in turn, radiated back to him from them.

Amélie's mother had predeceased him in June 1979 from a heart attack, her third within two weeks, at Maimonides Hospital. For the last few years of her life she had suffered from an enlarged heart. Two days before her death, Amélie had taken her father to visit her and will never forget the moving moment when she brought his wheelchair to her mother's bed and instinctively pulled the curtain around them so that they could share what was to be their last few moments of intimate conversation.

The cardiologist decided to allow her home on the Sunday following Shevuot, but Fanny Munk died on the Friday night.

Amélie was woken with the news at 2 o'clock the following morning and screamed in disbelief, having seen her mother a few hours before in 'wonderful, high spirits'. To this day she mourns the fact that she had not bade farewell to the eternally cheerful woman she describes as having been so full of life, although to die on the Sabbath is considered a special blessing for Jews. She was just seventy-two.

It was agonising for Amélie to wait until Sunday to bury her. As she died on Friday, they could not hold the funeral until then. 'Jewish teachings say that the physical body is a shell which houses the divine in each human being, which, we are told, ascends closer to the seat of the Almighty, while the body belonging to Him must be returned to earth as quickly as possible.'

Amélie and her siblings learned to cope with the loss of their parents – two such radiant individuals – because of the strength of their togetherness. 'My parents had a unique identity. They were exceptionally gifted with life-intelligence, which I am so grateful that my children have inherited.'

During the one week of mourning, *the shiva*, that followed her father's death, try as they did to be solemn and behave seriously, none of them could carry it through because they sensed their mother's joyful spirit refusing to allow them this sadness. 'I remember how we closed the windows so that passers-by would not hear us laugh as we related countless sayings, totally unique to our mother. I think there is a source of great comfort and strength in keeping your loved ones alive by quoting them as often as possible.'

Amélie wonders how people without her depths of belief manage their lives when something sad or painful happens to them. Her Judaism is a life-belt which 'you throw to somebody about to drown. You can hold on to it for security of mind and body.' And so she admits that she found it hard to pray at first in very large United Synagogue communities, mostly housed in huge, impersonal buildings. 'I always felt very lonely, because most of the women around me couldn't pray, and I had to concentrate very much to make contact with my prayers. It was not that they talked so much as the fact that they couldn't follow the prayer book because they had never had the opportunity to learn. So they didn't pray but either sat very quietly looking ahead of them into empty space or else chatted with their neighbours. But in retrospect it might have helped me to concentrate more fervently on my prayers.'

The New Age culture has opened up the meaning of prayer in more eclectic ways today as Amélie is well aware. For the majority of Jewish people, the mysticism of the Kabbalah remains quite literally a closed book, many taking the view that men should not study it under the age of forty and women not at all. Whisperings about the dangers of mental disorder that might spring from untrained study of the Kabbalah combined in past years to make it a no-go area. Yet such secrecy has also invested the subject with a sense of magical realism: something to which New Age travellers might be attracted without bothering to enter the long process of prior study which is the prerequisite of the Kabbalah. Yet the impact of ersatz groups offering Kabbalistic study programmes does not unduly worry Amélie. The life-span of such groups has always tended to be short. As the daughter of a student of the Kabbalah herself, she explains that the true study of the subject is to engage in the intricate depths of life's meaning. 'You need very great and thorough scholars to convey its science and there are hardly any left.' Admitting her own shortcomings in regard to serious Talmudic study, and having a practical side to her nature, she has always refrained from an involvement with the Kabbalah.

As for cults, however, that is a phenomenon that she points out has always ended in tragedy and runs counter to Jewish teaching. While a fair amount of work is being done behind the scenes within the community to combat it, Amélie is convinced that this work must remain discreet and not rebound into the area of public debate, which would be counter-productive. There are individual rabbis, she points out, who undertake this work almost as an undercover operation, never working in groups and always avoiding confrontation.

Amélie suggests that any Chassidic body which does not focus on missionary work to persuade other Jews to follow their line of thinking is neither cultist nor dangerous. 'They are all authentic groups whose teachers throughout the last two or three hundred years have taught Judaism in their own specialised fashion, but always within the confines of Halachic teachings. But those movements within Judaism which go out to missionise are rather unattractive to me.'

Loneliness has sometimes haunted Amélie: in the early days of her marriage, on moving to London, in the large, sometimes impersonal synagogues she has referred to, and in moments when she felt isolated among people whose sense of their own importance within their community was greater than their spiritual affinity with it. Ironically, she herself revels in plaudits when her husband's work invites it, but perceives the hollowness of pomp for its own sake.

While she remains a traditionalist at heart, and her long-held position on feminism does not waver, Amélie has always recognised the desire of women to hold public office within Jewish life, and would consider this neither inappropriate nor grandiose. It was during her husband's tenure that women were for the first time appointed to chair both Leeds and Manchester Jewish Representative Councils. Amélie also fails to understand the uproar surrounding the recent appointment of a woman assistant to a rabbi in Manhattan's Lincoln Square Synagogue. 'I could not quite fathom why this caused such a media turmoil, both in the USA and here,' she says. 'This lady has no *smicha* and was simply appointed to help the rabbi in his pastoral work, such as hospital visits, family and individual counselling and attention. This is halachically acceptable and has never encountered any objection from any rabbinic authority.'

One educationalist, who worked with Amélie some ten to twelve years ago on the issue of women being accepted on synagogue management councils, recalls how she steered them through some very rough waters, passionately expressing her view that women should have a place on the councils, while retaining her views on feminine modesty, particularly in the United Synagogue world.

No one, religious or secular, can enter public life without encountering both the best and the worst in others. But media overexposure can destroy personalities, Amélie believes, 'because if you are so familiar on the TV with the personality that you can see every hair on the person's head, then you can't have any respect.

I have tremendous awe to this day for the late Mother Theresa of Calcutta because she did not appear on the TV day in, day out. and therefore retained an aura around her. She was not in your bed-room or dining-room all the time.' Amélie is particularly inspired by one of Mother Theresa' s sayings:

> People are unreasonable, illogical and self-centred. Love them anyway. If you do good, people will accuse you of selfish, ulterior motives. Do good anyway. If you are successful, you win false friends and true enemies. Succeed anyway. The good you do will be forgotten tomorrow. Do good anyway. What you have spent years building may be destroyed overnight. Build anyway. People really need help but may attack you if you help them. Help people anyway. Give the world the best you have and you'll get kicked in the teeth. Give the world the best you have anyway.

33   Amélie – The Family

MOTHER THERESA's words attract Amélie because they embody the twin credos of selfless love with the drive for success: a true echo of Jewish values from the mouth of a dedicated Christian. As a nun, Mother Theresa's family was the world of the poor, whose suffering she chose to alleviate with immense compassion. Amélie has a family of her own, yet tries to extend herself wherever possible into the tragedies of others, in the hope of bringing support.

Public disasters, such as Israel's wars, the terrorist attack on Ambassador Shlomo Argov, or the assassination of Yitzhak Rabin in Israel in November 1996, may have given her an almost pivotal role, projecting her into the immediate tragedy of others. But far closer to home was the pain of losing her sister, Miriam, to cancer in 1994, which re-evoked the earlier death of her sister-in-law Lotti. Both events took place after her husband's retirement.

Miriam developed breast cancer in her early thirties shortly after the birth of her fourth child and endured the devastation of the disease for twelve years. Amélie describes her sister's extra-ordinary courage in caring for others while making light of her own condition. 'Her home was always open; people were always coming from abroad for medical visits. Often she would drive them to their appointments and then attend her own chemotherapy clinic which they knew nothing about.' While all the Munk children had inherited their mother's sense of humour, Miriam had the gift of spreading it more than any of them, according to Amélie. She was also considered the most academically intelligent and an extremely positive, controlled person. In the early years of her condition she once said, 'We all have a time limit on this earth and this passage of life. It is just that I know it a little better than you do. We all have a ninety per cent chance of living to the next day.' The other thing she said was, 'try to appreciate the infinite blessing of being unaware of your own body.'

Loss of her parents, the untimely loss of Miriam, all confirm in Amélie what has always been her essential message: the centrality of husband and family. She feels secure in the interaction of the generations. It is impossible to enter the Jakobovits household without meeting at least one of the daughters or grandchildren. Behind closed doors Immanuel Jakobovits might be in intensive debate with one of the dayanim; a granddaughter might be painting in the kitchen. Amélie will be there, as a mother or grandmother, with the tea and cakes, but her attitude is not grandmotherly: there is something feisty and vital in the air when she is around. And here is the sense of affirmation, that life goes on for them as it has always done, without family conflict or rivalry, without teenage rebellion, with total integrality. Amélie is also your best friend, no older than you, and she presents you with a Jewish home in eternal sunlight.

Yet Amélie will sometimes wonder aloud why her children have become so much more right wing than she is. Her daughter, Esther Pearlman, asks whether her parents would be members of the United Synagogue at all if it had not been for her father's position as Chief Rabbi. 'He is more right wing than his congregation, but wherever the rabbi goes into a congregation it is no good being the same. You cannot lead if you are totally one of them,' she observes. Perhaps Esther understands best where her parents' hearts really lie. 'Of the six children, some are very like their father in character and disposition, others are more like me,' Amélie believes. Perhaps it is proof of the value of a secure upbringing that has brought success to all the children in what they wanted to achieve.

Yoel synthesises his father's twin loves: Judaism and medical ethics. He married a childhood friend, Michelle (Micky) Tauber, and returned to America, where he took up medical residency and housemanship at Brooklyn's Maimonides Hospital. From there they moved to Yeshiva Lane on Yeshiva campus in Baltimore, Maryland, and he eventually qualified at John Hopkins as a gastroenterologist. Amélie considers her first son a virtual clone of his mother. He is quick, rather punctual, and even before getting up, he will mentally organise his day and only feel happy when he retires twelve to sixteen hours later, having completed his programme. He is also very emotional and impulsive. He has inherited the Munk personality – a joyful disposition – and fortunately married a girl who shares it. 'To this day our Micky, or rather Mouse, as her husband calls her, is a growing "teenager" despite being a mother of ten very active children!'

Amélie has a twinkle in her eye when she tells the following anecdote about her daughter-in-law, relating to her first meeting with Immanuel: 'I was convinced that it was Avraham Schreiber's idea that Mano should look me up in Paris. I subsequently discovered that he had my sister, Ruth, in mind. I always said I would get my own back one day, and I did, by taking his granddaughter, Michelle, as my daughter-in-law!'

Both Yoel and Micky are active in communal affairs and their home, according to Amélie, is a haven for children and teenagers needing a shoulder either 'to cry or laugh on'. Micky, much beloved by her mother-in-law, is administrator at one of Baltimore's major Jewish day schools.

Shmuel made *aliyah*, opting for an intensive study programme at the Ponovish Yeshiva, under the teachings of the Ponovish Rav Kahaneman, whom Amélie describes as 'one of the great, most humble and saintly men of post-war Jewish history'. Now a religious judge, a dayan himself, Shmuel married Esther Kahane of Detroit, whom he met a few days after his eldest brother's wedding in New York. On their first meeting, Amélie confessed to being awe-inspired by a young woman who, at twenty-four, was already Dean of one of Brooklyn's major schools for girls, as well as having obtained an MA in history. Amélie also found her very beautiful and secretly hoped that her son, Shmuel, would be equally impressed. As with Michelle, Amélie has a very affectionate relationship with this daughter-in-law. Esther is now a head teacher, counsellor and assistant director of the 3,000-pupil school, Bet Yacov. The couple have four children, two of whom recently married. Shmuel works tirelessly with different organisations at bridging the gap between the Orthodox and secular communities in Israel.

Shmuel's work has made him even better known in some circles than his father. 'Hardly a day goes by when someone we are introduced to doesn't ask, "Are you related to Shmuel Jakobovits?" And when we admit it, people seem to accord us enormous respect,' says Amélie, who is proud that her son has chosen to undertake this work and that, despite dealing with very difficult and thorny problems within the religious communities in Israel, he still manages to retain a good name within all sections. In many ways Amélie sees a reflection of her father, Elie Munk, in Shmuel. 'He is very sweet, gentle, patient, kind and thoughtful, yet forcefully determined to the point of occasional stubbornness to achieve his ambition.'

Esther has most of her father's characteristics, claims Amélie. 'She has his charm, his *chein*, and immense and very deep security. She has great leadership qualities which I already noticed when she was still an infant.' While still a teenager in London, Esther met Chaim Pearlman from Sunderland and, after renewing their friendship in Israel a few months later, they decided to marry. Esther was just seventeen and a half. Chaim was a Cambridge economics graduate, but also a gifted Talmudical scholar. He became the rabbi of the noted Machzike Adass, heir to a great Talmudical tradition, but also runs his own accountancy firm. Esther is an educationalist, presently increasing her qualifications, and the couple have raised eight children. They now have three grandchildren.

Shoshana – only three and a half years old when the family went to America – has most of her mother's personality traits. 'She is a very sensitive human being, caring deeply about everyone. Her greatest quality, which unfortunately I do not share, is her ability to stay in the same mood, extremely soft, sweet and kind. I cannot remember that she gave us a moment of anxiety or annoyance in her youth.' However, at the age of twenty-one Shoshana was 'swept off her feet' by mathematician Norman Turner, who had her 'completely enwrapped in his world'. An actuary by profession, Norman inherited his love of music from his father, Rev. Reuben Turner, a past chair of the Jewish Music Council, but he also teaches Talmud and related subjects throughout the community. Shoshana is a calligrapher, producing illuminated *ketubot* (marriage contracts), prayer texts for special occasions, table plans, etc. They have seven children. 'We always marvel at the particular

251

diversity of the Turners' children,' says Amélie. 'Each one has a totally different personality.'

The Jakobovits' fifth child, Aviva, attended the seminary in Gateshead and qualified as a kindergarten teacher. 'Aviva, like her sister Esther, inherited her father's inner calm and acute intelligence,' according to her mother. Always a very determined person, Aviva had very strong principles concerning the type of man she wanted to marry. 'She often said, "I will never marry a man any younger than twenty-five or twenty-six as I want him to be mature and grown-up."' Nor would she consider anybody who had not attended a yeshiva for at least five or six years, and a medical man was out of the question. Aviva was put off by her frequent babysitting stints for her sister-in-law, Michelle, whose husband was studying medicine day and night in hospital. And who did Aviva marry? A medical student who was barely twenty-two years old when he proposed to her and had spent only two years at a yeshiva. Amélie says that she will never 'forget hearing her tell a friend in New York on the night of her engagement to Yossi Adler, "Guess what! I've just got engaged to a twenty-two-year old medical student. Everything's wrong with him but otherwise he's perfect. So never say never!"'

Yossi, the third generation Adler to enter medicine, qualified at King's College Hospital and then took a two-year residency and housemanship in America, a medical option in a number of New York hospitals for religious medical students who do not wish to work on Shabbat and the High Holy Days. Aviva shares her husband's deep interest in medicine and has developed, according to her mother, a very solid understanding of medical intricacies. 'We are very much in awe of her when we are told by countless people how much they rely on her judgement.' The couple have nine children.

Like her mother, Elisheva, 'our American souvenir and youngest child', was nineteen when she married property surveyor Sammy Homberger, an active lay leader of the Golders Green community. 'Sami is particularly cherished because of his unfailing, positive and very cheerful interpretation and behaviour,' says Amélie. 'He takes great pleasure in spoiling his wife at every possible opportunity. As a mother I get such a thrill when he tells me, "You have wonderful daughters but mine is the best. You have done an extraordinary job. Just perfection itself."'

There is a gentleness in Amélie's tone when she speaks of this attractive youngest child. 'We adore her softness, her extraordinary ability to bring up her five sons and daughter. Elisheva totally concentrates on the greatest art of all, namely to be as perfect a wife and mother that she possibly can. She is also a most accomplished hostess and entertains a great deal. Although the mother of six, to her it is nothing to have twelve people at her table on a Friday night, followed the next day with seventeen for Shabbat lunch. She is the best cook in our family.'

34   The Bread of Affliction

IF HOME was the central focus, charity for Amélie was another extension of it. She had changed little in her long-held principles, developed in Ireland, that she should avoid taking office with any Jewish organisations, but honours were automatically conferred on her as soon as she arrived in Britain as the Chief Rabbi's wife. As president of a number of organisations, it occurred to her that maybe she should become a working president. One of them which particularly appealed to her was the visitation committee of the United Synagogue. This meant visiting not only the sick in hospital, but also Jews in prison. And this again led to relationships that were to expand her awareness of suffering.

'She never waited to be asked. She was always there with the right things to say. And you never felt embarrassed, as she is not intimidated by things. She would behave as a best friend, not necessarily from a spiritual point of view,' is Gail Ronson's view of Amélie's discreet yet energetic support during the Guinness Trials, which ended in her husband, Gerald's imprisonment. Charity is a literally embracing term and while it is said to begin at home, in the wider sense it embodies an entire attitude of sustenance to those in need. Amélie certainly sees it this way. She admires Gail for her strength and integrity – 'She is as beautiful inside as outside' – while Gail regards Amélie as an unpretentious person who 'understands everything' and believes she responds to the 'old-fashioned way in which I brought up my family'. The friendship of these two women is clearly not simply mutual but magnetic. Gail admires Amélie's uniqueness and inner contentment. Amélie, for her part, perceived more in the glamorous ex-model than the groomed socialite who graced the pages of the press. She would gently draw her out into helping people, perhaps in ways that Gail had not yet envisaged. There was the time for instance when she persuaded the reluctant Gail to visit a woman who was recovering from an operation and whose condition was unsavoury, to say the least. 'I had never seen skin that goes black. I must be honest. I wouldn't have thought of going down there. She was the second wife of someone who had done so much for Gerald. The woman was over the moon. It was awful, but to the woman it meant something that Amélie, more than me, also went down there.'

Ann Harris, wife of South Africa's Chief Rabbi Cyril Harris, recalls Amélie's more private good works, such as visiting the sick, making *challot* for 'the celebrating, the mourning, the ill', ensuring that every Jewish bride went to her wedding properly equipped, and the public works, such as the promotion of charitable causes and what she describes as 'indefatigable attendance at meetings'.

Others who have not forgotten personal kindness in hard times include Jewish educationalist Clive Lawton, who describes Amélie as 'driven by principles which one feels she is actively living out and you come across that in very few people'. Lawton compares her to Nelson Mandela, whom he regards as 'a man trying to live an ideal, not being just a nice bloke. I think Amélie is similarly not being just a nice woman, but trying to live an ideal and teach ideals in a fairly conscious way.'

Jean Marks, a Progressive Jew, recalls her car jamming one night when it was pouring with rain and Amélie refusing to leave her, despite having another appointment. 'She always had somewhere else to go – and we tried vainly to find an empty taxi, but finally we went by underground and there were all these winos down there and I saw the headlines in my mind, "Wife of Chief Rabbi Assaulted", but I mean she's an adventurer.' And her friend, Jackie Gryn, widow of Reform leader Rabbi Hugo Gryn, recalled Amélie's helpfulness with a personal problem some years ago when she offered to be her counsellor, if necessary. Interfaith promoter and benefactor, Sir Sigmund Sternberg, finds her 'on the whole a bit overwhelming', but praises her youthful exuberance, stamina and affectionate, passionate nature.

Amélie would also turn to doctors like Anthony D. Isaacs, Emeritus Consultant Psychiatrist at the Bethlem Royal and the Maudsley Hospitals, for help if she knew someone in trouble. 'She would deal with the problems of people not necessarily of prominence, just for purely altruistic reasons,' he says. 'She would help discreetly, always ready to meet the call of duty. She has the gift of spontaneity.'

'I have a friend who lost a son in the Lockerbie disaster and I know Amélie was wonderful to the family,' says Renata, wife of Henry Knobil, chairman of the Board of Governors at Immanuel College. 'I think she feels everything very deeply. I speak to her on days when she's terribly sad. I can hear she's depressed and will tell me about some terrible illness, and she does get very involved.'

Charity, Amélie recognises, is often most effective when conducted with a low profile. Once she volunteered to visit the Hospital for Nervous Diseases in Maida Vale on Thursday mornings in winter and Friday in summer. When she arrived, she chatted to the patients, introducing herself as Mrs Jacobs. 'I just didn't feel I wanted to show off by saying the Chief Rabbi's wife. I simply wanted to be Amélie.' When she took part in the march for Soviet Jewry, it received a great deal of media attention. On her next hospital visit, as she approached her patient, she saw that she was reading the papers. 'There was a photo of me with a synthetic fur hat on and I really did look like I was coming out of Siberia. Next to it was a picture of some of our women marching in that very cold weather. The patient said to me, "Aren't they wonderful, these women of our community? Imagine walking for three-quarters of an hour in that bitterly cold weather." Then she pointed at the picture and looked at me and said, "But you know what, this is not the Chief Rabbi's wife. I know her very well!"'

Sometimes, Amélie would be criticised for doing too much. In an effort to fit everything in, she had a tendency to arrive at a meeting late and remain there for only fifteen minutes. Whether it was out of a desire just to be there, to grace the meeting with her presence, or a genuine battle with time, is difficult to unravel. Some people found it an irritating habit, but most felt that she compensated by her sheer vitality.

One friend suggests that Amélie simply wants people to believe she still loves them even if she only has fifteen minutes to spare. Her detractors would argue that it is she who needs confirmation of their affection. Perhaps both contain elements of truth: there is something about her that is provincial and homely, and something else that has a touch of *grande dame*.

The charities Amélie supports or of which she is patron are legion. The work takes an emotional toll, but she seems able to sustain a cheerful front even when confronted with extreme pain or the proximity of death. 'Usually when people go to see somebody who has cancer, they put on a death signal before they get near you, but not Amélie,' says Frances Weingarten, who co-chairs with Susan Shipman Chai Lifeline, which supports cancer sufferers and their relatives. 'She was always trying to be positive and we immediately formed a very strong bond.' Out of that bond came Chai Lifeline, which is headquartered in Hendon and of which Amélie is patron.

In another personal anedcote, Mrs Weingarten recalls Amélie putting a hot-water bottle in her husband's bed while she awaited her own cancer operation in hospital. 'She was a very big support right through that period so I've experienced her healing messages. I would choose my time to ring her very carefully, between 8 a.m. and 8.15 a.m., but if sometimes I couldn't manage that, I would get a voice going *um,um,um,* and I would know that she was saying her prayers.'

Amélie's other charities include Ravenswood, British Emunah, Tlalim (established in Israel to provide educational support, including computers and software, for sick children enabling them to study at home), Yad Sarah, The Sarah Herzog Hospital, aiding elderly psychiatric patients, The Black-Jewish Forum, Cancerkin (a practical support group based at the Royal Free Hospital), Chai Lifeline (which offers emotional, spiritual and physical support to cancer patients), Heal (established at the Royal Free Hospital's Department of Haematology in support of leukaemia sufferers) and the Dysautonomia Foundation (helping to fight a genetic disease that afflicts new-born Jewish babies' autonomic and sensory nervous systems). Howard Weiser, DF's president in New York, praised Amélie for raising awareness about this dysfunction around the world. Others include the Institute for the Special Child, the Jewish Marriage Council, Ulpana Ruhava (launched twelve years ago with sixty children to help them overcome inferiority complexes and now grown to 500 children), and British Friends of the Israel Guide Dog Centre.

For this work Amélie receives hundreds of letters of praise and gratitude. Some of them can barely contain the emotion which spills over through the handwriting. Many people find her an enthralling speaker, who tells her life story with simplicity and pure sentiment. The very palpable love and affection they bestow on her in return is a sustaining force. One letter came from a doctor whose patient she had visited in the Holy Roman Hospital of St John and St Elizabeth in St John's Wood following a car accident. The woman was confined to bed and was unable to stand or even wash herself. 'It appears that you went to see her and touched her, kissed her and brought her some bread to eat,' wrote Dr David Levi of Wimpole Street. 'Since that time she has lost all her symptoms and is completely well. I must say that in a hospital where miracles are believed in, this is a pretty good miracle that you have worked, although the particular deity is a different one from the one usually invoked,' he concluded.

Amélie's work for these charities is tireless and too dense to be described in detail. She is a regular speaker at luncheons and seminars organised by the Federation of Women Zionists, for instance, or its international umbrella, WIZO, British Women's Organisation for educational Resources and Technological training (ORT), the League of Jewish Women, various lodges of the Bnai Brith movement, synagogue ladies' guilds, and schools and societies up and down the country. In some cases the organisations she supports derived from a single incident or inspiration, a tragedy averted and a longing to express thanksgiving.

Yad Sarah, for instance, was founded seventeen years ago in Jerusalem by a man whose mother, Sarah, had become very ill and for whom he could not find a wheelchair or other medical equipment anywhere in Jerusalem. After she died, he began a little centre in his own home for people who might require the loan of such medical equipment to make things easier at home. Because the district where he lived, Rohov Penina, is a relatively poor area, he decided not to charge anyone for the loan of the equipment and he found people would invariably return it. When he died, his son Uri, a close friend of Amélie's son, Shmuel, extended this room into a basement, and it has grown into a large organisation totally run by 5,000 volunteers. Amélie was very excited to share in its work as president of the English-speaking chapter of volunteers who raise money for expenses. The organisation also offers Russian immigrants a chance to work there, assembling the equipment. The charity has attracted considerable attention, recently from Scandinavia and Germany, which expressed a desire to go over and study its methods. Today there are some dozens of ambulances driving around Jerusalem bearing the name of Yad Sarah, and much is being done to raise money for sophisticated equipment. Amélie ran a function in Jerusalem to raise money for internal home communications, such as a device which will enable a parent to hear the cry of a sick baby immediately and which simultaneously connects to Yad Sarah's computer, which is manned twenty-four hours a day.

Tlalim was the brainchild of Atarah Rosen, a friend of Amélie whose husband Eli was a cultural attaché at the Israeli Embassy in London. She developed a unit to help supply housebound sick children with computers, connecting them to their school through a modem, which helped them feel less isolated. This was a programme that caught Amélie's imagination. She thought it a unique idea that nobody had been able to emulate. The programme was launched with eight pupils and now has 1,000 on its books, backed by a group of first-class volunteer teachers. It has also won support from the European Council.

Another Israeli involvement is Yeshiva B'nei Rem, created for boys who cannot stand the pressure of the very large yeshiva movement from which they have often run away. The story behind its origin could not fail to have stirred her. One Friday afternoon several years ago Rabbi Freeman and his wife, who had six children, heard their three-year-old son Jacob yell out from the fields near their somewhat primitive home, 'Abba! Abba! My sister has fallen into a hole at the bottom of the garden.' 'What are you talking about?' his father demanded. 'There's no hole there.' But the little boy tugged at his father's hand and pulled him to the end of the field, where they heard a cry coming from the depths of a hole which seemed to be an abandoned well with such a tiny circumference that nobody had ever noticed it. It was covered with grass and the child was only eighteen months old. The parents immediately called the police and the fire brigade, but nobody could get into the hole because they were all too big. Also nobody knew how deep it was. One of the firemen said he knew someone in Tel Aviv who could probably crawl down the hole, being very tall and very thin. The problem was that he had to arrive before the Sabbath set in. 'To save a life you may break the Sabbath,' retorted the rabbi. 'Get him here as quickly as possible.' The friend came and was lowered into the hole with a rope around his waist. By then there was no longer any sound from the pit, and a trauma-tised Mrs Freeman was beginning to come to terms with the terrible thought that she had lost her child. Suddenly the man cried out to be pulled up again, and when he emerged he was not carrying the baby as everyone had hoped, but a stone which was blocking his path. Everyone waited in tense silence as he was lowered about eight feet down into the pit and then was pulled up with the baby in his arms, fast asleep and perfectly still, without a scratch on her.

Rabbi Freeman consulted his teacher, Rabbi Moshe Shapiro in Jerusalem, told him the story and asked in what way he could thank the Almighty for saving the life of his baby daughter. 'It must mean', he reflected, 'that my wife and I have a very particular purpose in life. What is it?'

His mentor reflected and then told him that within the last two weeks two boys had run away from their yeshiva because they could not take the pressure. He advised the grateful father to launch a rescue scheme for boys like this which ensured that they were rehabilitated mentally, emotionally and psychologically, and taught a trade before leaving. So Rabbi and Mrs Freeman created Yeshiva Bn'ei Rem, and although it is still impoverished and largely housed in abandoned Russian caravans, Amélie continues her work to achieve more support from the Ministry of Education.

Amélie's pride in these Israeli initiatives is unmitigated by her concerns about so many issues which she considers wrong with Israeli society. She is mystified as to why Jews 'import more of the evils of the world than export the goodness of Judaism or the great lights of the luminaries'. She cites Israel, for instance, as having the second highest number of car accidents in the world after Ireland, which she blames on Israeli impatience and lack of road consideration, indicative of the general attitude of society, although as individuals they show incomparable kindness of heart.

Thus Amélie's charitable work often reflects her concern that failure to inculcate the love and knowledge of Judaism into the secular section of the community has eroded the moral strength of the Jews as a people. She is upset at the nearly 40,000 abortions calculated to take place in Israel every year, a potential loss of over one and a half million sabras.

Amélie also condemns the herd instinct in people, eroding the individual nature of 'thousands of the most wonderful human beings'. She reiterates a frequently expressed fear that people only demonstrate ethics and morality when threatened by outside forces to destroy them. This applies not just to the Jewish people but to human beings generally. 'I remember when we went through the war, people could not do enough for each other. But after the first couple of decades, since the late 1960s, you see a steady decline of ethics and morality.'

What does Amélie mean under this collective banner of ethics and morality? Personal kindness? Sensitivity? The ability to engage with one another and empathise? A religious revival of Jewish hope, invalidating the drug culture and sexual permissiveness? All of these, certainly. It is less clear how the great contemporary issues of homelessness, unemployment and degeneration can be handled in this particularly Jewish context. If they are part of the decline Amélie speaks of, her husband's dictum of Jewish self-help is her answer and the one that appealed so much to Margaret Thatcher's thrusting, sweep-all-before-it style of govenment. But can the disadvantaged so easily pick themselves up from the floor?

35   *Jakobovits Becomes a Peer of the Realm*

'I THINK it was a Tuesday in 1987,' Amélie recalls. 'We received a letter from No. 10, Downing Street, one day after we returned from a trip to Israel. I remember it came by hand. It was a blue letter in a blue envelope. In it, the then Prime Minister, Margaret Thatcher, said she was minded to propose to Her Majesty the Queen that my husband become a Baron, but would do so only with his consent. We looked at each other and read it again and again, and you know, the idea that a little refugee boy who came here in 1936 was going to be honoured thus and contribute so much to the law-making process of Great Britain, was so overwhelming that we just couldn't believe it. In fact no other rabbi had ever been received into the House of Lords, no other denomination is represented in the House of Lords except the Church of England, which has its Archbishops in the House of Lords and a number of bishops from all over the country.'

All the emotions – the curious tenderness in which Amélie saw her husband as a child, 'a little refugee boy', and the pride at having achieved the public honour that was to crown his life – rushed through her. Within a second she was both the child who had sung in the bread queues of Marseilles, and the Jewish mother of six whose husband had been suddenly catapulted to fame. They did not discuss the matter for the rest of the day. She found her husband very pensive and asked him what was on his mind. He did not reply then, but on his return from the office that afternoon he said, 'There are three things on my mind which somehow prevent me from giving an immediate and unconditional "yes" to the Prime Minister. The first point is: how would all the other denominations feel if a religious leader of the Jewish community had been invited to sit in the House of Lords? The next point is there are many things discussed in the Upper House which are really of no interest to me and to which I could contribute nothing, and the third point is that while many in our community would be thrilled, there is a small, vociferous minority who would not be happy to have the Chief Rabbi represented in the Lords; they would feel that, as Jews, we should keep a low profile.'

There was no one to advise them, so Jakobovits decided that he would simply go back and discuss it with the Prime Minister herself. She reassured him that he would not be expected to take part in every debate, but that she wanted him to join the Lords because of his ability to be a crystal-clear exponent of morality as taught by the Old Testament, which would add, she explained, to the public dimension of morality. She would be very grateful for that, she added. She also advised him not to concern himself with the misgivings of a few individuals in the community because she was sure that the majority would be happy, appreciative and proud of their spiritual leader sitting in the House of Lords. Further, she stressed, he was not invited for his position of Chief Rabbi but as Immanuel Jakobovits, who had the ability to expound on morality. There was nothing left but for him to accept graciously.

He chose Lord Young and Lord Mishcon to introduce him formally to the House of Lords. Both were personal friends. It was through Mishcon's contacts that the Jakobovits' had been able to celebrate the weddings of their daughters, Esther and Shoshana, at the Royal Festival Hall. He had sat on various Greater London Council committees and was a member of the National Theatre and South Bank building committee. Lord Young had been involved in the Department of Trade and Industry, was prominent in the community, and from the time of the Jakobovits' arrival they had been close friends, as they had been with his brother, the late Stuart Young, chairman of the BBC. They had spent time with him during the last days of his life. Lord Hailsham, who had been Lord Chancellor, also accompanied the new peer to the House, but could not introduce him because by then he could only walk with difficulty.

At the investiture they were invited to bring their children and a few guests who could watch in the visitors' gallery. Amélie recalls the 'wonderful ermine-trimmed coat', and her husband saying in his maiden speech that he was not really the first rabbi to be inducted into the House of Lords but the second, because the first was the one under whose picture he had been robed just a couple of hours ago, Moses.

'The Lord Chancellor, Lord Mackay, had indicated that he would like to see us both beforehand, so we met in his chambers and he opened a bottle of champagne, gave me the cork and said, "Keep it well."' They had to explain that they could not drink the champagne because, like wine, it had to be under rabbinic supervision. As a religious man himself, Lord Mackay said that he understood. Then Immanuel went into the interview room and Amélie joined their guests. When she saw Black Rod, he told her that it was the first time that the House of Lords had welcomed such a large family.

If there were a generic art form known as the Jewish Surreal, then Amélie's description of the formal proceedings that followed would have a key place in it. The image of her trying to explain the kosher dietary laws to Black Rod as they were offered lunch in the House with all their family and guests has more than a touch of Monty Python. Yet again Amélie saw this as nothing more than a demonstration of the strength of Jewish belief – in its power and its piquancy – at the high table of British public office. Amélie to this day recalls the kindness, the understanding, the hospitality offered by everyone concerned in the Upper House, which she describes as an eternal blessing.

They were forty-five people for lunch, including various dignitaries from the United Synagogue and the religious court, three of their grandchildren, and their eldest son Yoel with his wife, Michelle, who had come over from Baltimore with their three-week-old baby. Shmuel came from Israel as did Rabbi Fabian Schonfeld, Lotti's husband, who came from America. 'The House', smiles Amélie, 'had never seen anything like it.'

She giggles as she recalls the moment when it dawned on her that her husband became Baron Jakobovits of Regents Park, she became The Lady Jakobovits – and subsequently to her friends and acquaintances, Lady J. She simply sat in the gallery with their guests in a special seat reserved for spouses, praying that all the children would behave and not draw attention to themselves.

'It was a beautiful sunny day and we walked on the terrace with our guests and everyone wore a hat for the occasion. The girls found enough hats in our cupboard to match their outfits. Mine was blue to match my suit. At about 3 p.m., just before we dispersed, we did something the House of Lords had never seen before or since. With more than ten men present we were able to *doven** mincha, the afternoon prayers. It could not have been more auspicious than to do that in the House of Lords.' All the time Amélie retained the tender disbelief that this could really be happening to her life partner, her Mano, 'the little refugee boy who came to this country at the age of sixteen'.

From his unique situation Lord Jakobovits was able to have his say over the coming years on the 1991 War Crimes Bill, whose rejection by the Lords he passionately opposed: 'The security of the human race demands that we be unrelenting in the pursuit of justice against mass murder and repression.' On marriage and the role of schools in teaching how to preserve it; on moral anarchy and 'the inevitability of further retrogression'; on the Asylum Bill, urging the Government – as a recipient of asylum himself – not to withdraw benefits. He was giving the requisite nod to many of Margaret Thatcher's principles, even if she herself did not or could not, as a politician, express them. He was also able to inject some Torah wisdom into the arid ruminations of the Upper House at its business: 'An ancient Jewish source has it that when a young marriage breaks up even the altar sheds tears. Why the altar, my Lords? The altar is the vessel reserved for sacrifices. If a young marriage fails, we feel that the primary reason is that the couple were not prepared to make sacrifices for each other; and therefore the altar weeps. The altar has failed to teach its message.'

These were emotive words for those who would listen. But of course not everyone was to greet the Chief Rabbi's peerage with unreserved delight. Lord Janner, the ex Labour MP who was to lead the Nazi-looted gold campaign, sniffs: 'Lord Jakobovits' approach to British politics was that of a great Tory leader, and

---

*A Jewish term for prayer.

therefore he was considered Thatcher's theological guru. He was not, of course, appointed to the House of Lords because he was Chief Rabbi but because of his famous link with Margaret Thatcher in the sense of supporting many of her policies.'

Whatever conflict Lord Jakobovits may have experienced over this, no such tremors troubled Margaret Thatcher herself. At a dinner she gave for Chief Rabbi Jakobovits on his imminent retirement in February 1991, she was hardly less than effusive: 'No more than the office of Prime Minister does that of Chief Rabbi suit characters of the wilting kind. No Chief Rabbi has had so profound effect on the life of the nation as Lord Jakobovits.' She then admitted that 'one of the nation's worst-kept secrets is that he has had, through his thinking and writing, a deep effect on me as well. Though whether this makes me a Jakobovite or him a Thatcherite I would not like to say.'

Lady Thatcher praised Jakobovits' leadership for its unyielding commitment to principle, refusal to seek easy popularity at the expense of integrity and fearless statement of values symbolised beyond the life of the Jewish people, to the world. And in a tribute to Amélie she added: 'Lord Jakobovits has never made a secret of how much he owes to Amélie. Theirs has been that kind of partnership in which the qualities of each complement the other, the personality of each enhances the other, and the love of each strengthens the other. I believe, Lady Jakobovits, that you once remarked that a girl should always think twice before marrying a rabbi. I am glad not to have heard Denis's advice on those minded to marry politicians.'

36   *The Politics of Retirement*

CHIEF RABBIS never retire, goes the saying, they only die; and they die rarely. In fact, the truth is that rabbis retire, like the rest of the population, at the age of sixty-five, but then the United Synagogue decided that seventy would be an appropriate age for a Chief Rabbi to stand down.

The thought of her Mano facing retirement filled Amélie with sadness, because she felt that he still had so much to give. However, Lord Jakobovits decided differently. He felt it was time to stand down and give more time to the consuming passion of his life, Jewish medical ethics, a field in which he had by now become a leading authority and which he had developed, as a generic discipline, while still in Ireland. Today he carries the undisputed title, Father of Jewish Medical Ethics.

As a working peer, Lord Jakobovits also wanted to give quality time to the House of Lords. All this, plus a heart condition which had given him a couple of scares over the last few years, contributed to the decision to stand down in 1991. He was succeeded by the formidably gifted Cambridge don, Rabbi Dr Jonathan Sacks.

For Amélie, her husband's elevation to the peerage is the final accolade, the nod of state approval that crowns her husband's lifetime dedication. Yet if Lord Jakobovits had made his choice, it was harder for *her* to stare retirement in the face. You could say that she barely acknowledges the fact. The Chief Rebbetzin of Hamilton Terrace is now the châtelaine of Hendon, and from their elegant modern bungalow, whose luminous pastel shades evoke the pages of *Hello!* magazine rather than a house of rabbinic rumination, the show still goes on – all the concerns, the charities, the public face of high ecclesiastical office. She continues to run an ad hoc alliance of women from every religious spectrum, known as the Lady J Group, which keeps her informed and aware of current events and thinking within the community. She also remains close to Jackie Gryn, who is an active member of her Group.

Amélie was very interested in a visit by Cheryl Mariner, executive director of the Jewish World Relief, to three Russian communities in the Ukraine, where she was able to satisfy herself that monies being sent there in conjunction with the Joint was being well spent on youth centre developments and Jewish day schools. As a result of this programme,150 Jewish children now attend Jewish day schools in Odessa, and nearly 700 have joined the sole day school in Kiev. Amélie has great admiration for Cheryl, with whom she has worked, alongside Jean Marks, on a committee called Connection, aimed at supporting Jewish World Relief's programme. Within a matter of eighteen hours Amélie can be immersed in three totally different circles and community backgrounds, and on her return home she will make contact with her four daughters in London and their children, and meet her husband again at the end of the day.

Travel may have broadened Amélie's mind, but it has also given her the opportunity to get to know her own community better. She was much excited by her tour to China with a group of forty-six people in November 1986. This followed an invitation via Mrs Ruth Winston Fox (former Mayor and Alderman and doyenne of women's organisations) from the Federation of Chinese Women. Here *kashrut* found itself in a good-natured clash with Chinese hospitality. The group brought no less than 1,500 frozen kosher meals with them, which unfortunately must have inhibited the experience to some extent, since travel also depends on taste to create the full adventure. Their kosher dietary laws had to be explained to the Chinese Ambassador's wife in London and meant the visit was downgraded to a less official level since Chinese rules of etiquette always included invitations to official dinners and lunches.

When Amélie offered to share a room with Mrs Winston Fox, the lady was somewhat embarrassed because she did not know if she could attain Amélie's Orthodox standards. Amélie insisted that she was not to sleep alone. Mrs Winston Fox chuckled over the idea that the arrangement was rather like a good marriage. 'One of the likable things about her is the fact that she does prayers at regular times in the day,' Mrs Winston Fox said.

Writing about her group's experiences in the *Jewish Chronicle*, which referred to the trip as 'the great kosher Chinese takeaway', Amélie described a Friday night in Beijing-Xian in the middle of China, where they ate gefilte fish served by pencil-slim Chinese girls in cheongsams slit to the thigh. 'Afterwards we sang *zemirot*** and the peace of Shabbat came down upon us in this corner of the earth where nothing of Jewish value had ever been witnessed before.'

After walking up the Great Wall of China with an elderly member of their group who had been told she would never walk again, they travelled to Kaifeng, where a Jewish community had lived for eight centuries, and to Shanghai, where they found the graves of several Sephardi Jews. They then crossed to Hong Kong, which was then still part of Britain.

Why China? she was asked. 'Curiosity about other cultures,' she replied; a desire to develop a cultural understanding with Chinese women. Perhaps inevitably their communication was by the exchange of smiles and gestures, but the success of the group in penetrating areas few would have considered before has never been forgotten by its participants.

Amélie took a fact-finding mission to Israel and insisted, as always, on a Friday afternoon pre-Shabbat prayer visit to the Western Wall. They reached the Wall, where she pointed out a tradition that on Friday afternoon not only are the souls and memories of the Patriarchs, Abraham, Isaac and Jacob, present at the Wall, but also the Matriarchs, Sarah, Rebecca, Rachel and Leah. 'If you are attentive,' she told them, 'you will see that the Wall is visited by the real Jerusalem women whose families have been there for generations past, and who really know how to pray and cry out to G-d for help. There you can sense their devotion and their ability to create a unique spiritual atmosphere which takes

*Israeli word for songs, usually of a religious or liturgical nature.

you right into the Sabbath. There is no doubt in my mind that the Almighty needs the prayers of these sincere women as much as He needs the strength of the defence of our army.'

Retirement is one thing. Relinquishment is quite another. In their own ways, both Amélie and Immanuel tried to act as mentors to the new incumbents of their office, Chief Rabbi Jonathan Sacks and his wife, Elaine, a radiologist. It has been one of the more difficult relationships they have had to manage. Their successors are a different breed. Their demeanour is drier, shyer, more rarefied, in some ways less emotional. The present Chief Rabbi has proved in many ways more outspoken than Lord Jakobovits, lacking his feel for time and place, and in others, less sure-footed. He sometimes appears to speak more from expediency than conviction. At other times, it is the expediency and diplomacy you feel are lacking. Amélie considers Jonathan Sacks a brilliant thinker, but someone who has difficulty communicating one to one. She is a little upset that Elaine – a far more reserved person than she is – chooses to distance herself. Yet Elaine Sacks acknowledges Amélie's helpfulness in generous, if careful, terms: 'From the beginning Lady Jakobovits really put herself out to help me as much as she could. I know that she is always there to offer advice. A number of times I have called Amélie and said, "What did you do when …", and I always get a succinct and practical reply. Before my husband took on the position of Chief Rabbi, Amélie was kind enough to invite me round for coffee with two of her daughters and I was able to ask what it was like to grow up as the children of the Chief Rabbi, because, of course, I was concerned for my own family. It was very useful.'

The contrast in the style of the two women could hardly be more marked. Elaine Sacks demonstrates a clear demarcation line between her role and that of her husband; with Amélie, it is almost as though the distinctions are blurred. Sir Sidney Hamburger makes the succinct observation: 'As the wife of a Chief Rabbi she could have found adequate reason to detach herself from grassroots involvement, but she never did. On the contrary; in times of joy and even more in times of tragedy she was always there, bringing comfort and relief.'

How is the Emeritus Rebbetzin regarded in so-called retirement? 'A matriarch of the Jewish community and a paragon of Jewish feminine virtue,' gushes Rabbi Shmuely Boteach of Oxford University's controversial L'Chaim Society, a once Lubavitch outreach body which is now independent. 'Definitely the power behind the throne,' says Dayan Berger, 'and a great philosophic mind.' 'A human dynamo who has not slowed down in the slightest,' says Alan Greenbatt, executive director of the Chief Rabbi's office from 1990–1991.

Other people see a lighter, funnier side to Amélie's nature. 'Very bright and bubbly and fashion-conscious,' says actress Maureen Lipman, who loves her for having once upstaged her at a dinner with a knife-edge account of her trip to Russia. 'She makes you feel a lot older than she is.' 'She believes in fun and laughter,' smiled the late Lady Sieff. 'I could never believe that her hair was a wig. She has such with-it hairstyles.'

You know the story about her,' recalls Geoffrey Paul. 'A member of one of the leading Anglo-Jewish families was taken into a home. He had Alzheimer's, I believe. When she went to see him, she said he was still a ladies' man. As she turned to go, he tapped her flirtaciously. Yes, she has that charm. That's the Frenchwoman in her. You can't get away from that little sparkle. That little naughtiness.'

'I think she is still very excited about invitations to visit to the Queen or the Prime Minister,' observes a leading figure in the women's Zionist movement. 'It is apparent that she considers it very important to be invited, but you might pick up the wrong interpretation. It is an element which does not sit well. It suggests a different set of values from religious leadership values. Yet she has a freshness and sparkle as if it's the first time she has done something.'

Amélie has no intention of giving up a public role and does not think this should conflict with her successor's work. If it does, Amélie will rationalise it: it is just that their styles are different. One communal worker considers that the rather self-effacing Elaine finds Amélie somewhat daunting and possibly overbearing. The essential differences between the two women are that Elaine is involved in different things, in charities at a lower key, but does not have the same forceful nature.

'Amélie will see a gap and make sure something is done about it,' the communal worker says. 'But then I don't think Amélie became Amélie Jakobovits for quite a few years until she felt strong enough to come out and be herself. And the fact that Amélie is French helped her get away with a great deal because she could tell her little stories, which so endeared people to her. I think that when Elaine stepped into the Chief Rabbi's wife's role she knew that the worst cloud was that she was going to have a very hard act to follow and people are very critical; people aren't nice.'

Since retiring, Lord Jakobovits' work on medical ethics has borne fruit: a chair of medical ethics has been established at two Israeli universities, a timely move since the moral debate has been well extended within the field of genetic engineering and embryology. Lord Jakobovits has actively participated in many issues such as artificial insemination, surrogacy and animal cloning. He has also been praised for his writings on faith in the inner cities, which some observers consider contributed significantly towards the whole concept of interfaith awareness in Britain, an issue of universal concern in which Amélie is widely regarded as having encouraged him.

The inability to save marriages in the community and the resultant long-term effects of divorce continue to haunt Amélie, as does the perceived apathy of the church and its failure to encourage work on relationships. She is full of solemn anecdotes about marital break-ups – a young rabbi married for fifteen years with three children suddenly seeking a divorce on the grounds of his wife's silence, for instance. When she hears such stories, she is inclined to drop everything to help with counselling or anything else the family may need. Amélie is concerned at the tendency today to 'just walk away from a marriage at the drop of a hat', and will cite her Ten Commandments of Married Life in support of working on it – whether it is an instantaneous love-at-first-sight match or a relationship that needed to develop over time.

Of her own forty-nine-year marriage she describes her husband as a very gentle man. 'I was always surrounded by very kind people, my father, mother, people who instilled in me feelings of security and helped me avoid any arrogance.' My husband, she admits, is particularly modest, totally unaware of himself. 'I always knew I was in the shadow – no, I don't like that word – *by the side of* great, intellectual people, but I don't think of it perpetually. Many people ask how it is to live with the Chief Rabbi, with this great personality, but my genuine answer is that I don't live with the Chief Rabbi or this great personality, I live with a man.'

For a rabbi's wife, many people have remarked on her attractiveness; she is still a beautiful woman, very feminine, with generous features and unusual turquoise eyes reflecting her vivacity but also depth, a certain knowledge born, perhaps, of the war. She appears emotional, but confesses to envying people who cry easily. She is tactile, flirtatious, a nod and a wink away from the coquettish. One journalist said that he often felt he wanted to give her a hug or a kiss on the cheek and was almost sure she would not mind, but stopped himself at the last moment. It would have probably been too late anyway – she is so quick on the move.

Her feeling on becoming a grandmother was 'an overwhelming sense of my feminine extension through my daughter to whom I gave life, and now, herself, able to give life. It is beyond definition. I thought at first that the thrill of seeing your first grandchild can never be emulated. I find that now to be wrong. Each new-born baby is equally special.'

'Mano says I am a wonderful liver. I live very deeply.' He rarely loses his temper and never with his family. She sums up her husband as a rationalist and fatalist, as proved when he had his kidney operation in 1973 and his heart attack in 1989. 'His attitude is to take these things as G-d sends them, with total acceptance. It is unusual and I envy it. I am different. He tells me 100 times that I do everything a step or two beyond moderation. I do things to extreme.'

Amélie's comparisons between their respective natures sound like something Maurice Chevalier might have sung: his endless patience with her impatience; her tidiness with his untidiness, which, she concedes – like a mother rather than a wife – perhaps goes with scholarship. A precious relationship between husband and wife, parent and child, must be nurtured like a tiny seed developing into a plant, growing into a flower. As a paradigm she indicates the philosophy of one of the great thinkers of post-war American Jewish history, Joseph Baer Soloveichik, who developed the Brisk Talmudic discipline, which means that not everything you say has to be written and not everything you write has to be said.

However, given that marriages do break down and divorces follow, Amélie accepts that one of the great tragedies that the Jewish world must come to terms with is the plight of the *agunot* – women whose husbands refuse them a GET, a Jewish divorce, and who are therefore not free to remarry according to Jewish law.* She knows that her husband is haunted by the fact that his father could not find peace the night before his death because he could not help them. 'My son, I cannot die,' he said. 'My heart is so heavy with pains and agonising aches for all the *agunot* I could not help. I have the feeling that I cannot let life go before it gives me the opportunity to do some superhuman thing about the terrible tragedy of the *agunot*.'

Yet it seemed that some of the traditionalism of the United Synagogue must go before anything could be done to help them. This was something Jakobovits, in his time as Chief Rabbi, was unable to consider. 'The Pre-Nuptial Agreement (PNA) was already raised during my tenure,' he says, 'and I decided in the end not to pursue it because it was incongruous and may fail. What we are looking for here is to go for advice to a rabbinical authority. From there one hopes they [the *agunot*] will be guided properly. First of all civil law recognises synagogue marriage as valid. Therefore it is anomalous that the state should recognise that and not the need to dissolve both bonds, civil and religious, in the same way they recognise the making of that bond.'

Could Amélie herself have done more to persuade her husband of the importance of confronting rabbis with the issue of the so-called chained women before he retired? Brenda Katten, who has held the chair of the Zionist Federation and the Federation of Women Zionists among other communal roles, says rabbis can put pressure on husbands and feels that, while women have been very patient, the time for action has come. Amélie considers that, like her late father-in-law, 'any rabbi who is called a human being agonises over this question, but they cannot deliver if they can't

*Men can equally be refused a GET by their wives. Victims of this refusal may only remarry in a registry office.

get hold of the husband and make sense to him. There's a tremendous amount of emotional pain for rabbonim who cannot help as quickly as they would like. But I want to emphasise that there aren't thousands of *agunot* in the world. There are very few and for them it is, of course, very painful, but I get upset when these things are exaggerated. However, each individual case is so tragic that it hardly matters if it's one or a thousand. What does one say to any individual woman who literally feels herself chained, that she can't remarry and have a meaningful relationship with another man; she is virtually a nun. What does one say to her?'

37   The Women's Review

IT WAS not until Rabbi Jonathan Sacks took over as Chief Rabbi and launched his United Synagogue Women's Review that anything was done to address these and other questions relating to women's issues. In 1993 Jonathan Sacks announced that mandatory pre-nuptial contracts would be introduced for all United Synagogue marriages. While many women took Chief Rabbi Sacks' gesture as an opportunity to realise their protests in terms of public campaigns, Amélie stood fast by her principles of avoiding such activities on the grounds of modesty. Change must take place quietly and diplomatically, through the use of persistence and good taste.

In October 1995, when some fifty *agunot* organised a vigil outside the office of the Chief Rabbi, then also the site of the Board of Deputies, at Woburn House in London, many Jews signed a petition and gave support. The women who organised it were very successful; they produced banners and chains and were surrounded by supporters, but this did not appeal to Amélie.

Her attitude may have exasperated some women, particularly a younger generation who do not share her long-held belief in self-restraint, which they feel will get women nowhere and which they consider a reactionary stance in a woman occupying an influential position in Anglo-Jewry. Ros Preston, who headed the Women's Review, says of the demo: 'I think the sight of Jewish women on the street is entirely unique – and it is very high in the public mind at the moment, the whole question of marriage, divorce law, civil and religious law, women's equality or lack of it, women's human rights and lack of it, etc.' She acknowledges, however, that Amélie has beaten a path linking women of all denominations of Anglo-Jewry, both through the Lady J Group, which has a very broad agenda, and through the trips abroad on which she took them. Yet when Amélie heard about the work being done by the Women's Review, she insisted that this should not come from the Chief Rabbi's Office. It should come from a secular source, such as the Board of Deputies. 'She foresaw difficulties,' says Ros Preston. 'So, although the report was no longer emanating from her husband's office, she felt the same commitment, she still carried on as though it were. I knew what I was doing and had my agenda, and she saw it as a danger. She was trying to guard the office of the Chief Rabbi. I think she has as much feeling for women in this situation as anybody else, but I don't think she likes action.'

According to Brenda Katten, the only positive outcome of the Review was that many more people were talking about it, and women felt empowered by it, knowing they had the ability to do things, such as organise women's services. Women, she pointed out, were now on the committees of synagogues' boards of management. However, in order to address the issues, you need consensus: 'It's no good if there is a very fervent kind of woman who wants to rebel against male domination. In Judaism this would not be possible. I personally would not want to be chosen for a job because they said it is time to have a woman. I feel that is not what it's about.'

Mrs Preston regards Amélie as a traditionalist who understands the influence and the position of a woman as educator in the powerhouse. She personally made it work so successfully for her that she felt it was more than enough. 'One of the major things to come out of her era is that women had a greater religious knowledge and could become more spiritually fulfilled. She was partially responsible for this flourishing increase in learning circles.'

At least ten years ago the Association of United Synagogue Women was involved in early discussions on the issue of broadening the decision-making role of women in the community. Amélie was then put in an invidious position, according to Ann Harris. Amélie, a 'superlative clergy wife', had to be seen to support the position of her husband and his Beth Din, while all her friends and colleagues were taking sides. 'My impression was that because she, her daughters and many of her personal friends felt so secure in their place in the Orthodox community, she failed to warn the Chief Rabbi of the considerable groundswell of discontent among the ordinary United Synagogue women, particularly the educated and young with whom she came into contact far more than he did. Whether this was because she herself did not recognise it or wanted to protect him from it, I do not know, but I consider his views on the subject to have been greatly influenced by hers.' Women like Amélie, she continues, 'who feel comfortable in their spiritual status rarely see the need for change.'

But times, of course, are changing. Jonathan Sacks' Review has 'put Jewish women's rights higher on the political agenda and has opened the minds of women which before were closed through ignorance and lack of awareness,' according to Ros Preston. In her view, it has activated men as well as women and encouraged younger women to learn about Judaism. She feels that historically the battle between women and the religious establishment has now reached a new stage. 'Women are not prepared to sit back and wait.' Yet sit back and wait was exactly what Ros Preston and her supporters had to do because the Chief Rabbi took a long time to consider the Review's recommendations concerning the religious involvement of women in synagogue services and the question of the *agunot*. Mrs Preston understood that Sacks was torn between the politics of the religious establishment and the inability to achieve consensus, without which no support would be forthcoming. Yet with hindsight she considers the Review to have been 'an enormous success'.

Syma Weinberg, the educationalist who worked for Jewish Continuity before embarking on her career as Executive Director of the Chief Rabbi's Office, explains that the tension between Chief Rabbi Jonathan Sacks and the women happened because the women, having had the door opened, could not understand the Chief Rabbi's delay. 'We don't really understand what the Chief Rabbi's position is all about as ordinary people. He is juggling all the time and when he speaks to you very personally, you feel he's taken on your issue and he's going to do something about it in the next hour, but that's impossible. We are living in turbulent times, but it's part of the process of achieving this Decade of Renewal he's promised. Life didn't go that smoothly for the Jakobovits' either, it was just in the latter years that everything came together.'

So here are feminine voices for the future. And yet for Amélie the traditionalist, there is no feminist movement within Anglo-Jewry, no post-modern clamour of new demands; there are only eternal truths for women. Instinct is their major voice. Women, she insists, have that certain biological instinct – that French *je ne sais quoi* – and if they use it, they won't go far wrong. A simple solution? This feminine instinct, a term which has become unfashionable in the late twentieth century, implies an ancient, serpentine wisdom. It is knowledge with attitude. When she speaks of it, Amélie is saying that pressure groups and grassroots movements seeking change should just take it easy. Change will come at its own momentum. Today this once traditional view sounds almost unconventional.

The writer and journalist David Nathan describes Amélie as a woman who 'defies convention without giving ammunition to those who want to demonstrate that they are more pious than the pious, is flirtatious without any hint of impropriety and seems to have fun without giving anyone cause to believe that she is not serious'. He once asked her what she thought when she heard her husband thanking G-d every morning that he was not born a woman.* 'I think', she said, 'that he is referring to having been spared the pains and aches of a woman. I don't think that blessing is being said in a negative way. I really do think it refers to men having been spared the pain of bringing a child into the world and all that goes with it. And we women thank G-d for having made us what we are and for having been given the opportunity to reproduce ourselves.'

As for the *agunot*, it was finally Lord Jakobovits who won the day with a Lords amendment to the Family Law Bill permitting courts the right to withhold a decree absolute from any man refusing to grant his wife a GET – a vindication, no doubt, for the tormented soul of his father. But that move did not go far enough for many Jewish women, who felt that Jewish, not civil, law must

*A statement made in a man's morning prayers.

be addressed. The International Council of Jewish Women decided that the Halachah discriminates against women and have begun pressurising rabbis to change the rules of divorce. They plan to take their case to the European Court of Human Rights or the United Nations Human Rights Committee if they do not receive satisfaction from rabbinic authorities. A new project announced by ICJW chair June Jacobs pledged to monitor data on the violation of women's human rights in Jewish communities all over the world.

38   A Seismic Split

CHANGE WAS on the way. But if these once stifled feminine voices of Anglo-Jewry were at last being heard, so too was a clamour of a different kind. In an almost delphic replay of the events which brought Immanuel Jakobovits to the office of British Chief Rabbi, a new chasm between Orthodoxy and the Progressive movement threatened. Beyond the spiritual dimension alone, it had taken all Jakobovits' skills as a negotiator, politician and diplomat to maintain a respectful truce between all parties. But five years after Lord Jakobovits' retirement, the Cambridge-educated Jonathan Sacks was faced with a problem. Rabbi Hugo Gryn, the popular head of the West London Reform Synagogue, had died suddenly. Gryn was a man whose homespun Jewish wisdom had not only won the love of Britain's largest Progressive synagogue, but also illuminated Radio Four's weekly programme, *The Moral Maze*, transforming him into a media celebrity of magnetic charm and penetrating insight.

Would Chief Rabbi Sacks, a man not slow to show his colours when it came to his disdain for Progressive Judaism, attend his funeral? Sacks had less experience of religious politics than the Emeritus Chief Rabbi, yet oddly for a man of his intellectual gifts, he seemed disinclined to learn. His tendency then was to jump into the fray where sager men would stand back and reflect.

Almost from his first days in office, Sacks had taken to sniping at the Masorti movement, but he was aware how deeply British Jews of all persuasions felt about Gryn, whose death at the age of sixty-six seemed almost to have deprived them of a father-figure. Gryn was the archetypal man for all seasons, a person who had not merely survived the Holocaust, but grown from it. Gryn's nature was measured yet fiery, tempered by an innate good humour and true kindliness. He was mourned by those who sensed that his particular alchemy was to transmute Jewish suffering into a kind of renaissance, reclaiming light from the Holocaust darkness. It seemed as though two worlds met briefly in Gryn and then passed on – the cultivated but doomed Europe and the grittier Jewish-American dream.

Chief Rabbi Sacks, keenly watched by all factions within and outside the United Synagogue, was faced with a dilemma. To ignore a man of Gryn's stature would be to isolate the Reform rabbi's admirers among some elements in the United Synagogue. To attend the funeral of a man not even recognised as a rabbi by the Orthodox would inflame its hawkish, often narrow-minded right wing. Sacks sought compromise. He declined to attend Gryn's funeral personally, but agreed to address a secular memorial service where he praised Gryn as a Holocaust survivor without reference to his rabbinic status. But Sacks went further. He wrote a confessional letter to Dayan Chanoch Padwa, head of the Union of Orthodox Congregations, expressing his pain at having to honour a man he regarded as a 'destroyer of the faith'. It was the leak of this *mea culpa* letter to the press which drew blood, reopening all the old wounds of the Jacobs Affair which Jakobovits had tried to heal.

Amélie, a friend of Hugo and his wife, Jackie, could only watch in sorrow as the schisms gradually split the community. She was also privately saddened by Sacks' choice of words when he described the Reform leader as 'a wonderful survivor of the Holocaust'. There was more to Hugo than that, she considered. 'There's more to any human being than to describe him as a survivor.'

Amélie's demeanour when faced with controversy has always been to tread carefully, to avoid confrontation at all costs, whether with the very right or the very left; but if it proves unavoidable, then to diffuse it as quickly as possible. When it comes to a showdown, she believes in quiet dialogue and patience. Scarred by the fragmentation she found in Britain at the time of their arrival, Amélie recalls an emotive phrase used by her husband at that time: he described the community as 'frittering away its energies by insulting each other over the Jacobs Affair' instead of constructing something tangible. To those around him, Sacks seemed to act against his own best interests and of the community.

Lord Jakobovits, true to his principles, refused to intervene. He believed that any statement or advice from him on matters no longer under his control would devalue the office of the Chief Rabbi itself. 'Lord Jakobovits has been scrupulous in his desire to make himself available when the Chief Rabbinate felt they could call upon his expertise, but not to crowd his successor, and he has been true to his word', recalls Jonathan Kestenbaum, who ran the Chief Rabbi's Office under Sacks at the time. 'His counsel to me was arguably one of the most important voices that I heard after Chief Rabbi Sacks. He's been very discreet – one of his primary characteristics.'

Yet it was not easy for the quick-tongued Amélie to control the impulse to speak her mind to her husband's successor. Amélie had always loved to be at the pulse of life. Now she longed to be able to look Sacks in the face and advise him as a mother might a recalcitrant son. How hard it was for her to desist. However, she refused to betray the principles she shared with her husband. Her role at that time had to be a silent one.

Amélie realised, of course, that the letter written by Sacks in classic Hebrew to the ninety-year-old Rav Padwa and later leaked to the press was pivotal. It appeared to be the knee-jerk reaction of a man desperate to placate the right wing within central Ortho-doxy. It would have been Amélie's way simply to pick up the phone and make an appointment to discuss issues face to face with Padwa. Together in privacy, she considered, the two men might have reached an understanding about the most delicate way to handle the Gryn affair. At any rate neither of these things happened and the issue detonated like a bomb.

What has particularly upset Amélie is the unnecessary pain inflicted on the Gryn family, who maintained their dignity in the midst of media attention. But in her view the seeds of the anomaly that Sacks faced were in his induction speech describing his proposed Decade of Renewal. 'He spoke of inclusiveness,' she recalls; 'there would be an inclusive community. But was this really possible? Did Sacks indeed hand the Reform movement in that statement the false hope that they would be included in everything, irrespective of religious nuance and interpretation?'

Whatever Amélie's difference with Chief Rabbi Sacks, it is clearly more tactical than inherent. Her attitude reflects a certain dichotomy within her own character; she is able to develop relationships with Progressives whose Judaism she actually deplores. It is a characteristic that is as beguiling as it is unsettling. And so she offers Sacks a lesson on the power of words: 'We argue, yes, we argue. But we avoid using very strong language.'

When Chief Rabbi Sacks attacked the Masorti movement long before Hugo Gryn died, he called them 'intellectual thieves – destroyers of the faith'. Amélie's diplomacy, and by inference that of her husband, rejects the use of such language, 'because it would mean you can no longer have a dialogue. You have lost the opportunity of convincing your fellow Jew that he or she is mistaken in their beliefs.'

What was really important to the Jakobovits' was to be with the Gryn family the day after Hugo's death. They spent the day before the funeral quietly consoling the family at home, something on which the media did not focus since the formalities outweighed the concept of condolence. But like Chief Rabbi Sacks, neither of them attended Hugo's funeral, either.

This is an issue which surprises Rabbi Dr Louis Jacobs, who fails to see anything to prevent an Orthodox Jew from attending a funeral, no matter what the religious complexion of the deceased. In fact, both Elaine Sacks and Rabbi Dr Abraham Levy, spiritual head of the central Orthodox British Sephardi Community in Britain, were among those who paid their last respects to Rabbi Gryn at his funeral service at Golders Green Cemetery. According to Rabbi Jacobs, other Orthodox ministers in America had no problem with attending Progressive funerals. Once again the media had a field day. Chaim Bermant, writing in the *Observer*, urged Jonathan Sacks to resign, but retracted one week later in the *Jewish Chronicle*.

What would Emeritus Chief Rabbi Immanuel Jakobovits have done in Sacks' place? Arguably he might have written Gryn's obituary in *The Times* and nobody would have expected anything else. Either way, Rabbi Jacobs believes Lord Jakobovits would have shown more discretion over the whole issue, as does Geoffrey Paul, who goes so far as to say that even had Lord Jakobovits lacked the political nous, the trusty Moshe Davis would have guided him in the right direction.

'What has made me more sad than anything about this', says Amélie, 'is the soul of the departed, which could not find rest.'

It is a mistake that could cost Sacks dear. Representatives of the three Progressive synagogues – Masorti, Reform and the Liberals – were recently planning a joint platform on which to press their case for a Progressive Chief Rabbi of their own. That, in Orthodox eyes, would spell the end for any vision of Jewish unity in Britain today. Yet there are signs that all parties are considering ways of ending their conflict. *The Times* of 19 October 1998 reported moves towards a historic peace agreement between the Chief Rabbi, Masorti, Reform and the Liberal movement.

In the meantime, what is Amélie's advice for her husband's successor? 'If for the next two years he devoted himself exclusively to his "constituency" – the United Synagogue – and did nothing else, no writing of books, articles, no attending communities outside the United Synagogue proper, I think there might be hope for him to rebuild his authority.' She paints a rather moving portrait of Rabbi Sacks as a loner. Who advises him? He could participate in many councils, such as the European Council of Rabbis, but she thinks he cannot relate to people individually. 'Although he is a wonderful communicator, he is only secure when he is all alone on the platform and then he is brilliant. He gives something when he speaks, but the importance of leadership is to appreciate the nuances of the different interpretations. What is also important is the tone of language. *C'est la tone de musique*, we call it; if it is the wrong tone, you will not be understood. The tone changes everything. It is a question of a deep sensitivity to the other person. I don't think you are born with it. You have to develop it. My husband developed it. My mother had a wonderful saying. She called it "Search Aloud". If you are looking for something, say it aloud and you are more likely to find it.'

About one year before he died, Rabbi Gryn spoke prophetically about the religious divide which he felt that Amélie was able to bridge. 'Lord Jakobovits, for obvious reasons, could not do so. He is more subtle than his successor and wiser, but there are certain things he can't do. Amélie is much more open and able to break down those barriers within Anglo-Jewry. She has formed herself into a one-woman band, visiting hospitals, supporting the bereaved and vulnerable, quite without demarcations, and quite right. Amélie is a harmoniser. I divide the religious into two: polarisers and harmonisers. I don't think there is anything in the middle, other than people who are just asleep. [Amélie] expresses herself forcefully, rapidly. If she has to choose between being diplomatic and being honest, she would be the honest person. She's funny. She's got a wonderful sense of humour, the kind that dissolves tensions, which is an intellectual and emotional gift, and I think in situations where you can play up either the tragedy or the comedy, she would go for the comedy.'

In private conversations with Rabbi Gryn, Amélie had voiced her regret that Lord Jakobovits had not always been treated in the way they would have liked. But in this loyalty Rabbi Gryn perceived the quality of the tigress, and voiced his affection for her. He recalled the day Margaret Thatcher resigned and Rabbi Gryn had taken part in the launch of a group in the House of Lords. Amélie 'totally riveted' him as well as the entire audience with her history and experiences. 'If you take [Amélie's] history, she has every licence to be cynical, to be narrow, to be at the very least a critic of life and of peoples' intentions, and she isn't and that's the tribute.'

39   *The Lord's View*

'I WOULDN'T say I had a romantic feeling. I was basically a really romantic girl but Rabbi Jakobovits was already too much of a personality for me to be romantic about him. I had an inner voice – we call that in the Hebrew language, *Batkol*, a voice from the Divine, from something you can't reach, which kept on telling me in my intellect – he is the man for you.'

Nevertheless in its way theirs was a romantic story. She was only twenty; he was twenty-seven. She, a lively, young French beauty; he, tall, slender, with the tender obeisance of an oak to a sapling. His eyes were blue and perceptive. It was less easy for him to express feelings and there was a certain charming gaucheness, an old-fashioned courtliness about him in the early days, appealing in a clerical gentleman.

'Suddenly I meet someone who is Chief Rabbi of Ireland – so we had to get a magnifying glass from the concierge downstairs and eventually found that little tiny island behind England. I always had this arrogance – a real cheek – to only want to live my life with a man of great intellect. This attracts me more than any other quality in a human being.'

'She has been quite an exceptional partner,' Immanuel told David Nathan in a *Jewish Chronicle* interview on the twentieth anniversary of his appointment as British Chief Rabbi in 1987. 'I am biased, but with her vivaciousness and her inexhaustible energy, she has a major share in whatever little success I've had in this office. She has been adviser and critic. People don't always feel as free as she does to say, look, this time, your sermon, or lecture or address didn't come up to standard.'

Their relationship symbolises the successful bonding of energy with contemplation. When telephoned out of the blue by SKY TV asking him to take part in a programme on the Divorce Bill, Jakobovits pondered for a moment and replied, 'The problem is the media are purveyors of brevity and I am a purveyor of eternity.' It sounds pompous in print, but in fact his words – a soundbite in themselves – came over with a kind of reflective innocence. He wonders why we always want instant answers. 'Snappy decisions have to be made on matters that should be of considered thought. We have all these gadgets forcing us to give instant replies.'

But who is Lord Jakobovits? What measure of man is he? It is too easy to see Britain's Emeritus Chief Rabbi as a distant and ruminative figure, even though the products of his discourse do, indeed, come from long and deep consideration. For him to decide something will take whatever time it takes, and Amélie is used to him going into the silence of gestation in order to gather his thoughts. Although his demeanour is full of gentle bonhomie, he wears his seriousness on his sleeve. It is hard to equate her buzzi-ness with his stillness; difficult not to think that her bustle might sometimes grate on his nerves. Yet they are air and earth together, a life force that interflows. After all, this is the man who loved to drive off in a caravan like an explorer into unknown territory. It is not merely a life lived on the pulpit. And if his words tend towards the ponderous, there is his dry, self-deprecating humour: 'She was optimistic. She took the plunge with a great deal of courage.'

They were both the eldest of seven children – an important Kabbalistic number, but Immanuel resists the inference, he is not much given, he says, to Kabbalistic thought. Immanuel met Amélie after two previous introductions which never reached 'any resulting state of intended commitment'. He had already promised his Dublin congregation that he would get married. 'Of course there are always moments in a marriage where one wonders, did I do the right thing? But not in really critical respects. She is supreme in personal relationships, in befriending people. She loves the social conviviality of that. I do not love it at all. I am very reluctant. I do not have it on the social level to mingle with people as she does. She is constantly on the go, on the phone, and that makes her entirely different. We sometimes have arguments, and she pushes, I resist. She is completely at home with everyone. She is an extrovert. I haven't got this love of people which she has.' He has always maintained that without her he could not have achieved so much. 'But right from the beginning, once she was there, she took over.'

Their arguments tend to be based on whether or not he should attend a particular cocktail party or reception. If she feels it important, she will manage to persuade him. However, Lord Jakobovits is far less reserved and wary of people than he likes to suggest. His convictions are firmly yet quietly borne, his tone is light and spirited – although when upset it can sound strangulated – his intellect approachable. Friends will say that Amélie teased out this ability to communicate; his eyes too can sparkle with fun. He is grandfatherly, fond of a joke and though sometimes portrayed as a formal, quaintly anachronistic figure, he is more of a realist, more in touch with popular sentiment on some issues, than many are aware.

But this is not to diminish the influence Amélie has had in more important matters than those of social quarrying. Ann Harris points out that she was an excellent public relations officer for her husband and must take a great deal of credit for his career advancement. 'She also intervened discreetly to prevent controversial issues involving her husband from escalating and becoming public.' Mrs Harris adds, 'Read your *Barchester Chronicles* and think of Mrs Proudie as a really well-meaning person.'

Lord Jakobovits' daughter, Esther Pearlman, reflects that her father would not be where he is without her mother. 'He is what he is because of her. He was shy. She was much more ambitious than he. She would bring out the warmth and emotion; she also knew how to deal with people.'

From his handwriting, graphologist Allan Conway analyses Jakobovits as a profound and lucid thinker, a man of great perseverance, his judgements based on reason and objectivity. He also sees him as meticulous and loyal with a sense of duty conforming to his own principles. For good measure Conway also describes his acute intelligence.

Although Amélie is notorious for not being able to stand any criticism of her husband, she has always upheld his views and had to put up with the brickbats they inevitably brought down on his head. 'The disagreements I had with Amélie were on the domestic front,' recalls Jakobovits. 'When I spoke out about the plight of the Palestinians, urging Jews to express their views on this point, I was disowned by rabbis. She never disagrees with me on deep rabbinic issues. She was a great support, even when I got involved in the Israel crisis because of the Arab refugees. I always said – imagine Jews having to live in these conditions. And for us Jews to oppress others!' Thus Hamas terrorism was an evil – a perversion of religion – just waiting to happen. 'You cannot deny two million people their most basic rights and just expect them to go away.'

Oddly, he regards as his greatest triumph in twenty-five years as Chief Rabbi, not his amendment in the House of Lords on the Family Law Bill, not his work in the field of Jewish education or medical ethics, not the courage it took to become a lone, dissenting voice on the Palestinian issue, but his ability to move so many at the Albert Hall in the freshness of his days in the post on the outbreak of the Six Day War. It seems he surprised himself: 'I am not so easily moved by emotions.'

And yet it took all the powers of persuasion of the Zionist leadership in Britain to divert him from fulfilling a prior arrangement, a pastoral visit to Newcastle to discuss abortion, one of his *causes célèbres*, instead of addressing the rally. Rev. Reuben Turner describes his almost futile attempt to convince him of his priorities, while Jakobovits kept pulling out volumes of Maimonides, etc., and talking about abortion. 'Amélie was there all the time, coming in and going out, bringing coffee, etc., and in the end I just left. I had all my family in the car outside, and I said, I leave it to you now. There's no more I can do.' Rev. Turner is sure that it was Amélie who managed to convince her husband to go the Albert Hall and deliver what was his first major speech since taking office. 'It was a highly emotive speech. Everyone was taken aback by his eloquence and by the way he became emotionally involved in the whole thing.'

It is in the deadlocked settlement with the Palestinians that Lord Jakobovits probably sees the greatest failure of Orthodox Judaism to make a difference, to sound the clarion call of moral and spiritual activism. Because the call never came. Instead there are carrion men, those who preach death to optimism, to peace, and beyond that to the search for true religion in the world. It grieves him –

Jakobovits will indulge words like this – that transcendent moves towards harmony come from the secular rather than the religious side: '*We* should be active towards a political settlement,' he insists. 'Orthodoxy should be the experts on spiritual decisions, giving a spiritual interpretation of the essence of Judaism.'

However, the rabbi who became a lord is hopeful. Although a solitary and often harried voice within Orthodoxy, his call for a just settlement of the Palestinian issue is an article of faith with him; he does believe his thinking will catch on. In 1995 he called for part of Jerusalem to become a self-governing Palestinian enclave as part of a peace settlement. Certainly he would welcome some form of investment for the Palestinians, a complete autonomy, some economic progression. He admits a lot of money goes into the setting up of a Palestinian 'substructure', towards which Israel has contributed and funds have been raised in America to obtain major allocations for the Palestinians. 'The situation is very volatile. How we do it? I cannot pronounce on that, just as I cannot on the political expediency of the various moves. I just look at the overall scene.'

To Lord Jakobovits that overall scene is a changing landscape of confused idealism. The prayer for a just society that has focused his life is something of a mixed blessing. Good deeds come from the most unexpected people. His world has become less certain. In the real world he was bewildered to admit that 'the secular are closer to the promotion of peace'. For him, it was a sobering experience to see Yael Dayan, the daughter of the late flamboyant General Moshe Dayan, and 'possibly one of the ringleaders of the anti-religious movement', effectively campaigning for peace.

Does it matter where this call for peace comes from? Yes it does. 'Just living in peace as the seculars want is not sufficient. There are particularly special Jewish insights and Jewish values that must be employed, too.' He believes that many people would have turned to religious teaching but for 'the unacceptable face of the Orthodox'.

If religion is sometimes seen in the world as Fascist and obsessive, he suggests that it is not religion that is offputting, but the money, the horsetrading and general dissidence which accompanies the National Religious Party in Israel. These things he would be happy to see go. In fact, he does not believe in the

291

National Religious Party at all. For him, religious values should penetrate all the political parties. What does he expect from Orthodoxy? 'That they should concentrate on the spiritual aspects of the Jewish state.'

Soul-weary with the public level of morality in Israel today, Lord Jakobovits' distaste for a media-fed, sex-obsessed, materialistic society comes out in the derogatory language of despair: 'the high divorce rate, the smut, the cohabitation!' It is as though he seeks a metaphor here for the divisions he finds so unacceptable between faith and state itself: the promised image of spiritual purity sullied by contact with the material place.

Thus it is with an almost innocent surprise that he discovers that Israel is no more moral than the rest of the world. And – because to be that pure one must also combine a child-like naiveté with an angelic maturity – he then suggests that we cannot afford to be impatient with these things. The sort of society he envisions will take time to evolve. After all, he says, it took 400 years from crossing the Jordan to start the occupation of Canaan until Jerusalem, then another generation for the Temple to be built. So Lord Jakobovits, part cleric, part politician, part visionary, does not despair of messianic hope catching on. It will do so, he believes, because people will gradually become disenchanted with an empty, materialistic life devoid of spirituality.

But despite this stalwart optimism, he is given to parading a sense of personal hurt or injury. His *Jewish Chronicle* interview in 1987 contains a reference to congregants who do not observe the Sabbath or eat kosher food: 'I sometimes feel that they do not sufficiently recognise the grief I suffer in having often to deal with and relate to people who do not share my convictions and my commitments.'

Lord Jakobovits is a friend of Margaret Thatcher but denies being a Conservative. He considers himself closer on many issues to Labour than the Tories. 'I have never seen myself as right wing. I believe I am a moderate. Moderation is an article of faith. The willingness to see both sides and always be very concerned about compromise; to see the opponent's side, the sense of commitment out of which they acted.' He adds that this moderation is a principle of Maimonides, yet at the same time he has been undeniably regarded as an important influence in the crystallisation of Thatcher's Victorian values, because she found moral support in his preaching denied her by the established church.

Lord Jakobovits has been associated, of course, with some very Conservative causes: the Trust Hospitals, for instance. 'I did not know enough to pass judgement, but the notion that you spread the burden of responsibility among a wider group of citizens appealed to me. I am a great believer in the Beveridge Report and most of all the responsibility of the state for the least privileged, who are entitled to support. Which form is more efficient? I am not sure I can always see that, but in principle I do believe you should train other citizens to be responsible for themselves. I have from time to time come out on such issues as apartheid, human rights in South Africa, housing situations in Britain. I feel that each one should contribute to society what he is most competent to confer on it.'

Rabbi Shmuely Boteach says that he has 'immense respect' for Lord Jakobovits. 'But he places emphasis on education as being most important. I disagree. Jewish unity is more important than Jewish observance.' Amélie does not agree with this view and takes exception to the comment.

Dayan Berger sums up the Jakobovits years differently: 'During his regime the community has changed from emulating Christianity and preaching love and kindness and nothing else. The whole community faced change. People who had not been in England for eight or nine years and then returned just could not recognise their own shul. This is largely the influence of Lord Jakobovits. He blessed us with a sense of Judaism and turned it away from trying to emulate the Church of England. Judaism is the mother of all religions and Christians do not appreciate Jews trying to emulate them.'

Despite his amendment in the House of Lords to make religious divorce contingent on civil, Lord Jakobovits is more noted for speaking out on the sanctity of marriage. As the founder of the Jewish Marriage Council in the 1940s, he may have heard the dying words of his father on the situation of the *agunot* as a duty devolving on him, but in reality he finds divorce repugnant. His idea is less that you lock the doors so that you can get in but can't get out, than to make the 'interior of the marriage so exciting that there is no desire to get out'. For instance, 'It never dawned on Amélie and myself to have an opt-out clause in a marriage contract. That makes it far too easy to throw up the sponge.'

His lament that Britain has become the divorce capital of the world with 170,000 annual divorces has become a threnody for his life. Training at school, pre-marital instruction, all these ideas he throws out are like flares in the dark that shed no light on the deeper, sadder impoverishment of society, although he sees them only too clearly. His views on the causes of marital breakdown will not endear him to feminists, as he blames it partly on the new role of women. 'They no longer feel fulfilled in making marriage a primary commitment as a wife and mother. They want a life outside the home so that the home is an afterthought. A woman can be replaced in her job, but she cannot be replaced as a wife and a mother.' He does not seem to consider the financial difficulties many women face bringing up a family on their husband's income alone, or those of the single mother.

Yet his daughter, Esther, recalls her father preferring to work quietly behind the scenes on women's issues rather than going to the media. It seems that her mother's traditional voice is confirmed in her when, speaking on behalf of her sisters, she suggests, 'We feel that anyone who really understands religious Judaism understands women's issues. A woman's role is behind the scenes and we are very content with that.'

Lord Jakobovits has equally shocked the gay community for his outspoken homophobia, and these attitudes may mark him in some ways as a reactionary force in the late twentieth century, no matter how much sensitivity and progressive thinking he has demonstrated elsewhere.

'My father caused confrontation but never looked for it,' remarks his daughter, Shoshana. 'He has certain views on certain issues that he will not change. He sleeps every night. He is very much at peace with his conscience.'

Yet if Lord Jakobovits aroused no controversy, he would be less respected for his integrity. The living embodiment of Rabbi Hillel's words – 'it is not your duty to complete the work but neither are you free to desist from it' – Lord Jakobovits believes he is misunderstood: 'They know me for things that would otherwise not have been said.' It sounds inadequate, simply not enough to describe a man who has thought so hard, given so much time to moral perplexities. Perhaps thinker and philosopher are the best words to describe him after all. Sometimes, but not always, thoughts incarnate into deeds. Sometimes those deeds, inspired by the thinker, are undertaken by others.

He is modest when he says, 'I cannot help solve all the problems that afflict the world. We should make some relevant contribution, but where this is merely amplifying other voices, I do not think my contribution is all that important. I believe that each individual human being must contribute something unique to the enrichment of the world. Just to join the bandwagon of popular causes is not good enough. We must sometimes be prepared to be lonely and make statements that may alienate people, but yet make them because we believe them to be right.'

40   *In the Time To Come*

ON ISRAEL's fiftieth anniversary, in May 1998, Amélie joined the United Jewish Israel Appeal on a celebratory visit to the Jewish state. There she was much troubled by the secular spirit which she felt had taken over the country. Although she had expressed these fears before, it was as though the shock had hit her for the first time. 'There's nothing Jewish here,' she kept protesting. 'Nothing of the *ruach* [spirit] of Israel. Nothing!'

True enough, there was no hint of it in the Yom Hazikaron solemnity of tributes to the fallen, which took place without a Kaddish for the dead at Latrun; no hint, of course, in the triumphalism of the Israeli air force anniversary flypast next day in Tel Aviv. And least of all was there any hint of a holy presence at Jerusalem's Givat Ram, Israel's fiftieth anniversary Jubilee Bells showpiece, where the colour of khaki brushed lapels with the Prime Minister and foreign dignitaries, including America's Vice-President Al Gore, and blared out its apology for the Bat Sheva Dance Company, which refused to tailor its act to suit religious sensibilities. But there was no religious sentiment in the first place. Instead, an oversized white plastic dove floated in the air, almost carrying a small boy with it, as the plaintive song, invoking peace, '*Ose Shalom Bim'Ramov*', wafted in pursuit.

Perhaps what Amélie is really searching for is gratitude. Grace. Is there not something humbling in the experience of the Jewish state having reached its half century after the pillage of the Second World War? But is grace synonymous with the eternal battle for security?

Watching the show with a similar despair was the tense, slight figure of Rabbi Shmuely Boteach, the American outreach Chassidic rabbi, who hopes to bridge the perceptible religious gap with media-friendly goodwill and Jewish sex-guides. The disappointment of both was tangible. Neither could completely express it. Perhaps disappointment was inevitable. So much had happened in these intervening years – how could any of it be encapsulated? Boteach, a man of his times with a wannabe attitude, was waiting for something of a spiritual nature to happen. Amélie, a woman of hers, with a romantic view of religion, was staring into the past.

She found it at Yad Vashem and in the adjoining Valley of the Lost Communities, which forms a map of Europe. As you walk there you can find an entire wall devoted to each European country which suffered the blow of Nazism. As she walked through this reconstructed Valley of the Shadow, she did not expect anything to happen to her. But suddenly, near Nuremberg where her mother came from, she saw the name Ansbach, her home town, where her father had been a rabbi before being forced to flee to Paris. 'Then I was stuck. I felt something happen to my body, and I felt that what happened to me was not physical but Divine.'

Thus, symbolically, on Israel's fiftieth anniversary, Amélie found herself having come full circle. She was staring at an engraving of her German home town, Ansbach, whose rustic beauty belied the terrors that would shortly overtake it, yet which would one day deliver the State of Israel into the hands of persecuted Jewry. So many turbulent memories were evoked by that name: her beloved and martyred grandfather, the bullying by her teacher, the gradual restrictions imposed on a young girl playing in the woods, too young to comprehend the bald anti-Semitism which condemned her. It seemed now there was a diurnal aspect to the Jewish spirit, nurtured for centuries in inhospitable soil and then returned to its birthplace in Israel.

Amélie went on from there to talk to the crowds gathered at Yad Vashem, and what she told them was the story of the fifteen-year-old girl from Paris she had known, who had been taken to Auschwitz and whose new-born baby was killed before her eyes. Maybe they had heard this story before (it appears in Chapter Five). Maybe they had not. It was a shocking, yet entirely fitting parable, and evoked for Amélie, as it did for anyone else, something that has not quite been bridged between Israel and the diaspora.

As the Millennium dawns, the *fin-de-siècle* years sometimes invoke a cloying, almost helpless nostalgia. Amélie recognises that some of the changes that the new century will bring are already present within the heart of the State of Israel. From the early, often devastating pioneer years of Zionism half a century ago, she is now looking at a country split by rivalry and by an obsessive, self-regarding attitude towards that vexed question: who or what is a Jew? Sometimes it seems to Amélie that the tenet with which she grew up – that Jews should be a light unto the nation – is still barely understood. Certainly, as Israel in its fiftieth year tries somewhat arrogantly to ascribe its meaning purely to the nation state, it seems to miss the point that Judaism, for its own sake – whether in Israel or in the diaspora – might just have something to do with it.

In recent months Amélie has learned of a Russian child bomb victim in Jerusalem who was refused Jewish burial because his mother was not Jewish and of a controversy over whether a religious court did or did not order an Orthodox man to divorce his raped and traumatised wife, mother of his nine children. Amélie agonises over a view that the secular have taken the moral high ground in Israel from the religious, and is reminded of the bitter, divisive arguments which twice led to the destruction of the Temple and the state in Biblical times, and whose tremors are once again felt within Anglo-Jewry.

On that night of Yom Ha-Atzmaut in Jerusalem, I asked Shmuely Boteach, a man who is trying with unorthodox methods to bring about the consensus that Amélie herself is seeking, what the Messianic age means to him. It means, he replied, the merging of opposites. And I asked Amélie the same question. Rabbi Elie Munk saw the Messianic age as a gradual process through a general awareness of higher values and morality. His daughter accepts this, but believes that this can only come about through a change in ethical and moral awareness. Born into the horrors of the Second World War, she had hoped and prayed that purer values would evolve from that dark age. She could not have predicted that conflict, greed and materialism would rise instead in an eternal cycle of violence. Yet true religion must foster optimism, and Amélie is ever-hopeful.

She recalls Baroness Thatcher once asking her husband at a

reception, 'Why is it that whenever we take two steps forward in technology and the development of science or medicine, in human relations we seem to go back three or four steps?' He replied: 'There are two things in the world that are badly distributed. One is the appreciation of religion and the other is the distribution between the haves and have nots, and it is difficult to catch up.' 'Either things will get worse and decline into a Sodom and Gemorrah situation, or something catastrophic will happen – a jerk like an electric shock treatment – to bring the world back to its senses,' says Amélie.

Emotion, she feels, has guided Israeli politics since the foundation of the state. None of its politicians have had the will, the time or the maturity to work out ways of handling the future in a more reasoned way. In this Amélie sees a reflection of the American political scene where US politicians conduct affairs of state more through emotion than intellect. She refers to the melodrama of so many ephemeral, insignificant events which receive an inordinate amount of attention, while the energies of world leadership should go into working day and night to averting world catastrophes, such as the threat to peace by unstable leaders like Saddam Hussein.

So, does Amélie Jakobovits look forwards or back? *Aliyah*, emigration to Israel, which translates in religious terms to a literal *ascent*, eluded her. But the radiance of the Jewish state seems like a mirage. Some of this may have to do with a perception that those who are not obviously religious are indeed secular – in other words agnostic or even atheist. There is a clear unwillingness to accept more subtle, internalised forms of Judaism, which are no less spiritual or effective. Undoubtedly extreme religious fervour in one religion can spread into others, and the fallout from Islamic fundamentalism in Iran during the era of Ayatollah Khomeini cannot be disregarded. But if Amélie mourns the lack of religious sensibility in Israel, she equally abhors 'this internal disarray' among the Jewish people, as she does the presence of 'the most extreme form of Torah interpretation', while Israel is denuded of any leader of magnitude, either religious or national. A report which states that sixty-four per cent of the ultra-Orthodox population are in favour of turning Israel into a theocracy only reinforces her fears.

Ideally Amélie would like to place Israel as the central base, the heart of the Jewish people, from where all religious, cultural and political inspiration should emanate. But despite all her misgivings, she was much cheered by a recent visit to Israel where she noticed that there were many religious Jews willingly 'stretching out their hands to the secularist citizens of the State'. This is a serious beginning in which her own son, Shmuel, is playing a pivotal role, ensuring the survival of the Jakobovits values.

But Europe, too, must play its part, not least in the confirmation of social harmony and inter-faith tolerance. When she returns to Paris, the city where she grew up, it must be impossible not to be struck by the contrast between the almost seedy elegance of a city which capitulated so easily to foreign tyranny, with the towering glass edifices of La Defense, a post-modern statement of economic power, whose Grande Arche constructed in marble and glass stares the Arc de Triomphe straight in the eye. The new arch commemorates the French Revolution and is dedicated to human rights.

One positive aspect of the last half century is the prospect at last of some financial restitution for victims of Nazism. The suspicion that Amélie felt about the Swiss during the war right from the time of her family's escape has been fully vindicated: the picture clearly suggests that Switzerland used its so-called neutrality as a cynical cover for large-scale profiteering, enabling it to emerge from the war as one of the richest countries in the world. On the issue of the Swiss gold, the Eizenstat Report, commissioned by the Clinton administration to assess the post-war distribution of the Nazis' stolen funds, claims that Switzerland bankrolled the Nazis, enabling Germany to buy arms and other commodities, while at the same time providing an Allied base for spying. The report adds that only a portion of the $580 million in gold pillaged from Nazi-occupied territory (today worth some $5.6 billion) was recovered, while up to $400 million in German stolen gold remained in the Swiss National Bank at the end of the war. Only $58 million was returned.

As inter-governmental feathers flew over the discovery of Switzerland's pot of gold, it seemed a bizarre and bitter end to the tragedy in Europe. Amélie and survivors and refugees like her witnessed the protracted agony of the Holocaust disintegrating into the financial pickings. Suddenly European cities, caught in the Nazi stranglehold during the war, became vultures encircling the dead.

In Britain Lord Janner, chairman of the Holocaust Education Trust who led the drive in Britain for financial restitution, sharply criticised the Swiss Government for its delay in handing over 100 million Swiss francs belonging to victims of Nazism, accusing it of having renegued on its promise to relinquish funds to the World Jewish Restitution Organisation, despite Switzerland's agreement to back a conference of all the powers which handled the Nazi gold. The first monies released by a new fund (July 1997) went to Holocaust victims in former Communist East European countries, who were due to receive over £7 million.

However, all the restitution in the world cannot eradicate memories of the Holocaust. The scars, physical and psychological, are continued manifestations within the Jewish soul. And for many the poet, Abba Kovner's exhortation that the victims should not go like lambs to the slaughter is branded into the psyche – perhaps for Amélie, too. With some Jews the idea of passivity does not sit well. The question of Jewish vengeance against the Nazis emerged with the publication in 1998 of Ort leader, Joseph Harmatz's book, *From the Wings*, which reveals the plot of a group of Jewish partisans to kill one German for every Jew slaughtered. The issue of Jewish revenge adding to the eternal cycle of violence is something causing Amélie further inner turmoil when she speaks of her desire for purification.

Amélie sees some reflection of Israel's struggles with those of that other beleaguered region, Northern Ireland, with its eternal spiral of violence. Her memories of living in the South when her husband was Dublin's Chief Rabbi cannot help but foster affection and concern for that beautiful island, even though she had no experience of the troubles in the North. Amélie has described her personal admiration for the last British premier, John Major, and his wife, Norma, praising the persistence this low-profile premier showed in pursuing his aims. She had much sympathy for Major's pioneering work in establishing the first, tentative peace talks with Belfast and is disappointed that he did not see his ambition crowned with success before the last general election, which, in her view, would have made him 'one of the greatest Prime Ministers we have had'. Amélie was concerned that respect for John Major's groundwork could be submerged in his acrimonious defeat amid accusations of sleaze, Europhobia and weak leadership. Now that New Labour's indefatigable Northern Ireland Secretary, Dr Mo Mowlem, is building on Major's foundations, she was gratified to see that Major's groundwork achieved full recognition by Tony Blair's New Labour Government.

Epilogue

IF THERE had been no Amélie Jakobovits, you could not have invented her. The woman they call Lady J is a unique personality in a role which could have condemned her to obscurity. For Amélie, the absoluteness of her time and place invests her with a message; she is in harmony with her listeners, but she is also quicksilver, on the move, forever alert to a greater need. Amélie has all the qualities of the charmer; she does not hang around long enough to be fully grasped. And in another sense she is always *there*. As with all incandescent people, she is fleeting and evanescent, but where others may be shallow, she leaves something magisterial: a presence, a kind of magic. 'Many daughters have done worthily,' says the Proverb, 'but thou excellest them all.' Perhaps it is her faith in a world which has lost its right to believe which makes her so attractive. At a time when head teachers battle with churches as to whether it would be insensitive to preach Christianity in schools, Amélie's case for Judaism goes on. But no one can alleviate her sadness that the questions of the twentieth century, in which Jewish nationalism rose from the ashes of persecution, have not been answered.

There will be other great women married to great rabbis. They will plead their cause and those of their husbands. Unlike Amélie, rebbetzin will continue their own careers and make a clear distinction between their work and that of their husbands. And the battle for the soul of woman will continue. Amélie – still far from retiring – is confident that she can contribute to the advancement of many community projects. She is open to change, but realistic about what that might be.

Personal changes are less likely. Still confessing herself a feminist – in its broadest sense of seeking self-realisation – she says that

303

while there is no such thing as an organised feminist movement, such eclectic women's initiatives as the Rosh Chodesh groups, where women choose to pray on Rosh Chodesh (New Moon) according to Halachic standards, function well on an individual community basis, as they do in America. Yet her own code of strict religious observance has 'never posed a contradiction to her life of public service', according to Esther Sterngold of the Institute for the Special Child.

Amélie is concerned about her people and, as she admits, often wounded by their attitudes, their frailties. According to Ita Symons of the Agudas Yisroel Housing Association, she remains 'undaunted by cynics' as she is by 'fleeting fashions of the day.'

'With most well known people,' adds Mrs Symons, 'the closer one gets to know them the more cracks are seen in their personality. In the case of this lady, the reverse applies.' Clearly, Amélie wants to make a difference, to create her own resonance in the world – and, of course, to leave something behind. A retinue of grandchildren to perpetuate the Jakobovits line is her most obvious heritage, something others may take for granted, but for her it is one of the main tenets of Jewish continuity. This is pointed out by Ellen Adler, who refers to the admiration and respect Amélie arouses in 'her extended family world wide', quite apart from the love of husband, children and grandchildren.

Amélie never desists from speaking her mind and will do so in the most unexpected places. She recently addressed a Brussels conference of Jews in favour of the continuation of the peace process, the only rebbetzin present and certainly the only one called to speak. She spoke *'passionately, passionately* in favour of the peace camp', said Geoffrey Paul, 'and had the audience totally enthralled.'

For me, a most enduring image of Amélie comes from her visit to Israel with a group of women at the time of the Gulf War. During the air-raids at night she comforted them with the intensely moving *tefillot* prayer – that deeply enduring heritage of belief passed down from Rabbi Elie Munk, her father, to her children and grandchildren. Deep in Amélie's heart at that moment were thoughts of her family as well as her late parents, grandparents and sister, Miriam.

But there is another, even more potent image of the life and times of Amélie Jakobovits. It is a picture of Amélie dancing at the wedding of her first granddaughter, Zipporah, where, in accordance with customary Orthodox practice, she joined the women of the family in a bridal dance. As the excitement of the moment dissipated and the bride drifted away with the other women, she found herself dancing alone with her sister, Ruth. It was a moment of intense rapture as they celebrated their closeness and the continuum of traditional family life it mirrored. A moment later they stared deeply at one another and collapsed in tears into each other's arms. Someone was missing from this celebratory group. It was their younger sister, Miriam. Amélie and Ruth went outside to cry alone for their so recent tragic loss. But then they remembered words which only their mother could have said to them: Enough of tears. Let's rejoin the world of life and laughter.

Perhaps the spirit of Maman Munk, with all her celebrated *joie de vivre*, was indeed standing there, just watching.

Index

Index

Index

Romanian Jews, 210, 211; and Russian Jews, 209; Six Day War, 72, 121, 201, 215, 290; views of Amélie on, 260–1, 296, 298, 299–300; views of Immanuel Jakobovits on, 200–1, 290–2; visits by Amélie to, 72, 200, 209–10, 269–70, 296, 304; work of Shmuel Jakobovits in, 250–1; Yom Kippur War (1973), 92n, 200, 201, 202–3; mentioned, 138, 171, 187, 213, 223, 240, 248, 272, 301

Israel Bonds, 148

Italy, 35, 36

Jacobs, June, 280

Jacobs, Rabbi Dr Louis, 123n, 177–8, 179, 180, 181, 182n, 182–3, 184, 284, 285; *We Have Reason to Believe*, 177, 178

Jacobs Affair, 177–84, 192, 283

Jakobovits (née Munk), Amélie: personality, xiii, xv–xvi, 194, 235–6, 256–7, 303; birth, 4; early years in Germany, 4–11; relationship with grandfather, 8–10, 11; childhood in Paris, 1–2, 13–18; journey from Paris, 18–20; as refugee in France, 20–49; escapes to Switzerland, 49–57; in Switzerland, 58–64; returns to Paris, 65–72; ideas about love and romance, 73; meeting with Immanuel arranged, 74–7; second meeting with Immanuel, 78; declines invitation to induction in Ireland, 79; corresponds with Immanuel, 79, 80, 84; meets future mother-in-law, 80–3; meets Immanuel in Manchester, 85–7; feelings about proposed marriage, 87–8, 89; goes to Dublin for engagement reception, 89–90; wedding, 90–2; honeymoon, 93–5; visits Zurich, 95; parting from parents, 96; early married life, 97–106; and mother-in-law, 101–4, 116, 117, 132; and Lotti, 101, 102, 131, 134, 136,143, 145–6; birth of Yoel, 105–6; social activities in Ireland, 107, 108, 110; birth of Shmuel, 109–10; growing family, 110; beginning of interest in care and community work, 110–11; and children, 112–16, 118; and public affairs in Ireland, 119–24; enjoys life in Ireland, 124–6; and proposed move to America, 127–8, 130; birth of Aviva, 130; finding home in New York, 130–1, 134, 135–6; departure from Ireland, 131–2; arrival in New York, 133; and material wealth, 136–8, 139; involvement with family, 138, 139–40; change in style, 139; recollections of Wouk, 141–2; in role of Rabbi's wife in New York, 144–5, 147–51; views on women, xiv, 153–8, 246, 276–8, 279; Ten Commandments for successful marriage, xiv, 159–64, 272; holidays, 165–72; and invitation to Britain, 174, 185; and invitation to South Africa, 175–6; birth of Elisheva, 185; moves to Britain, 185–92; role as Chief Rabbetzin, 194–6, 241–2; educational interests, 195, 208–9, 214; and family responsibilities, 196–7; and Immanuel's Albert Hall speech, 199, 290; first visit to Israel, 200; and Yom Kippur War, 201, 202–3; and death of mother-in-law, 204–5; and security, 205–6; and Russian Jews, 209; further visit to Israel, 209–10; meets Romanian Chief Rabbi and wife, 210; and Moshe Davis, 212, 213; entertaining and social skills, 215–20; and Conservative Party, 222, 225–6, 227–30; and kosher caterers, 226–7; and Royal Family, 231–8; and media, 239, 246–7; and travel, 239–40; and prayer, 242, 244–5; and death of parents, 243–4; and Kabbalah, 245; and cults, 245; and death of sister Miriam, 248–9; centrality of family, 249–53; charitable work, 254–61; views on Israel, 260–1, 296, 298, 299–300; and Immanuel's peerage, 262–6; activities since Immanuel's retirement, 267–74; and *agunot*, 274–5, 276; and schisms, 282, 283–4, 285–6; relationship with Immanuel, xiv, 154, 160, 161, 287–90; and Israel's fiftieth anniversary, 296–7; and Northern Ireland, 301–2; images of, 304–5

Jakobovits, Aviva (Amélie's daughter), 110, 130, 133, 135, 145, 168–9, 185, 187, 252

Jakobovits, Cessie (Amélie's sister-in-law), 109, 110

311

Index

Index

Index

Sternberg, Sir Sigmund, 255
Stratford College, 99
Streicher, 6
Sturmer, Der, 6
Succot, 136n, 202
Swiss Humanitarian Fund for Holocaust Victims, 59n
Swiss National Bank, 300
Switzerland: Munk family escapes from France to, 49–57; Munk family as refugees in, 58–64; and Nazi wealth, 58, 300–1; role in Second World War, 58–9; Amélie returns to visit, 74; Amélie and Immanuel honeymoon in, 93–5; mentioned, 65, 68

Tabernacles, festival of, 136n, 202
Tagore, xviii
Talmud, 155, 156, 167, 245
Tauber, Michelle (Micky) *see* Jakobovits (née Tauber), Michelle
Tel Aviv, 296
Temple Emanu-El, 129, 130
Texas, 168
Thatcher, Denis, 218, 224, 225–6, 230
Thatcher, Margaret, xiii, 206, 215, 218, 220, 222, 223, 224, 225, 226, 229, 230, 261, 262, 263, 265, 266, 286, 292, 293, 298–9
Theresienstadt, 19, 65
35s's Group, 206
Times, The, 190, 191, 234, 284
Tisha B'Av, 200
Tlalim, 257, 259
Torah, 123, 156, 178, 180, 265, 299
Toulouse, 20, 28, 29, 31
Trust Hospitals, 293
Turner, Norman, 199n, 251
Turner, Rev Reuben, 199, 199n, 251, 290
Turner (née Jakobovits), Shoshana *see* Jakobovits, Shoshana

Ukraine, 268
Ulpana Ruhava, 257
Union of Orthodox Congregations, 282
United Hebrew Congregations of Great Britain and the Commonwealth, 174, 183, 191
United Jewish Appeal, 120
United Jewish Israel Appeal, 215n, 219, 296; *see also* Joint Israel Appeal; Joint Palestine Appeal
United Nations Human Rights Committee, 280

United States *see* America
University College Hospital, 187
United Synagogue of Great Britain and the Commonwealth, 173, 178, 179, 182, 184, 186, 191, 197, 244, 246, 249, 254, 264, 267, 274, 276, 278, 282, 285; Women's Review, 276–7, 278; *see also* Anglo-Jewry
University of Cardiff, 126
Unterman, Rabbi Maurice, 201
Updike, John, 185

Val Fleuris reception camp, 56
Valley of the Lost Communities, 297
Vichy, 36, 68, 70
Vietnam War, 174, 181

Walesa, Lech, 229–30
Waley-Cohen, Sir Robert, 179
War Crimes Bill (1991), 265
Warshawski (née Metzger), Mireille, 16
Waterford, 99
Weidenfeld, George: *Remembering My Good Friends*, 210–11
Weinberg, Syma, 278
Weingarten, Frances, 257
Weiser, Howard, 257
Weiskopf, Rabbi, 13
Weiss, Dayan, 85
Wesker, Arnold, 141
Western Wall, 200, 269
West London Reform Synagogue, 281
Windsor Castle, 231
Winston Fox, Mrs Ruth, 268–9
WIZO (Women's International Zionist Organisation), 121, 226, 258
Wolfson, Sir Isaac, 173, 174, 176, 180, 181, 182, 185, 186, 187, 192, 197–8
Wolfson, Leonard, 197
Wolfson, Lady, 187, 189, 190, 191, 195, 197
women, xiv, 153–8, 163–4, 193, 246, 276–80, 294, 304; *see also agunot*; feminism; marriage
Women's International Zionist Organisation (WIZO), 121, 226, 258
Women's Liberation movement, 157, 158; *see also* feminism
Women's Review, 276–7, 278
Wood, Natalie, 141
World Jewish Congress, 69
World Jewish Restitution Organisation, 301

317

Index

Wouk, Herman, 130, 141–2; *The Caine Mutiny*, 141; *Marjorie Morningstar*, 141; *This is My God*, 141

Yad Sarah, 257, 258–9
Yad Vashem, 297
Yalibez, Sarah, 70–1
yartzheit candle, 65, 65n
Yellowstone Park, 166, 168
Yeshiva B'nei Rem, 259–60
Yeshurun youth movement, 16, 42, 43, 67, 68, 69, 72, 73, 151–2
Yom Kippur, 242

Yom Kippur War (1973), 92n, 200, 201, 202–3
Young, Stuart, 263
Young, Lord, 263
Young Israel communities, 143

Zionism, 98, 99, 100, 127, 128n, 290, 298
Zionist Association, 4
Zionist Federation, 199, 274; Synagogue Council, 199
Zonnenberg, Aviva, 156
Zurich, 59, 62, 95